**OFFICIALLY
DISCARDED**

AVIATOR
EXTRAORDINAIRE

AVIATOR EXTRAORDINAIRE

My Story

By
Air Commodore G J Christopher Paul, CB, DFC

Pen & Sword
AVIATION

First published in Great Britain in 2012 by
PEN & SWORD AVIATION
An imprint of
Pen & Sword Books Ltd
47 Church Street
Barnsley
South Yorkshire
S70 2AS

Copyright © G J Christopher Paul, 2012

ISBN 978 1 84884 901 3

A CIP catalogue record for this book is
available from the British Library

Printed and bound in England
By CPI Group (UK) Ltd, Croydon, CRO 4YY

Pen & Sword Books Ltd incorporates the Imprints of
Pen & Sword Aviation, Pen & Sword Family History, Pen & Sword Maritime,
Pen & Sword Military, Wharncliffe Local History, Pen & Sword Select,
Pen & Sword Military Classics, Leo Cooper, Remember When,
Seaforth Publishing and Frontline Publishing

For a complete list of Pen & Sword titles please contact
PEN & SWORD BOOKS LIMITED
47 Church Street, Barnsley, South Yorkshire, S70 2AS, England
E-mail: enquiries@pen-and-sword.co.uk
Website: www.pen-and-sword.co.uk

CONTENT

ACKNOWLEDGEMENTS

The Publishers are indebted to:

AIR VICE MARSHAL SIR JOHN SEVERNE KCVO OBE AFC DL

AIR MARSHAL IAN MACFADYEN CB OBE

MOLLIE PAUL

This book is sold for the benefit of the Royal Airforce Benevolent Fund.

FOREWORD

CHRISTOPHER PAUL   31 October 1907 – 11 January 2003

Christopher was not only a good friend, but I had always admired him for his enormous enthusiasm for aviation in general and for the Royal Air Force in particular.   However it was not until I started asking around, and then read the remarkable book which he had written for his family entitled *My Story*, that I realised that here was someone who had spanned an incredible period of aviation history, the like of whom we shall probably never see again. I will try to pick out some of the highlights of this most extraordinary career.

His first recollection of flying was in 1911 at the age of four, when he was taken to an air display to see Pégoud, the Frenchman who was the first pilot to loop an aircraft in public.   There were no less than three Admirals on the two sides of his family and he chanced to overhear the one who was uncle and godfather say: 'Of course the boy must go to Dartmouth'.   Christopher subsequently wrote: 'Such being my perverse streak of obstinacy, this decided me that whatever else I did, it would never be Dartmouth!' Later he was not exactly encouraged at Cheltenham where most of the boys were going into the army because the RAF was considered 'not quite the career for gentlemen'.

It was, however, at Cambridge, reading mechanical sciences that he realised more than anything else that he wanted to fly. So he joined the recently formed University Air Squadron in 1927, going solo on the Bristol PTM (the Primary Training Machine) after five hours, gaining his wings after a mere thirty-six hours and, after his degree, a regular commission in the RAF in 1929. In the same year, at Spithead, he watched Flying Officer Waghorn of the Central Flying School win the Schneider Trophy for Great Britain for the second time.

After completing the course at No 1 FTS at Netheravon he joined his first squadron in 1930, No 13 Army Cooperation Squadron, equipped with Armstrong Whitworth Atlases.   His disappointment on being told, after only six months on the squadron that he was posted to the Fleet Air Arm at Gosport was compensated by his final report from his squadron commander. Christopher wrote: 'He awarded me that coveted and rarely given pilot assessment of exceptional, a rating which I was proud to retain in every subsequent pilot report so long as they were made on me.' this was remarkable.

Fleet Air Arm postings were not popular; the only way out being to volunteer for the five year Japanese interpreter's course; he decided to stick with the Fleet Air

Arm whose pilots were roughly 50/50 RAF and RN. He flew from the carriers *Courageous, Furious* and *Glorious*, rather disrespectfully referred to by the RAF as Outrageous, Curious and Spurious. He flew most of the seaplanes and flying boats of the day and the list includes a number of aircraft I have never even heard of. Of the Fairey IIIF amphibian he reported 'water performance poor, deck performance frightening'.

Pre-war RAF officers were expected to specialise, and when, in 1932, the Air Ministry realised he had an engineering degree they sent him on the two year engineer officer's course at Henlow. He didn't enjoy being away from flying, but he did enjoy getting to know one of his fellow students, Frank Whittle. He also seemed to spend most of his spare time scrounging flying from friends in such wonderful aeroplanes as the Hawker Fury. During this period he joined the London Aero Club at Stag Lane and obtained his civil licence, No 1179, on a Cirrus Moth at 15/- an hour. After the engineering course he rejoined the Fleet Air Arm at Lee-on-the-Solent where he was responsible for the workshops which serviced all the Fleet Air Arm aircraft, and, as their test pilot, naturally he had to fly them all.

He was promoted Squadron Leader in 1938 to take command of 90 Squadron at Bicester, recently formed with Hawker Harts, but about to become only the second squadron to re-equip with Blenheims. Then during the RAF Staff College course at Andover, which he completed just before the Second World War started, he managed to fly a Spitfire which had just come into service at Duxford. Christopher wrote: 'it became, in a magic way, one's own wings'.

The day before war was declared he was sent to his war appointment, the Advanced Air Striking Force at Rheims. His job was to prepare for the arrival of the ten Fairy Battle Squadrons supporting the British Expeditionary Force. He was the camp commandant based in Madame Pommery's champagne factory. Poor fellow!

In December 1940 he took command, now as a Wing Commander, of 150 Squadron flying Wellingtons from Newton. He describes an incident in *My Story* which tells us much about Christopher. He was acting station Commander at the time when they were tasked to attack the *Scharnhorst* and *Gneisenau* at Brest. The bomb load specified by Group was such that the crews would be dangerously short of fuel on their return if the weather was bad. He argued to have the load reduced or to have a diversion specified in the south of England, but was met by incomprehension from the staff and was firmly told to 'obey orders or else'. In the event, one of his crews ran out of fuel and they were all killed. Christopher felt that he should have put up a much more determined fight, regardless of the consequences, for what he knew to be right.

In 1943, as the RAF member of the Directing Staff at the Army Staff College at Camberley one of the RAF students, Bob Braham, by then a famous night fighter pilot, sent Christopher solo on a Mosquito. After landing he thought the Mossie to be one of the most delightful aeroplanes he had ever flown. By now I'm sure you have come to realise that nothing could keep Christopher out of the air.

And now to what I presume was the most critical period of his life, his four month tour in 1944 commanding 98 Squadron flying Mitchell medium bombers from Dunsfold. Their targets were the softening up of the German defences before the allied invasion of Europe. He flew thirty-nine missions, mostly leading his squadron with up to twenty-four aircraft. He was then awarded his DFC (Distinguished Flying Cross) which had an unexpected beneficial effect. Until now his father had never overcome his disappointment at Christopher joining the not quite gentlemen's brigade, but as soon as he won his DFC he suddenly became a good chap! He had already been awarded the Czech Military Cross in 1939 and the Belgian *Crioux de Guerre avec Palme* the next year. Subsequently he was also mentioned in dispatches.

After the war the 98 Squadron Association was formed and he was elected an Honorary Life Member. Until shortly before he died, he used to send the secretary a cheque to cover the cost of the port for the members to be able to drink the Queen's health. He was also involved with the creation of the 90 Squadron Association, becoming its chairman and later its President and Patron.

The war is now over and it is the 11 March 1946, which he wrote was a very significant date in his life. It was while commanding 13 Operational Training Unit with Mosquitoes at Middleton St George (now Teeside Airport), that he used to fly, first thing in the morning, a Tiger Moth. To the entertainment of the airmen he used to land it on a small patch of grass in front of the hangar and, at the end of the landing run turn towards the hangar door, switching off the engine just before it free wheeled silently into the hangar. This required approaching very low over the roof of a hut. Unfortunately he hadn't noticed that, since his previous flight, a co-axial aerial had been erected only three feet above the roof, and this he collected with his undercarriage, the aerial acting as a very effective arrester cable. This brought the Tiger to a grinding halt, but about 20 feet up. He survived the resulting crash, but with two badly bruised eyes. In writing his own station commander's comments on the accident report he said: 'The pilot was showing off and is entirely to blame.' Unfortunately some years later, as a result of the crash, he lost the sight in his left eye.

Shortly afterwards he experienced his first flight in a jet aircraft, a Meteor at Molesworth, describing the flight as: 'a delight beyond description, so much so that I got completely lost!' It was also at Middleton St George that he became seriously involved with gliding by setting up the first RAF gliding club in England on his station. This interest continued with his next posting to the British Air Forces of Occupation at Buckeburg where, as Group Captain Air Training, he was responsible for all the many RAF gliding clubs in Germany, most of which were based on ex-Luftwaffe schools.

He had flown to Germany on this tour with his own Mk VI Mosquito and he used this aircraft on all his staff visits for the following two years. There had been a good bit of muttering about his refusal to allow anyone else to fly it, but shortly after his departure for a tour in the USA to attend the USAF War College course, the chief mutterer decided to fly the aircraft, swung badly on take-off and finished up in a rubbish dump; who said aircraft don't have personalities?

On his return to England in 1949 he found himself in the Intelligence Department of the Air Ministry. During that tour he founded the RAF Gliding and Soaring Association. He felt strongly that it was important for other ranks to be able to enjoy flying in much the same way as Naval ratings can enjoy sailing dinghies with the Royal Navy's Sailing Association. Initially there was no enthusiasm from the RAF Sports Board for official backing – the Secretary saying to Christopher: 'You can't kick it, you can't throw it, you can't hit it, you can't shoot it – so it can't be a sport'! But he and some friends decided to go ahead anyway. The actual event is recorded on a plaque of the Founders Trophy which he presented in 1964. It is inscribed: 'The RAFGSA was founded on 15 December 1949, by H.G. Forbes, D.D. Martin, R.P. Hanks, T Page and G.J.C. Paul in a taxi on the way to a Chinese Restaurant. Also at the birth was a policeman, who tried to stop it on the grounds of overloading the cab and the driver who pressed on regardless.' Christopher became the first chairman and made the first flight in a RAFGSA Prefect glider from Detling in May 1950. He later became their Life Vice President.

After a year at the Imperial Defence College he achieved his life-long ambition in 1954 of becoming Commandant of the Central Flying School, as an Air Commodore, at Little Rissington. CFS is the oldest flying school in the world, its first Assistant Commandant in 1912 being one Major Hugh Trenchard who founded the RAF in 1918.

It was a time of great change, not least of which was the introduction of helicopters to CFS. He described his first helicopter solo in a Dragonfly thus: 'It was quite an experience, and I never thought it possible to recapture for a second time, the amazed mixture of delight, apprehension and triumph when one's instructor, as always, unexpectedly gets out and says: now do three circuits and landings yourself!'

He sums up his time at CFS thus: 'For Rosemary (his first wife), as well as for myself, it was, I think, the best two years of our life in the service.' For his work at CFS he was awarded his CB (Companion of the most honorable order of the Bath). Later he became President of the CFS Association.

After CFS he was posted to Aden as the Senior Air Staff Officer. It was 1956 and the time of the Suez Crisis. The consequent build up of British Forces in the area resulted in his one transport squadron of Valettas being hopelessly swamped with tasks. So he requisitioned Aden Airways and their Dakotas which, he said, did the work most efficiently. I wonder how many other RAF officers have requisitioned an airline?

After a year at Aden he was posted home to the Air Ministry as Director of Operational Training. But before taking up his appointment he attended a Meteor refresher course at the Flying College at Manby. He was so impressed with his instructor that he wrote: 'I think this was the moment when I first conceded that the new generation of pilots were better than me. My instructor gave me a certain belief that the present pilots in the RAF are, as indeed they must always be, superior in every way to their predecessors. My much loved RAF is indeed in good hands.'

In 1958 he took early retirement at the age of fifty-one. The very next day he started work as the Secretary General of the Air League, an organisation pledged to improve the nation's air-mindedness. The job required him to visit many civilian airfields and so, to compensate himself for the loss of service flying, he bought a Turbulent for £650. The Turbulent is an ultra light aircraft weighing only 3cwt and is powered by a Volkswagen car engine. He even wangled a personalised registration – G-GJCP. As part of the job he was manager of the Air League's magazine, *Air Pictorial*, writing many articles himself reporting on some of the aircraft he flew. During his thirteen years as Secretary General his name had become synonymous with air education and he helped with the creation of the Air Education and Recreational Organisation (AERO) for which he was awarded the League's Scott Farnie Award of 1970.

He parted company with the Air League in 1971, but by then had become very involved with the light aircraft movement in general and in particular with home-built aircraft represented by the Popular Flying Association, of which he had become President three years earlier. The writing of the so called Presidential Flying Tests in the PFA magazine gave him the opportunity to fly yet more different aircraft types. He organised the first of the big PFA rallies at Sywell in conjunction with AERO of the Air League. He called it the F3 Rally – Flying For Fun. Ten years later he wrote a good book on the fifty year history of Sywell.

He was an active member of the Tiger Club and in 1963 he became the first secretary of the British Seaplane Club. He flew the initial test flight on the Sea Tiger, but before doing this he had to get a civil licence to fly seaplanes and also an instructor's endorsement, for which he tested himself and awarded himself, would you believe, an exceptional category.

After Rosemary died in 1975 he continued flying because he found it therapeutic. But in 1978 the doctor's caught up with him and failed to renew his civil licence. He said they condemned him as having an irregular heart beat, only one eye, and various bits missing including parts of his left arm, and being decrepit. He was seventy-one. He consoled himself by remembering that he had been an active pilot for over fifty years and by finding out that his civil licence was the oldest still current when it expired. He had flown the astonishing total of 276 different types of aircraft. Not a bad record.

So many people have told me of his professionalism, his charm, courtesy, helpfulness, sense of humour and above all, his friendship. One summed him up by simply saying 'he was a lovely fellow'. How right he was.

One of the many people who wrote to his wife Mollie ended his letter by saying: 'A great man has passed on, his presence will always be with us'. And so it shall.

Air Vice-Marshal Sir John Severne KCVO OBE AFC DL

INTRODUCTION

Air Commodore Gerald John Christopher Paul died at the age of ninety-five in January 2003. In his latter years he compiled and wrote *My Story*, which was a personal account of a remarkable RAF career, followed by an extremely unusual civilian career in aviation. The original manuscript was produced for his family and close friends. It comprehensively covered his military and civilian career.

We were approached by Pen and Sword, who had been contacted by Air Vice Marshal Sir John Severne, to edit and slightly reorganise the original autobiography. We were pleased to do so, but it was not until we began to read *My Story* that the full importance of this singular character and his involvement in some of the pivotal periods of RAF and aviation history became clear. It was indeed an extraordinary career.

Simple facts, like being an active pilot for over fifty years and discovering that his civil licence was the oldest still current when it expired only begin to explain the span of Christopher Paul's career. He flew a truly astonishing selection of aircraft since first gaining his pilot's licence in the 1920s. There is virtually no iconic or, for that matter, obscure aircraft that Christopher Paul did not fly in the next fifty years.

Such was the quality, vibrancy and obvious enthusiasm with which Christopher Paul explained his experiences on each of the 276 aircraft that it was unnecessary to change his words. Hence the vast majority of the words are his and rather than being a biography, this is truly an autobiography. At times we have taken slight liberties with sentence structure, or inserted explanations of technical terms, or historical events.

Christopher Paul was born on 31 October 1907 and educated first at Cheltenham College and then at St John's College, Cambridge. It was at Cambridge that he began his early association with the RAF, in the Reserve of Officers, learning to fly with the University Air Squadron in 1927. He was commissioned in the RAF in 1929, but in the following year found himself serving onboard HMS *Courageous*, the ill-fated aircraft carrier that was sunk by U-29 on 17 September 1939.

By then Christopher Paul had already rejoined the RAF, to serve with 90 Squadron on Blenheims. At the outbreak of the Second World War he was attached to the Advanced Air Striking Force HQ in France. After France fell he commanded a Wellington Bomber Squadron, was closely involved in training crews and then took over command of the B-25 Mitchell Bomber armed 98 Squadron. In the period centred round the crucial Operation Overlord in June 1944 he led his squadron against innumerable targets, which would earn him the DFC, the Belgian *Croix de Guerre* and the Czechoslovak Military Cross. He was also mentioned in Despatches. He would fly some thirty-nine missions.

In the post-war period Christopher was posted as part of the occupation forces in Germany. This introduced him to a new flying passion that would continue for many years to come. He helped form the RAF Gliding and Soaring Association, where he learned to love powerless flight. He then spent time in the United States and then in the Air Ministry's Directorate of Intelligence.

In 1954 he achieved one of his lifetime ambitions when he became the Commandant of the Central Flying School. Two years later he was awarded the appointment of Commander of the Order of the Bath in the January 1956 New Year's Honours List. He was then sent to Aden as Senior Air Staff Officer. This was during the build up to the Suez Crisis and it is a measure of his adaptability that he effectively requisitioned an entire airline to operate as an impromptu transport unit.

Following his tour in Aden he returned to the Air Ministry and finally retired from the RAF in 1958. He was just fifty-one years old and had a whole new career in civilian life ahead of him. Whilst being involved in civilian flying and gliding, the Royal Aero Club, the Popular Flying Association and the Tiger Club his main duties were as Secretary General of the Air League. This was a post that he would hold from 1959 until 1971.

Even after this he still continued to be a frequent flyer, both as a pilot and then after he finally lost his civil licence, at the age of seventy-one in 1978. By that time his sundry ailments and age had caught up with him. But he remained a strong aviation advocate for the rest of his life.

For virtually all of Christopher Paul's RAF career he was married to Rosemary and had two sons and a daughter. Rosemary died in 1975, but twelve years later he married Mollie Samuels. It is obvious from *My Story* that Christopher was a loving and dedicated husband to both Rosemary and Mollie and very much a family man. In the original *My Story* there were many examples of occasions and reminiscences that would only have resonance with family and close friends. As a result these have been either edited out or have been reduced in scope and length. What remains, however, is a detailed account of his career, but more importantly, an opportunity to see, perhaps uniquely, an account of aviation in its broadest sense across an enormous span of time. Christopher Paul was fortunate in as much as he began flying on First World War vintage aircraft, yet decades later, now a highly experienced yet still supremely competent pilot, was flying in jets. What certainly comes across on every occasion where he recounts clambering into an aircraft is the sheer joy and enthusiasm he felt each time.

My Story is chronological in its approach. Interwoven with his own career progression and experiences are world events and situations. Coupled with this we can clearly see the development of aircraft over a period of more than fifty years.

Christopher Paul clearly identifies some of his favourite aircraft and is never frightened to identify the shortcomings of even some of the most famous and successful aircraft that have ever been produced.

My Story is also accompanied by three appendices that Christopher Paul compiled. The first is his record of RAF service, spanning from 25 June 1927 to his last posting as Director of Operational Training with the Air Ministry, a post that he held when he retired on 6 October 1958. Christopher Paul interestingly sets his final retirement date as July 1978, after which he has not made any additions to his career CV. This is, perhaps, largely due to the fact that this was the fateful year in which he lost his pilot's licence. The second appendix is a fascinating extract from the log book of Flying Officer I.M. Williams, who flew as the navigator and bomb aimer on all of the sorties with 98 Squadron against German targets in France from 20 May to 17 August 1944. The final appendix is another fascinating list, in chronological order, of every aircraft type that Christopher Paul flew throughout his flying career. In itself it is a roll of honour of every conceivable aircraft, not just British built, across arguably the most important period of aviation development. Hidden amongst the list are the truly iconic aircraft, such as the Fairey Swordfish, the Hurricane, Spitfire, Wellington, Maryland, Mosquito, Tempest and Gloster Meteor. Even for those with more of an interest in civilian aviation, all of the key aircraft across these notable decades have been flown and subsequently rated by Christopher Paul.

Christopher Paul was a pilot during a period of aviation history second to none. He had an absolutely extraordinary career. He had been just four years old in 1911 when he had been bitten by the aviation bug at an air display. Despite family pressure to join the Royal Navy it was always going to be the RAF.

The likes of Christopher Paul may never be seen again, hence, and quite rightly, the title suggested by friends and family of this adaptation of *My Story* is *Aviator Extraordinaire*.

Jon Sutherland and Diane Canwell

CHAPTER ONE
LEARNING TO FLY

At *Cambridge*, as an undergraduate of St John's, I realised that, more than anything else, I wanted to fly. This started when I read in *The Times* that the Royal Air Force was about to begin direct recruiting of pilots into the Reserve of Air Force Officers. This was in late 1926. Up until this point the Reserve had comprised only those who had first served as regulars. I applied, was accepted, and at the same time accepted for entry into the University Air Squadron, with effect from September 1927.

I learned to fly at Filton in the RAF Reserve School run by the Bristol Aeroplane Company. This was during the period June to August 1927, having been commissioned as an Acting Pilot Officer on Probation, Reserve of Air Force Officers, with effect from 20 June 1927.

Our course at Filton was the first of its kind, and we were all undergraduates from Oxford, Cambridge or London. There were ten of us and most of us lodged in the house of a small garage located exactly on the threshold of what is now the eastern end of Filton's huge runway. In those days Filton was, like all aerodromes, all grass. It was owned by Mr Nash, who welcomed us and introduced us to the only other lodger, an ex-Royal Flying Corps Sergeant pilot on reserve training.

For our first week the weather was foul and nobody flew. We met our instructors, all ex-RFC and veterans of the First World War. Mine was a smallish Scot, named Jock Campbell. Dour at first meeting, reserved and very Scots, he had reddish hair and could be very forthright with a splendid economy of words. He was a superb, patient and gifted instructor, who sent me solo after just over five hours dual with the parting words 'Remember your ambition ought to be to become, not a brave pilot – just an Old One'.

The other two instructors were Shaw, of whom I saw very little; and Cy Holmes, a happy extrovert who appointed himself social mentor to our gang from Cambridge and introduced us to all those delights of old Bristol.

The first aircraft we flew was the Bristol Preliminary Training Machine (PTM). It was strong, fully aerobatic, had no peculiarities that I can remember, and was powered by a three-cylinder 100hp Bristol Lucifer. Very early in our training we were taught spins, and recoveries, and on every subsequent flight, dual or solo, we practiced at least one good spin; and generally one each way. One point of this was that a spin initiated suddenly in the same direction as the rotation of the engine could stop it, in which case it had to be restarted by diving. But most important was to regard spinning as a normal, everyday manoeuvre.

After qualifying on the PTM we moved on to the Jupiter Fighter. This was a truly beautiful aeroplane. Its wings and empennage (tail section) were identical to the Bristol Fighter with a 275hp Rolls-Royce water-cooled engine. It had, however, a 450hp nine-cylinder Jupiter radial engine, a plywood fuselage and Frise ailerons, which conferred a degree of lateral control previously unknown. Its performance was as good or better than most contemporary RAF fighters; at that time the Grebe, the Fleet Air Arm Flycatcher, and Hawker Woodcock. In fairness to these, it must be added that the Jupiter Fighter carried no armament, and no drag producing fitments like external bomb racks. The smaller fighters could obviously out-manoeuvre it, but the Jupiter fighter performed all normal aerobatics well and, in our enterprising but inexperienced hands, some unusual ones as well.

I completed my course at Filton on 19 August 1927, having flown a total of twelve and a quarter hours dual, and twenty-four hours and five minutes solo.

A year later to the day, I received Air Ministry authority to wear RAF pilots' wings. It is interesting to note that the authority was signed by Cuthbert Dearlove, later to be my Commanding Officer at RAF Bicester; and the covering letter by Squadron Leader Leslie H. Slatter, captain of the victorious RAF Schneider Trophy Team of 1927.

After a carefree summer holiday, travelling mainly by motorcycle and staying with friends first at Mullion Cove and then Cadgwith, I returned to Nottingham, and then to Cambridge. By this time my motorcycle was a rare Packman and Poppé. It was an the P & P that I took every opportunity to visit the RAF Aerodrome at Duxford, where the Cambridge University Air Squadron (CUAS) flew. This enabled me to get a good deal more flying in at Duxford than my share, to the neglect of my degree studies, but to my own complete enjoyment and satisfaction. I was able to cut many lectures, having come to a suitable arrangement with the various lecture theatre attendants, whose duty it was to ensure that attendance sheets were signed.

The CUAS Chief Flying Instructor was Foxy French. He was tall, lean and quiet, but never seemed to be quite serious about anything, but underneath a genial exterior was a most acute mind which missed nothing. His assistants at Duxford were Nuttall, who for many years held the RAF high jump record; Edmund Hordern, one of Cranwell's (officer training school) first products; Rupert Nash; and part-timer Mouse Fielden. Fielden would later train Edward Prince of Wales and become the First Caption of the Queen's Flight. During the Second World War, Fielden, then a Group Captain was in command of RAF Station Tempsford and from here he controlled all flights to drop agents into, and to pick them up from enemy occupied territory, using Lysander aircraft. At Duxford, however, Fielden was a pilot in the meteorological flight, flying Hawker Woodcocks. The flight was commanded by Jeffrey Quill, who would go on to be Supermarine's Chief Test Pilot and was closely involved in the development of the Spitfire.

In 1927 I also became a member of the London Aeroplane Club, based at Stag Lane in Edgware, London. This gave me my first taste of Club flying and light aircraft, in the form of the then relatively new de Havilland Cirrus Moth. I paid fifteen shillings an hour to fly at Stag Lane and, having been checked out by the Club's Instructor, Clem Pike, was able to fly there whenever I had the cash, and my P & P would take me there. Stag Lane was the headquarters of de Havilland. They also ran a Reserve School similar to the one at Filton. The primary trainer was the Avro 504 and their advanced trainer the DeH9J. It was here where I first obtained my Civil Licence (Number No 1179, dated 19 September 1927). Looking back, I had become a fully licensed civil pilot nearly a year before achieving my RAF Wings.

The high spot of the summer of 1928 was the CUAS camp at Old Sarum, near Salisbury in Wiltshire. The squadron was divided into three sections, each about twenty strong, and each spending three weeks under canvas. We became accustomed to the life of a busy RAF station, which, at that time, housed the School of Army Cooperation (aircraft used for reconnaissance, air photography and liaison). The school was commanded by Wing Commander McEwen a tall, gaunt Scot, who joined the RFC from a Highland Regiment and later became an Air Marshal. The Commandant of the CUAS was Wing Commander Vernon Brown, who had joined the RAF from the RNAS in 1918. The Adjutant, Victor Goddard (later Air Marshal Sir Victor Goddard) had been an airship pilot.

I was promoted from AVRO 504s to the Bristol Fighter, the ancestor of the Jupiter Fighter which I had already flown the year before at Filton. Although lacking the power of the Jupiter it was a superb aeroplane. It was reasonably aerobatic, and comfortable with a good view all round. In those days it was considered bad form to use the engine during the approach to land – every landing was done as though it were a forced landing. On grass aerodromes without runways the universal rule was that the aircraft lowest in the circuit had right of way. Following aircraft landed on the right of the one ahead, came to a halt before turning, and then turned off to the left. This was for the prevailing left hand circuit. I cannot remember any aerodrome that used a right hand or variable circuit. There was, of course, neither radio nor air traffic control. But with good pilot discipline, quite a small grass aerodrome, like Old Sarum, could handle large numbers of aircraft simultaneously, and it was not uncommon to see a dozen or more 504s and Bristol Fighters together on circuits and landings. The engine off landing originated from RFC days, when engine failure was frequent.

Before being allowed loose on a Bristol Fighter, there was a requirement to make three landings, engine off and finishing within a chalk circle of 50 yards diameter marked in the centre of the aerodrome. Needing an engine to get in was known as 'Rumbling'. Anyone needing to rumble had to buy the beer that night. We used to start flying before breakfast, usually by about 6.00 am.

It was at Old Sarum that I first met Corporal Lever. He was one of the kindest of men, large, grizzled, tough; an old soldier who knew every fiddle and who had a heart of gold. My particular chums at that time were Bruce Cooper, Pat Fraser (later Air Marshal Sir Pat Fraser) and Harry Burke. Corporal Lever looked after the

Bristol Fighters and by way of appreciation we sometimes took him into Salisbury where, over beer, he regaled us with stories of Iraq, Egypt and similar places. In return, he and his friends invited us on the last evening of camp to the Corporals' Club. It was that evening that I knew beyond any doubt that the only possible future for me was in the RAF. In fact all four of us came to that decision and for me at least, Corporal Lever was, I think, if not the only influence, certainly one of the most decisive. We served together again, for Corporal Lever joined me later as my Rigger in my first squadron, and again in the same capacity in the Fleet Air Arm. Although I never saw him again, the last I heard was that he had perished in 1942 as a Sergeant Air Gunner in a flying boat in the Indian Ocean. He was a gallant and loyal friend, to whom I owed a great deal.

After Old Sarum, and a spell at home, where I flew Cirrus Moths at Hucknall with the newly formed Nottingham Flying Club, I was sent to Coventry to do my annual Reserve Training, having been attached to the school run by Armstrong Whitworth, at Whitley Aerodrome. The aerodrome took its name from Whitley Abbey, and had been built in 1917/18 by German prisoners of war as a RFC stores depot. It was bought in 1920 by Armstrong Whitworth, and in 1923 the Reserve Flying School was formed there, with most of the aircraft production facilities formerly at Parkside in Coventry being moved there. It later gave its name to the 1939 Whitley twin-engine bomber.

In 1928 everything was still concentrated in wartime buildings located within the inner angle of what was still a small and inconvenient L-shaped grass aerodrome. The longest run in any direction was about 800 yards, and hazards included a small hill at the heel of the L (opposite the hangars) and a perimeter bounded by the rivers Sowe and Sharbourne, which were liable to floods. An overshoot into this area could result in the aircraft tipping onto its nose. The Chief Test Pilot and Chief Instructor was Alan Campbell-Orde and his deputy was Bennett-Baqqs.

I had the option of flying either the Armstrong Whitworth Wolf or the Jaguar-engine DH9 (DH9J). The Wolf, had been designed as a replacement for the Bristol Fighter. It stood very high and entry to the cockpit of its box-shaped fuselage was by means of a metal step ladder permanently attached to its port side. Of the six Wolves built, three disappeared into test programmes at Farnborough, and the others became part of the Whitley Reserve School. I opted for the DH9J, with its powerful 325hp Armstrong Siddeley Jaguar engine. It had a good take-off and climb and a landing speed of around 45mph at touchdown. Elevator and rudder controls were normal but lateral control I regarded, after the Bristol, as bad. Its principal defects were a heaviness which demanded two hands for any speedy rolling movement at more than 100mph, and an almost complete lack of feel at anything below 60mph. In the RFC DH9 this may have been less important, for with war load, external bomb racks, and gun ring, and other paraphernalia, landing speeds, and therefore approach speeds were higher because greater drag soon killed any tendency to float. With the DH9J drag was greatly reduced, resulting, in conjunction with a high tick-over speed of the Jaguar, in a marked tendency to float and, in the confines of Whitley, the absolute necessity of a dead accurate approach at a speed where aileron control retained little feel despite being still effective. It took me some time to master the aircraft, but it gave me my first serious lessons in really accurate flying. By the time I left I could manage the normal approach, without use of engine, and having maintained my speed on approach within 2 or 3mph of the optimum finish my landing run on the edge of the tarmac by the school hangar. The rest of that summer I spent flying whenever and wherever I could.

It was during the winter holidays of 1928 that I found an SE5A at Hucknall. Known as the Spitfire of the First World War, there was nothing, absolutely nothing, I wanted more than to fly it. It belonged to Major Savage, who owned a sky writing company. I got myself introduced to the pilot and ingratiated myself to him at the cost of many gallons of beer in local pubs. I succeeded in extracting a promise from him that after sky writing he would land back at Hucknall, leave the engine running for me, and let me have a go. When the great day came, I was on the tarmac wildly excited as the SE5A came into land. I watched the beer-sodden clot hit the boundary hedge and roll it up in a ball, which is how I lost the only chance I ever had to fly that most wonderful of all First World War single-seat fighters.

I was gratified to find that the RAF Reserve had assessed me as 'above average'. This enabled me to spend my final year at Cambridge doing a good deal more flying than might otherwise have been permitted.

My CUAS flying was all on Bristol Fighters at Duxford. At weekends, I continued to fly with the London Aeroplane Club at Stag Lane, and in the intervals did some work. This was essential because entry into the Regular RAF with a permanent commission required a degree, which I eventually achieved, in engineering, labelled 'Mechanical Sciences'.

It was during this final year that I first visited Martlesham Heath, first by air from Duxford in the autumn term and on several other occasions by air or by car. Martlesham had been established in 1911 as the Aircraft and Armament Experimental Establishment (AAEE). All RAF test flying was conducted at either Martlesham or at Felixstowe, where the Marine Aircraft Experimental Establishment (MAEE) was based.

A new generation of single-seater fighters were arriving at Martlesham for performance and other tests. These included the Avro Avenger I with a Napier Lion; the Westland Wizard, with the earliest Rolls-Royce Kestrel, and following these the Hawker Hornet, later for RAF service, renamed the Fury, and the Fairy Firefly. These two also used the Kestrel.

To us these were the most beautiful aeroplanes we had ever seen. We were privileged to climb in and out and all over them, and came to know each one intimately. And, of course, we saw them fly. It was here that I first met George Bulman, Hawker's famous Chief Test Pilot. To his superb skill, and profound understanding of pilots' needs, Hawker owed the fine handling of all their aeroplanes, from Woodcock to Hurricane and it was in the end the fact that it was a pilot's aeroplane that gave the Hawker product the edge over its otherwise evenly matched competitors. When, a few years later I flew the Fury and its Fleet Air Arm derivative, the Nimrod, I understood why Martlesham liked the little Hornet. It was an aeroplane that did not seem to require to be controlled. Rather it gave the feeling that it had become one's own wings, so that one had only to think a manoeuvre to be doing it. A bird no doubt flies with the same lack of conscious effort. The enjoyment of such flight is complete and known, I fancy, only to a limited few.

Martlesham at this period was a wonderful place. Museum pieces from the First World War shared hangars not only with the latest fighters, but one or more of nearly everything that the RAF possessed, or which it had on test. One such, a monster too big for any hangar, was the Beardmore Inflexible. This appeared at Martlesham, where it was assembled in March 1928, and was the toy, if the word can be applied to such a beast, of Squadron Leader Jacky Noakes. It had a span of 157.5 feet, weighed 16.5 tons empty, and was propelled by three Rolls Condors of 650hp each. Historically it is of great interest, being the first attempt by the RAF to obtain an all-metal heavy bomber. It was a narrow chord high-wing monoplane whose structure, almost entirely of duralumin, was based on the wartime work of Dr Rohrbach in Germany, and successfully applied to the construction of all metal flying boats for the German Navy. The deep mono-spar wing, with torsion stresses taken by the all metal skin anticipated the construction of the Spitfire, and other later aircraft including modern sailplanes. Some lift bracing, however, was provided, in the form of enormous stranded steel circular cables, one each side, of a size more suitable to a suspension bridge. Jacky Noakes, cavorting in an Avro 504 round trees and buildings needed to be seen to be believed. I later served twice under his command, and had the privilege of flying with him.

In early 1929 the RAF High Speed Flight was reforming at Felixstowe prior to its move to Calshot in order to defend the Schneider Trophy. Having visited Felixstowe I was invited to visit the flight at Calshot in the summer of 1929. Here I met Dick Atcherley, Squadron Leader Orlebar who was the flight commander, the engineer, Flying Officer T.H. Moon, as well as D'Arcy Greig, Stainforth and Waghorn.

Initially, the flight used a Fairey Flycatcher on floats, and two of the Gloster IV biplanes built with Rapier Lion engines for the 1927 contests at Venice. The Gloster IV I consider the most beautiful looking biplane ever built. But 1929 was the year of the monoplanes, and when we visited Calshot we were shown the Supermarine S6, with its Rolls-Royce 'R' engine, the direct ancestors of the Spitfire and the Merlin. Larger, and less graceful than the 1927 S5 which used the smaller Napier Lion, the S6, in retrospect, was the ultimate in single-propeller engine seaplanes. In its final development as the S6B, it retained for Britain the 1931 Schneider Trophy and, by giving this country three successive wins, permanent possession of the trophy.

In 1929 the Regia Aeronautica was our principal rival for the Schneider Trophy. The United States and French entries did not arrive at Calshot. The Italians relied upon the beautifully built Castoldi-designed Macchi M67, a development of the earlier Macchi M52 of 1927, but enlarged, and powered by the new Isotta-Fraschini eighteen-cylinder engine with its cylinders arranged in three banks of six. Painted a rich red they appeared in vivid contrast to the blue sea and sky, and the white spray and foam during take-off and landing. Macchi development under designer Castoldi followed very similar lines to that of Supermarine under R.J. Mitchell. The historical difference is that, whereas British development led directly to the Spitfire and the Merlin, Italian engine development faltered, and the few effective Macchi fighters were powered by German Daimler-Benz engines, and lacked the performance of either the Spitfire or Me109.

The Italian team was led by Lieutenant Colonel Bernasconi, and comprised of Captains Canaveri and Motta, Lieutenants Monti and Cadringher, Warrant Officer Dal Molin, and Sergeant Majors Agello, Gallone and Huber. Of these two were killed in training on Lake Garda, and Monti, Cadringher, and Dal Molin flew in the race. It was won for Britain by Waghorn at a speed round the triangular course of 328mph. Later, Orlebar, flying an S6, raised the World Speed Record to 357mph.

It is worth recording that in 1931 Ramsey MacDonald decided that it was not worth defending the Trophy; however the patriotism of Lady Houston, who put down the cash to pay for the defence, should be remembered. Without it, the continuing development leading to the Spitfire and Merlin would have been abandoned, with results that might have turned victory in the Battle of Britain only nine years later, into defeat.

During the eventful summer of 1929, having attended my second CUAS camp at Old Sarum and done a good deal more flying on Bristol Fighters, I was able to enjoy a sort of pilot's summer. At the Easter pageant at Lympne, I was given the job of looking after Dutch visitors who arrived in three most attractive little Pander sesquiplanes (fixed wing biplanes with one pair of wings longer than the other pair). It was powered by 80hp Walter five-cylinder radial engines. This was my first experience of a foreign aeroplane, and our generous Dutch guests allowed me to enjoy it to the full. Other visitors included the delicate little Klemm from Germany, with its seven-cylinder Salmson 40hp radial engine, which was very quiet, and the Blackburn Lincock.

Lympne was a port of call for trans-channel air traffic, including a huge twin-engine Farman biplane. My recollection of this conveyance is having seen twenty-four passengers embark through a large aperture in the side of the fuselage, watching with amazement whilst the cabin steward replaced a fuselage strut, which had been removed to make the entrance. He hooked up and re-tensioned the necessary wire cross bracing that held everything together. The Farman then took off for France.

Another pleasant interlude was a similar pageant at the Suffolk's Club at Hadleigh. Here I was re-introduced to the Blackburn Bluebird, a charming little side by side two-seater with an Armstrong Siddeley Genet engine. The Chief Instructor was George Lowdell. He returned to active service in 1939, and retired in 1946 as Wing Commander George Lowdell, AFC.

Yet another visit was to Conington Fen where the Cambridge Flying Club held a meet. For this I borrowed a Cirrus Moth from Hucknall. Thinking proceedings somewhat dull, I used it to give an unauthorised aerobatic display. Looking back I realise what bad manners this was, to say nothing of unexpected performances by inexperienced pilots without previous practice. On landing I was taken into a quiet corner by Wing Commander Vernon Brown, who happened to be there, and received the dressing down which I richly deserved. Shortly after this he gave me the recommendation which secured for me a permanent commission, complete with a year's ante-date of seniority in the RAF. The rocket he gave me came at exactly the moment which I think many young pilots go through at about the 300 hour stage of experience. One thinks one knows it all. With experience of some ten different types, and being somewhat spoilt by the privileged reception often accorded to CUAS members, I was grossly over confident. Some pilots don't survive this stage. Vernon Brown ensured that I did, and for this timely dressing down I owe him as much as for the good recommendation he subsequently gave me.

It may be useful here to say something about flying conditions in the 1930s. No aircraft had voice radio and few had W/T (Wireless Telegraphy). There was no such thing as Air Traffic Control or Airways, or Controlled Air Space and safety, mainly in visual flight conditions, relied upon sensible local rules at aerodromes and pilots seeing and being seen when flying. The air was not crowded, and collisions were almost unknown. If one wanted to go somewhere, one just went, just as by car; or perhaps more accurately, as small boat sailors go today. There were no landing fees except at a few places, like Croydon, and to arrive at a Club aerodrome, like Hadleigh, for example, or Hamble, the home of the Hampshire Flying Club, was to be welcomed as a privileged and honoured guest. The same applied at most aircraft makers' aerodromes, and notable examples in this respect were Glosters at Hucclecote, Handley Page at Cricklewood, and Blackburns at Brough, all of which gave a special welcome to pilots from the CUAS.

CUAS members flew in grey flannel trousers and a blazer which constituted our recognised 'uniform'. Except for those few of us who were Reservists, we had no service obligations and rank and service regulations had little significance to us. The declared purpose of the Cambridge and Oxford University Air Squadrons when they were formed was not to recruit for the RAF, but to indoctrinate those selected undergraduates who, in their future careers, might be expected to rise to positions of industrial or political power, in which they could be expected to understand and to support the needs of the still infant RAF. This was the plan of the great Lord Trenchard (Chief of Air Staff). The fact that the two squadrons provided many officers for the RAF was, at first, a by-product of the scheme.

In these circumstances we mixed easily with everybody concerned with flying and were guests, as I have recounted, at places like Martlesham, Felixstowe and Calshot, as well as of Frederick (later Sir Frederick) Handley Page, and Rolls-Royce at Derby. Equally we were welcomed at Old Sarum in the Corporals' Club and our range of friends and acquaintances was very wide. I at any rate felt privileged to fly about the country in a variety of aeroplanes with no particular restrictions, and little supervision. I enjoyed myself hugely!

Thus it was that in company with Sheraton Swan, latterly a director of Swan & Hunter at Wallsend on Tyne, I watched the 1929 Schneider Trophy race. I reported for duty to the Adjutant at No 1 Flying Training School, RAF Netheravon on 1 September 1929. I was in uniform for the first time, as a Pilot Officer in the RAF, and became one of the smallest cogs in a big wheel. I was subject twenty-four hours a day to RAF discipline as described in *King's Regulations* and *Air Council Instructions*, and all the more detailed and legal provisions detailed in the *Manual of Air Force Law* (MAFL). The change in status was much the same as leaving prep school as a prefect to become a junior fag at a public school. My first task in the RAF was to incorporate all the overdue amendments in the old copies of *King's Regulations*, *Air Council Instructions* and *Manual of Air Force Law*, which were the first text books issued to me by a welcoming RAF.

CHAPTER TWO
JOINING THE RAF

Netheravon was one of the oldest and most historic stations of the RAF, and before that the RFC. It had been an RFC camp since 1913, and in June 1914 was the scene of a concentration of the Royal Flying Corps in anticipation of the move to France two months later when war broke out.

When we arrived in September 1929 it had changed little from its wartime aspect. There were two post-war steel and brick hangars but the majority of buildings were 1913 RFC pattern. These included the Officers' Mess, over the entrance of which were mounted RFC wings. Adjoining the Mess, and on two other sides of the square bordering a rose garden and tennis courts were square bungalows, each containing four rooms for officers; bathrooms and lavatories, and a batman's room. These were well built in brick, and were put up in 1913. The four of us from the CUAS, Pat Fraser, Josh Braithwaite, Robert Harston and I were all fortunate enough to be put into one of these comfortable bungalows. One batman looked after the occupants of each bungalow, putting out clothes, pressing and cleaning, and caring for laundry. They were all old hands at the business, and for the most part took great pride in seeing that their charges were smartly and properly turned out, and never late for early morning colour-hoisting parades. Colour hoisting was at 0800, wet or fine; and only the foulest weather, when the Padre's prayers were blown to the skies, or drowned in torrential rain caused parades to be cancelled. On these occasions the rough weather ensign was hoisted at 0800 by the Duty Corporal, assisted by the Duty Sergeant and the orderly Officer Under Instruction, the latter always a pupil from the Flying Training School (FTS). Normally the whole station attended these parades, which were conducted with considerable ceremony.

From the parade ground, at the lower end of the camp, everybody then marched to work. On Saturdays FTS pupils remained on the parade ground for drill, under the orders of a small team of drill sergeants. In turn we marched, slow-marched, and wheeled as members of a squad; or, standing isolated in the far corner of a wind-swept parade ground, bellowed unheeded orders to about turn, as a squad of our fellow pupils retreated into the distance; and on at least one occasion marched out of sight and beyond recall across the plain. On these Saturday mornings I had some slight advantage, having risen to the lordly rank of Platoon Sergeant in the Officers' Training Corps (OTC) at Cheltenham. At Cheltenham military precision, both with small arms and marching, was an important subject at a time when half its pupils went either to Sandhurst or Woolwich.

Our course senior pupil, Charles Gill, had served in the Royal Canadian Mounted Police. He stood well over 6 feet and had an air of authority and command of language that disarmed even the toughest Drill Sergeant. Gill, however, was the kindest of men; he was content and exercised his authority by diplomacy. He was universally liked and respected.

Our course, Number 14, comprised of thirty-four pupils. The whole course, including two month's leave, lasted for twelve months. At any one time there were two courses running at Number 1 FTS. New arrivals trained on the Avro 504 but after six months the survivors moved onto the senior flying course using the Atlas. The whole twelve months resulted in a total of between 120 to 150 hours of flying time per pupil. Depending on the pupil's rate of progress, between a third and a half would have been dual flying.

At the end of the year the pilots would receive their wings and were then posted to squadrons. With the average intake on a course at around forty, about two-thirds would normally qualify. The four of us from the CUAS, already having gained our wings as reservists, joined the senior term of Number 14 course and flew the Atlas. At this time entry into the RAF as a pilot was either through the Cadet College at Cranwell, direct from school, and corresponding to entry into Sandhurst. This was the route designed for a full career in the RAF, but was supplemented by university graduates, who entered as we did through one of the five Flying Training Schools then in existence.

The principle task, however, was to train both officer and NCO pilots who engaged upon a five year short service engagement. At the end of their five years the very best who applied were selected and could obtain a permanent commission, and so join the select band who had arrived via Cranwell or a university. The remainder then received a lump sum gratuity and undertook a further period of reserve liability. The scheme was the brainchild of Lord Trenchard and without it the great expansion of the RAF prior to the Second World War would have been impossible.

Many of the FTS pupils were fitters and riggers already serving in the RAF. They became Sergeant Pilots, and many were later commissioned. Perhaps the best evidence of the success of Lord Trenchard's forward planning was that by 1947 most of the Air Council and nearly all the most senior commanders, including Commanders-in-Chief, had originally entered the RAF on a Short Service Commission.

Our Number 14 course at Netheravon was a splendid mixture of people. I remember Cooke and Bishop. They bought a retired Fokker seven to eight seat monoplane from KLM. Another friend was Reggie Beaton, brother of Cecil Beaton. I visited London with him on many occasions in his Alvis 12/50 two-seater. Frequently we would only return from London with just enough time to change into uniform for morning parade. In those days Number 1 dress was breeches and puttees; white shirt and hard, starched white collar; cane and leather gloves. This uncomfortable and inappropriate rig had been designed as a combination of naval and army uniform, in order to satisfy both elements of these services. Eleven years later, when I joined, we were still suffering from this inept compromise and continued to do so until at least officially the RAF medical service condemned breeches, puttees and hard collars as likely to restrict circulation at high altitude.

The four of us from the CUAS, because of our previous experience and qualifications, were not required to do the whole year's course. We joined No 14 at the half-way point when it became the senior course at Netheravon and began to fly the Atlas. The Jaguar engine was already familiar, being similar to the earlier model fitted to the DH9J. The Armstrong Whitworth Atlas, which I had first seen at Bagington had been the successful competitor in a competition to find a replacement for the venerable Bristol Fighter. It was also all-metal, using mainly steel strip and rolled sections, the whole being fabric covered. Having been accepted for Army Cooperation duties, a two-seater dual-control version followed, and this was the equipment of the advanced training flights at Netheravon.

The Atlas was notable for its solid and rather heavy feel. It seemed to have no particular vices, but was generally sluggish on controls; with a span of 40 feet, and an all up weight of 4,000 pounds. Its 400hp Jaguar engine gave it a top speed of 140mph at sea level. It was very strong, which was just as well, for we made it do everything possible. This included some unauthorised and certainly unorthodox aerobatics. It was the first aeroplane in which I blacked myself out. At first, being unable to see, I thought I had gone up into a grey cloud that I had not noticed, but it then got darker, at which point I abandoned my attempted manoeuvre and let the Atlas sort itself out. It did and I regained my sight in an earthward dive, though not going very fast and, fortunately, with plenty of height between me and Salisbury Plain.

On another day three of us decided to see if the Atlas would do a bunt. A bunt is, in effect, half an outside loop starting at the top; at the bottom one is, of course, upside down, and regains the normal upright position by means of a half roll. We had seen this manoeuvre at the Hendon Air Pageant when the pilots were flying Genet Moths. Realising that the Atlas was not quite like a Moth we approached our attempts with some caution, deciding that the best procedure would be to reduce to stalling speed, with the nose fairly well up, then push the stick firmly forward, and hold it there. This worked, though for my part I had a bad moment looking at the excessive airspeed when getting well over the vertical. I persevered on realising that to change my mind and pull back would result in even higher speed. After that it worked, though when we taxied in, at least one Atlas looked a bit droopy with some re-tensioning of anti-lift wires needed. But this and other experiments gave us great confidence in the Atlas and, more importantly, experience in recovery from what are now termed as unusual positions. The bunt, and the complete outside loop are now, of course, standard manoeuvres in any kind of competition and display aerobatics.

For some reason my instructor did not like aerobatics, which was one reason for the solo experiments. Flying Officer Willie Watt, who was a superb pilot, showed me how to make the Atlas do things safely that I would have thought impossible. Before he left to become staff instructor at Central Flying School then at Wittering, he paid me a singular compliment. One day, at the completion of our course, he flew me over to Upavon, the home of Nos 3 and 17 Squadrons, both flying Bristol Bulldogs. I duly admired the Bulldogs and was astonished when he said quite quietly 'Would you like to fly one now?' Twenty minutes later I was airborne in my first genuine single-seat fighter. It had all the handling qualities of the Jupiter Fighter and the rumble of its own 490hp Jupiter engine was sweet music after hours of clattering Jaguars. With a span of 32 feet and all up weight of 3,500 pounds it was smoothly agile. Its top level speed was 174mph, easily exceeded in a dive and this was the first time I exceeded 200mph. Forty minutes later I landed; or more accurately the Bulldog landed me, doing it gracefully and easily as though anything untidy were impossible. The slightly humped fuselage, cowling sloping down to the engine, and the pilot's eyes nearly level with the trailing edge of the centre section confirmed marvellous visibility and a sense of control. I taxied in, and walked on air for the rest of the day. I wanted nothing more than to be posted to Bulldogs at Upavon and it was only later that I realised that Willie Watt, bless him, had arranged all of this and it was all part of a generous and kindly pilot to get me into his old squadron. No instructor could do more for his pupil. Sadly, as I will relate, the Air Ministry had other ideas.

Willie Watt later represented Britain in the first international soaring contests held at the Wasserkuppe in Germany just before the Second World War. He flew one of the Kirby King Kites built by Slingsbys to Mungo Buxton's design (later Group Captain) and as a member of Air Intelligence in 1945 retrieved and flew the first Me262 jet fighter back to England. Watt took command of a Hampden squadron at Waddington when the Second World War broke out. Tragically a defective instrument landing beam in zero visibility led to him losing his life when his aircraft hit the closed steel doors of a hangar.

When the time came to leave No 1 FTS I achieved a reasonable place of third in the passing out list. I was pipped for second place by Leading Aircraftsman Rose and by Pat Fraser, who had a clear lead with a ninety-six per cent pass mark. Rose was promoted to Sergeant Pilot and was transferred to 101 Squadron. Pat Fraser went to India for five years. Robert Harston, who finished in fourth place, went to Iraq, Josh Braithwaite and I were both posted to No 13 Army Cooperation Squadron on February 12 1930. We would fly a variant of the Armstrong Whitworth Atlas.

I was posted to A Flight, commanded by Flight Lieutenant Wadbrooke and Josh to C Flight. The squadron commander was Squadron Leader Cole-Hamilton. It was a very happy squadron and equipped with the Army Cooperation version of the Armstrong Whitworth Atlas. As the squadron was based at Netheravon I was able to keep my old room in the mess, and already knew my way around. Almost best of all was to be intercepted on my way to report for duty on my first day with the squadron by my old friend Corporal Lever of the CUAS days. He informed me that I was to be posted to his flight and that he had arranged for me to have the newest Atlas allotted for my use. He added that he would be in charge of it, and would always fly as my gunner. Those were the days when the Air Gunners' Badge was a winged bullet, worn above stripes of rank on the left sleeve. The qualification was rewarded with extra pay, and all such gunners were recruited within the squadron from among its fitters and riggers. They trained and qualified in the squadron and anyone so fortunate as to have his gunner in charge of his aircraft, and an old hand at the game as well, was indeed well placed.

On Saturday mornings there was no flying, and we all polished our Atlas together, till it shone, as did the drip tray placed beneath the engine lest a drip of oil blemish the swept and chalked hangar floor. At 1100 inspections began. First the Flight Commander, accompanied by the Flight Sergeant; nothing escaped that eagle-eyed pair; a bit of mud still clinging to a tail skid could earn the pilot of the aircraft an extra orderly officer duty. So, by the time Squadron Leader Cole-Hamilton, accompanied by the Adjutant, Geoffrey Simonds, and the Squadron Warrant Officer came round everything was spotless and immaculate. Crews stood together, pilot in clean, white overalls, his crew in blue in front of their aircraft, lined up with exact precision along either side of the hangar.

After inspection the weekend began. Reggie Beaton and I usually went off to London in his 12/50 boat-tailed Alvis. Tragically around this time Reggie fell disastrously and impossibly in love. No one will ever know the true story, but Reggie's life ended under a tube train on the Piccadilly Line. The coroner recorded accidental death and I lost a much-loved friend.

Once a month, the whole squadron had to attend Church Parade. In best blue, which in those days meant breeches and puttees, hard white collars, gloves and cane, we paraded regardless of religion or lack of it on the Netheravon parade ground. The parade was compulsory for all. However on arrival at the church the command was given 'fall out the other denominations'. The ODs were allowed to hang about outside the church until after the service. They then rejoined the parade and marched with it back to camp. The station warrant officers were known to take the names of those who waited outside, with a view to checking that their service papers identified them as authentic ODs. Those that avoided church service on false pretences appeared as defaulters on Monday mornings.

All this discipline we endured together. We swapped tales about it, laughed at those who suffered and enjoyed listening to those that had cleverly got away with something. We were in fact a very close family and led by Cole-Hamilton and his three flight commanders, Wadbrooke, Searle and Paul Tankerville Chamberlayne, we were welded into a happy and efficient unit. With twelve aircraft, our crews and our complement of administrators, cooks, butchers, and batmen, we totalled about a hundred all told.

An Army Cooperation pilot was expected to know a great deal about the army.

Close reconnaissance and with it recognition of troops on the ground, artillery spotting and control of shoots, air photography and occasional strafing with small bombs and the front gun were all required tasks. There was no R/T (radio transmission), all communication was by W/T (wireless transmission) in Morse and we spent many hours perfecting our tapping and reading. The gunner's job was to ensure the safety of his pilot whilst engaged on these jobs.

The gunner had a Lewis gun on a Scarff ring mounting in his rear cockpit. He also, when rare occasions demanded it, acted as a high level bomb aimer; and was responsible for reeling out and later hauling in the long, trailing W/T aerial on which our Morse code communications depended. When right out this extended some 100 feet below the aircraft and had a lead weight on the end of it.

Normally an Army Cooperation pilot was not deemed to be qualified until he attended and passed the three months course at the School of Army Cooperation at Old Sarum. Josh Braithwaite and I escaped this chore and qualified on the job.

One of my first expeditions in 13 Squadron was when our flight went off on its own in the early spring of 1930 to work with units of the Army's Eastern Command. We were entirely self-contained, lived in our own tents, and although we were actually located on the grass aerodrome at Henlow, we lived away on the far side of it, and were not allowed to use any of the permanent facilities, even to get a bath. There were two good reasons for this; the first of course, was that we were expected to be able to follow the Army into the field, and to look after ourselves wherever they required us to follow. I remember well constructing, with spade, buckets and seats supplied from stores the flight lavatories, following exactly the instruction contained in the RAF's quite superb Field Service Pocket Book.

It was a kind spring, and we flew from dawn to dusk. Our cooks were good, and we all enjoyed this expedition, except for one thing, for it was to test under field service conditions, the RAF's field dress.

This requires some explanation. In 1930 we were still in the age of puttees, inherited from British India, and universal in the Army in 1914 to 1918. However the RFC had departed from strict dress regulations to cope with the cold and altitude, as well as the requirements of freedom of movement. By 1930 the emphasis was upon strict observance of dress regulations; and for reasons which remain to me a complete mystery, the field service dress for the RAF was identical to that for Church Parade. Every day at Henlow, having washed and shaved in our canvas basins, made up our camp beds, and dressed as for Church Parade, we went about our work with Eastern Command. As a result we were able to render an utterly damning report on the unsuitability of the current field service dress, and every man who, since then, has been able to fly in more suitable dress owes to us some thanks for what we endured.

Later in the spring, the whole squadron moved into camp at Odiham. There were no permanent buildings and the aerodrome was a grass field. The mess was a large marquee and we all lived in bell tents. The only one who did not was the squadron doctor, who lived in his ambulance, where he also maintained a well stocked bar much favoured by those of us who had returned too late from London to catch the transport from Hook Station, which was timed to arrive back at the camp before the mess bar closed. At Odiham, together with 4 Squadron based at Farnborough, we came under the operational control of the GOC Aldershot.

Each spring began with individual training, progressing to training first small, and then in increasingly large formations up to battalion level. In the late summer we would carry out manoeuvres with large forces consisting of several divisions. After that everyone went on summer leave for a month.

A major excitement during this leave period with 13 Squadron was to be allowed to borrow for a weekend that superb 'mini-fighter' the Blackburn Lincock; with a 285hp Lynx engine, no guns or equipment, this compact little biplane was an aerobatic delight. I remember my special pride in being able to demonstrate, to what I hoped were admiring friends, two successive upward vertical rolls, followed by a stalled turn and further similar tricks. It was the first truly aerobatic aeroplane I flew. I loved it, and was sad indeed, when, after a weekend of displays, I had to return it to its owners, the Blackburn Brothers at Brough-on-Humber. I flew home to the squadron in my staid old Army Cooperation Atlas.

It was in 1930, between camps at Henlow and Odiham that I first flew a Hawker Hart. This was J9945, which Jerry Sayer flew down to Netheravon from Brooklands, when he was testing and demonstrating for Hawkers under George Bulman, their great Chief Test Pilot. Jerry Sayer, a young man of great personal charm: as well as flying skill later became famous as the first British pilot to fly a jet. This was the Gloster Whittle E28/39 which made its first flights in his charge in May 1941 from Cranwell. Sadly Jerry Sayer later lost his life in an accident. In 1930 he was taking the Hart round the Army Cooperation Squadrons to get pilots' opinions on its suitability as an Atlas replacement. The eventual result was the Audax. To all of us who flew it the Hart was a revelation. It handled like a dream, and its Rolls Kestrel engine gave it a top speed 50mph more than our Atlas. Its aerodynamic cleanliness resulted in some difficulty in losing speed, whereas with the Atlas, closing the throttle resulted in an immediate slowing down, the Hart seemed to go on and on. In landing, the effect, after the Atlas, was reminiscent of that earlier described on the DH9J. But once one got used to it, and in particular to the precise control maintained right down to the stall, the Hart could be put down from the conventional engine off glide just as precisely, and in no more space, than the old Atlas. A new and intriguing noise was the full-throated roar from the Kestrel's twelve, short exhaust stubs, and the crackle and popping when the throttle was closed. The Audax, when it appeared, was rather less exciting. In the course of development it had acquired long exhaust pipes; a message picking up hook, and other Army Cooperation paraphernalia, and added a good deal of weight; but it was still a great advance on the Atlas.

After this excitement the squadron went to practice camp at Sutton Bridge, on the Wash. Here we spent one month at front gun, rear gun and bombing practices on the ranges. Normally, all this was at low level, and we seldom flew higher than

1,000 feet. We used plenty of live 303 ammunition and dive bombed with small practice bombs filled with stannic chloride, which, on bursting produced quantities of white smoke. The Atlas was a poor front gun platform, being difficult to hold steady on the large balanced rudder when diving onto a ground target. Aided by Corporal Lever, I fitted to my Atlas a large aluminium plate, which was carried by two spruce spars extending 2 feet beyond the designed trailing edge of the rudder. This made my Atlas stable in a dive, and vastly improved my shooting. This illicit modification was roundly condemned by a visiting engineer staff officer, and had to be removed; but not before I had achieved a score which my brother officers, too late to copy my rudder, were unable to equal.

The climax of my month at Sutton Bridge was the day on which Corporal Lever and I were allowed to drop a live bomb. This was a 20 pound cooper bomb, left over from 1918. To do this we were required to climb to 13,000 feet, and to aim at a target well out on the mudflats in the Wash. Corporal Lever aimed and released the bomb from the back cockpit, using a bomb sight fitted in the floor; he directed me, his pilot, by instructions through the voice pipe, known as the Gosport tube. It was one of those misty days when sea and sky merge, and the land is visible only in a small area below; not a problem with modern instruments, but in the Atlas of 1930, relying on Air Speed Indicator, altimeter, compass, and bubble cross-level, not easy to fly accurately. However, having clambered up to 13,000, we finally managed a successful run up to the target, release the bomb, and in great excitement circled to see our target demolished. For all that happened our bomb might have floated quietly away across the North Sea. Nobody, not even the ground markers ever saw sign or trace of it; it just vanished. It was ten years before I dropped another live bomb. And then it was for real.

On our last weekend at Sutton Bridge I was allowed to borrow the station Moth to fly to Hucknall, to spend the weekend with my parents in Nottingham. On Monday, the NW wind was so strong at Hucknall that when my wing tip walkers released the Moth, and I opened the throttle, it climbed almost vertically and, turning downwind, covered the journey back to Sutton Bridge at 140mph. Sutton Bridge were alert and ready, and the ground crew caught hold almost as it landed. The next day we returned to our tented camp at Odiham. Everything ended with a bang on the last day of June, when the Adjutant, Geoff Simmonds, informed me, sorrowfully, that I was posted to Gosport, for Fleet Air Arm conversion training with effect from 1 July. There was a compensation that made up for almost everything. In his final report my Squadron Commander awarded me that coveted and rarely given pilot assessment of 'Exceptional', a rating which I was proud to retain in every subsequent pilot report so long as they were made on me.

CHAPTER THREE
FLEET AIR ARM

On 1 July 1930 I reported to the station Adjutant, Flight Lieutenant Hayworth-Booth, at RAF Gosport. He quickly passed me on to E Flight, under Flight Lieutenant Anderson; ex RFC, redheaded and a charming irascible extrovert.

Gosport aerodrome was pretty much as it had been in 1918, except that some new hangars had been added. The Officers' Mess was in the old moated Fort Grange at the southern end of the aerodrome, and the Sergeants lived in Fort Rowner, a similar construction at the northern end. These were two of the chain of forts constructed during the Napoleonic Wars to protect Portsmouth. My cabin, entirely underground and without much natural light, was actually very comfortable. It opened out into the inner courtyard of the fort. The earth-covered top was overgrown with dense brambles and shrubs, and was the home of flocks of nightingales whose nightly serenade seemed to be stimulated rather than discouraged by human noise from the fort. To get out of the fort one passed through a tunnel below the earthworks, through great wooden gates, and over a drawbridge. Nearly all the mess staff were ex-Royal Marines, and each day my batman would enquire if I would be going ashore after duty, and if so what clothes to put out.

Gosport at that time was one of the main bases of the Fleet Air Arm when ashore. When I reported at Gosport, it was still best known by its 1914-18 name of Fort Grange. I have also noted that my daily rate of pay as a junior Flying Officer was eighteen shillings and eight pence a day, and that I had managed to accumulate rather more than 400 hours total flying time.

My initial stay at Gosport was brief, for within a week I was sent to RAF Station Leuchars, near St Andrews, Fife to do my conversion training on to the Fairey IIIF, at that time newly introduced as successor to the Fairey IIID as the standard deck landing Fleet Spotter/Reconnaissance aircraft. Leuchars at that time was, like Gosport, a purely grass aerodrome whose buildings had remained unaltered since 1918. All pilots intended for the Fleet Air Arm went to Leuchars to convert to the type they would fly from carriers. At that time the Fleet Air Arm was made up of RAF and RN pilots in about equal proportions, with a few Royal Marine officers as well. All Observers and Telegraphist Air Gunners (TAGs) came from the Navy; all servicing and maintenance was done by the RAF. When ashore, the whole organisation was under RAF discipline and when afloat it was under Navy discipline.

At Leuchars there were three flights; the fighter conversion flight, with Fairey Flycatchers; the torpedo conversion flight, with a mixture of Blackburn Darts and the newly introduced Ripon; and the Spotter Reconnaissance Flight, commanded by Flight Lieutenant 'Farmer' Brill. My course-mates were Spendlove, Geoffrey Fairtclough and Sanderson, all destined for Flycatchers; and Rees, Heyworth-Booth and Beynon, for IIIFs. Sanderson and Heyworth-Booth (from Gosport) and Beynon had all fought in the 1914-18 war, in which the first named had gained a DFC, and the second both a DFC and MC. The rest of us were post-war products, Spendlove and Fairtclough from Cranwell and Rees on a five-year short service commission. There were several other conversion courses in progress, which included between twenty and thirty RN and RM officers straight from training at No 1 Flying Training School at Netheravon .

The Fairey IIIF with its 570hp geared Napier Lion enclosed in a good streamlined fairing, had a maximum speed of 120mph and a loaded weight of 6,300 pounds. The crew comprised pilot, observer, and TAG, who spoke to each other by means of the still prevalent Gosport tube. The two-bay biplane wings had the Fairey camber changing flaps, and could be folded for stowage in the carrier's hangar. The span was 45 feet 9½ inches, reduced to a bare 13 feet folded.

I recall the IIIF as a pleasant aeroplane, with heavy aileron control which became increasingly noticeable as the camber wound on because the ailerons as well as the flaps were included in the camber changing gear. I never liked this, because at the low end of the speed range where a delicacy in feel is advantageous, it was lacking. The pilot's cockpit was comfortable and warm. To maintain engine temperature the under-slung radiator was retracted out of the slipstream into the fuselage, thus providing the pilot with warmth. The observer and TAG, on the other hand, lived in a cockpit like an open bath, and were constantly windblown and frozen.

In early August, having completed my IIIF conversion, I moved on to Calshot for floatplane training. All Fleet Air Arm aircraft at that time could be put on floats, so this was an essential part of a carrier pilot's training, just as much for pilots flying off catapults in other kinds of ship.

At Calshot we were the last course to go through the old Fairey IIID. In general the IIID might be termed an unsophisticated, un-streamlined, slower variant of the IIIF which replaced it. From the pilot's point of view one big difference was the engine cooling plumbing. There were two non-retractable radiators with shutters, one on either side outside the cockpit. There seemed to be a profusion of hot water pipes about the place, and carelessness could result in scalded fingers. The IIID was the last floatplane in the RAF to use a tail float in conjunction with two short main floats instead of the later practice which employed just two long main floats and no tail float.

After Calshot, and some summer leave, we returned to C Flight at Gosport, to complete the final stage of Fleet Air Arm training, that is Aerodrome Dummy Deck Landings (ADDLs, pronounced Addles) followed by the actual thing. Addles at Gosport were conducted by placing two prominent upright boards, representing the end of the deck, out on the aerodrome, and requiring the pilot to touchdown accurately a few short yards beyond them. A constant stream of Darts, Ripons, Flycatchers, AVRO Bisons, Blackburns and Fairey IIIFs were engaged in the roundabout at Gosport in the weeks before the arrival of HMS *Courageous* for the great day towards the end of September, before she embarked her regular flights for the autumn cruise.

All of us, including the sailors among us anticipated deck landings next day with some apprehension. Nor were we wrong, for when the aircraft which we were to use were flown out next day from Gosport to the ship, now off St Catherine's in the Isle of Wight, the first to land on, with an instructor piloting, broke its undercarriage and, waved off, returned to Gosport. The next aircraft, an AVRO Bison, broke its undercarriage, and remained, flat looking, in the middle of the deck. It took two hours to clear the deck and get remnants below. After lunch we landed on the remaining training aircraft, and called it a day, anchoring off Bembridge for the night. Early next day training landings began. The drill was that each pilot completed at least two approaches, and overshoots. If these were satisfactory, he was allowed to attempt his landings. To qualify, three successive good landings were required and, in those days, we had no hooks or arrester gear nor were there any dual controls in the aircraft we used. The pilot was alone. On touchdown on the deck the aeroplane was caught by a crew who grabbed wing tips or any other part of the aeroplane they could reach.

First away were the Blackburn Darts, all without trouble. Next the Flycatchers, two of which were finally waved off and sent back to Gosport, depriving us of two of the three single seaters for the rest of that day. Next morning it was the turn of the IIIFs. Mine was second turn, and went through without problems. So did number three. Number four swung on landing, capsized over the palisades, and sank in three minutes. The pilot was considered to have failed to qualify. And so it went on for five days during which time we lost two IIIFs overboard and damaged several other aircraft.

On Friday we re-entered Portsmouth and having disembarked returned to Gosport. In the event this wait at Gosport proved to be a long one. It was Air Ministry practice at this time to keep ready at Gosport a pool of ready-trained RAF pilots so that should a sudden vacancy arise the RAF should never prove unable to fill it. Fleet Air Arm Service was not universally popular in the RAF and it was widely believed that the only escape was to volunteer to take the five year course to qualify as a Japanese interpreter.

After a tedious initial wait life in C Flight at Gosport became rather fun. There were a wide variety of aircraft there and eventually I was allowed to fly all of them, as well as some of the strange things that did not belong to C Flight at all. These included the Fairey Flycatcher; the Blackburn Dart Torpedo carrier, and its replacement the Blackburn Ripon, the huge and hideous AVRO Bison, and the equally odd Blackburn Blackburn. The two latter were spotter reconnaissance aircraft built to an Admiralty specification which provided the naval observer with an enclosed cabin. The pilot sat high up in front of the leading edge of the top centre-section; below him was the Napier Lion engine, and his feet were almost on top of the centre cylinder block. The view was, of course, superb but the performance of these monstrosities was minimal. The AVRO Bison was alleged to be capable of a maximum level speed of 110mph, and the Blackburn 100mph, but none of those which I flew were able to get near it. Most remarkable of all was a Blackburn Blackburn equipped at Farnborough to carry, pick-a-back, a target glider. Released from the parent aircraft, it was then controlled by radio by the naval observer, and used as a target for naval gunfire. I collected one of these from Farnborough and found that its already poor rate of climb was further decreased, presumably by the additional weight of extra gear now fitted. It was barely 500 feet a minute and to achieve this brought the Napier Lion close to the boil. Fortunately it was raining hard most of the time and every time we passed through a good rainstorm, the engine cooled off. But it was a nasty trip with lots of low cloud, and to avoid high ground we followed the old railway line. I was glad when we got to Gosport.

It was also at Gosport that I had my first blind flying course. For this purpose a flight of three Hawker Tomtits arrived at Gosport in charge of Flight Lieutenant V.B.J. Jackson from CFS. Instruments comprised turn and slip indicator, the usual ASI, altimeter, and magnetic compass. A large part of the instruction comprised correct interpretation of such things as the vagaries of a magnetic compass under the influence of northerly turning error, and understanding the performance of ASI when recovering from dives and unusual positions. The final test comprised a forty-five minute flight in which the pupil pilot taxied out under the hood, and remained there until, by his own dead reckoning, it was hoped, his accurate flying returned on time at 1,000 feet, over the aerodrome. Several of us actually succeeded in this; but most of all I remember V.B.J. Jackson as my first encounter with the superlative skill of a CFS Staff instructor, and the Tomtit as quite the most attractive small trainer I ever flew.

On 1 January 1931 I was posted to No 446 Flight, Fleet Air Arm, for duties on HMS *Courageous*. She had been laid down in 1915 as a light battle cruiser. The *Courageous* emerged in 1928 with a deck 570 feet in length.

My cabin, right down aft was in what was known as the sub-officers flat. I was fortunate not to be in a hammock like several of my friends, because we were a crowded ship, our normal complement of around 1,200 being swelled by others taking passage with us to Gibraltar where they were to join HMS *Eagle*. I shared my cabin with an old hand at deck flying, Lieutenant Commander Byass, known throughout the Fleet Air Arm as 'Boozy' on account of his family connection with the world famous sherry of Gonzales Byass. He proved a charming and considerate cabin-mate, and brought home to me the fact that whatever battles between RAF and Navy might be in progress in Whitehall, no such conflicts existed afloat. The flight Commander was Lieutenant Commander Joe Malleson. His senior pilot was Lieutenant Dick Pugh and the third naval pilot was Lieutenant J.C.D. Little. Then we had two Royal Marines, both called Martin, and myself. As the only RAF pilot in 446 Flight, I was allocated the Senior Observer, Lieutenant Commander John Harvey.

At the time I joined her, *Courageous* carried two Flycatcher flights, Nos 401 and 402; two of Dart Torpedo Bombers, Nos 463 and 464; and our two flights of Fairey IIIFs, Nos 44 and 446. Some years later, the flights of six aircraft each were joined in pairs to become squadrons of twelve aircraft each. Thus 401 and 402 became 800 Squadron and the two Dart flights 810 Squadron and the IIIFs 820 Squadron.

In the years between the wars it was the practice for the Atlantic Fleet to assemble in January at Gibraltar, whilst the Mediterranean Fleet assembled at Malta. After a month or so of individual exercises of increasing complexity, the spring training culminated in a wargame in which the two fleets opposed each other. After this, both Fleets assembled at Gibraltar for a week or ten days of analysis, accompanied by a good deal of festivity.

The climax of this training came in March when the Mediterranean Fleet defended the approaches to Malta against incursion by the opposing Atlantic Fleet. These exercises were somewhat unrealistic, because Government policy restricted all ships, except the two opposing carriers, to no more than economical cruising speeds. Once we had found the Mediterranean Fleet and its various components, everybody knew it could not move fast or far, and the opposing Admirals planned their Jutland type encounter of big ships in slow motion.

In the end, the Mediterranean Fleet were deprived of their carrier *Glorious* when she rammed an American cargo ship the *Florida* in a sudden sea-fog. Her aircraft, having flown off before the fog were all aloft, mostly far away from the accident. Her Flycatchers, however, were due to land and could see her down through the fog. They saw the *Florida* too. But without radio and no way to communicate they were helpless observers of the impending collision, and its rending impact, in which *Glorious* rammed the *Florida* broadside on. One RAF Flycatcher pilot more alert than the rest, did what he could. He landed in the sea, through the fog, ahead of *Glorious*, in an attempt to make her stop. But *Glorious*, attempting to get out of the fog so as to land her aircraft, ignored him, and he was picked up by the attendant destroyer. The two fleets then sailed for Malta, where we spent a fortnight.

On the way home we did some flying. One of my tasks in the Bay of Biscay was to tow a drogue target for the anti-aircraft guns of the Battle Squadron. The drogue, behind us on nearly two thousand yards of wire, made our IIIF a slow aeroplane. We flew a sort of race track pattern, so that all the guns on one side could have a go, and then returning on the other side of the ship, all the rest that could bear. It was a most impressive performance. Each time we turned, the wire with the drogue at the end of it followed rather as though glued to a track of rails, with ourselves as the labouring engine and the drogue the end van on the train. I found that, if we made the turn quite small, we then passed our drogue quite close and still going in the opposite direction. Fascinated by this, Corporal Lever, on this occasion acting as drogue operator, suggested that an embellishment would be to fly through the loop, and so tie a knot in the wire. This I declined but evidently the gunners were already confused, because there was a sudden bang, and the IIIF, freed from wire and drogue, fairly leapt ahead. On winding in Corporal Lever found the wire severed only ten feet beyond our rudder.

On returning to England *Courageous* was due for a refit at Portsmouth, which left me surplus to requirements. I was sent to Invergordon. The aerodrome was on the edge of the waters of the Cromarty Firth. The aerodrome itself had one small hangar. Next to it ran a little stream over which two foot-bridges led to the eight wooden huts that provided living quarters for the entire complement of the aerodrome. The Officers' Mess, whose tiny garden ran down to the stream, was two of these huts. My job was to fly a IIIF spotting for big ship shoots at towed screen targets. The spotting would normally have been the task of a naval observer but, as none was available, I did it myself and wondered why the Navy always insisted upon a dark blue to do it. It seemed to me not vastly different, and certainly no more difficult, from conducting a shoot by the Army.

In August I returned south for leave, and to Gosport, whence I was able to visit Calshot and see something of the 1931 Schneider Trophy team and their racing seaplanes.

My final expedition with 446 Flight was in the summer of 1932 when we flew from Netheravon to Catfoss for armaments practice camp. Catfoss, just inland from Hornsea and not far south of Bridlington, was a smallish grass airfield with wooden buildings and canvas Bessonneau hangars, by no means unlike many old airfields of the earlier Royal Flying Corps and Royal Naval Air Service days. Firing and bombing ranges were on the adjacent coast and, like Sutton Bridge and other ranges, were wonderful bird sanctuaries.

We were at Catfoss for a month but when we eventually left in drizzle and low cloud this was to be my last flight with 446 and my last with Corporal Lever. In the autumn I went into hospital for a nose operation and I returned to Gosport to become part of C Flight in November 1931. This in fact became a very enjoyable posting. For one thing I lived in considerable comfort in the newly opened mess, now the wardroom of HMS *Sultan*, and more important flew everything that Gosport had to offer. Being a spare pilot B Flight always had room for me to fly a IIIF doing Telegraphist/Air Gunner Training. A Flight, who provided towed and glider targets, sometimes needed a pilot. In the Torpedo Experimental Flight I had a very lucky break flying the first Hawker Horseley allocated to Gosport. There was also a good deal of ferry flying from Blackburns at Brough, Hawkers at Brooklands, and Faireys at Hamble and sometimes to ships at sea.

One unique experience at Gosport was my first amphibian, the Saunders-Roe Cutty-Sark. It had a flying boat hull, a monoplane wing, and above it a pair of Cirrus engines mounted on struts. Although rather underpowered, it was fun to fly, and handled nicely on the water. On land it seemed less happy. As far as I know only one or two were built, and it was succeeded by the similar but larger and more powerful Saunders-Roe cloud.

By this time I had accumulated over a thousand hours flying experience on a wide variety of types, and most important of all to me, kept my pilots assessment as 'exceptional'. However the Air Ministry rediscovered my engineering degree in August 1932 and I was posted to the RAF's two-year specialist engineering course at the Home Aircraft Depot at Henlow in Bedfordshire.

Henlow camp was built during the First World War by the Royal Flying Corps as the Home Aircraft Depot complementing the two depots in France: No 1 at St Omer and No 2 at Candas. Henlow's aerodrome was less in area than that covered by the workshops of the depot, which was intended to be able to overhaul and repair every type of aircraft used by the RFC, and later the RAF. In 1932 the wartime buildings were getting a little old, but all were still in use, including the wooden huts in which everybody lived. Besides the still active depot, Henlow stored aircraft and was the home of a Parachute Development Unit, using the last Vimy, flown by Mongoose Soden and ourselves, the Officers Engineering Course. Entries to the two year course were made each August, so that there were two courses present at anyone time, amounting to about sixty students. We got our severely rationed flying on Saturday mornings, in Moths although few students had their own aircraft. My own flying was enlivened by visiting my friends at Clubs; the London Club at Stag Lane, the Suffolk Club at Hadleigh, and the Nottingham Club, which about that time moved from Hucknall to the new aerodrome at Tollerton, on land provided for it by Sir Albert Ball, father of Albert Ball VC. Here I had experience of all the current British light aircraft, a field in which our country then led the world. They included the Avro Avian, the Blackburn Bluebird, and the BA Swallow, the British development of the delightful German Klemm monoplane. The Klemm had a 40hp seven-cylinder Salmson air-cooled radial engine which decorated the front of this graceful monoplane like a jeweller's brooch. The Salmson even at full power, made little more than a whisper of noise, and the Klemm handled like thistledown. It was among my favourites. But, best of all was an occasional visit to Harry Burke, still with 25 Squadron at Hawkinge. Here I was privileged to fly the squadron's Hawker Furies.

When I reached the end of our two-year stint I was among the most fortunate, being posted to the School of Naval Cooperation at Lee-on-the-Solent. I took up my new post on 1 August 1934, as a flight lieutenant. The base had been built by the RNAS in 1915 as part of their chain of seaplane stations. In 1934 some of the buildings were demolished and the base expanded inland, so by 1935 it was the only RAF station in England operating both land and seaplanes.

Lee-on-the-Solent, besides Area HQ, and the School of Naval Cooperation, the role of which was to train Naval Air Observers for the Fleet Air Arm, was the base for all catapult aircraft in HM Ships. This I found was my major responsibility. When a ship was commissioned, or re-commissioned, my job was to see that it got its seaplanes. At first these were mainly Fairey IIIFs and Ospreys, though later they included Sharks, Swordfish, the Fairey Sea-Fox, and Walrus. At first these arrived from Gosport by road, but in 1935, when the land aerodrome opened, I collected them from the base at Gosport if they were landplanes already in service or from the makers' aerodromes if they were new deliveries to the service.

However, my first task on arrival at Lee was to spend a fortnight across the water at Calshot, refreshing on floatplanes. The Fairey IIIDs had long since gone, but in their place I found the Fairey IIIF floatplane, the Avro Sea-Tutor, and in some ways the most interesting newcomer, the attractive little Fairey Sea-Fox with its 395hp Halford Napier air-cooled sixteen-cylinder engine.

In between engineering and testing I was able to get in a certain amount of routine flying in the training fliqhts at the School of Naval Cooperation. This was mainly on IIIF Seaplanes and in the course of this flew with many naval Observers who later attained either fame, or high rank, or both. I knew them well, of course for we all lived together in the Mess at Wickham Hall. Among them was Bill Beloe, eventually the last Admiral of the Nore.

When the aerodrome ashore was opened, the Telegraphist Air Gunner training came over from Gosport to Lee, and I flew with them too, first with IIIFs and later with Shark landplanes. But they were not such fun as the seaplanes, and flying round the sky trailing a long aerial inhibited any kind of adventure.

A most important and far reaching event in my life took place during my last year at Lee. It all started when I prepared an Osprey seaplane early in the year for the 10,000 ton Country Class cruiser *Dorsetshire* to take with her to the Far East; the China Station, and Hong Kong. The pilot was Lieutenant John Lane and from the start he took more than a usual interest in the preparation of his Osprey. John Lane had previously flown Flycatchers from HMS *Furious*; he played rugby for the Royal Navy for three years in a row. More significant, as it eventually turned out, his sister Rosemary was devastatingly lovely. We met first in May 1935 when I finally handed over to John his Osprey, and he took it away to Devonport to embark on *Dorsetshire*. John's three sisters, his mother Rachael Lane, and I stood together at the end of the cliff overlooking the Lee slipway to see him away. I never saw him go; I saw nothing but the loveliest person I had ever beheld. I expect I was incoherent and for the rest of the day, I thought of all the arresting things I might have said; my failure to invite them all to tea in the Mess and every sort of faux pas I imagined I could have committed to damn me for ever. By this time I was seriously in love and disturbed by the thoughts of a hundred and one other young men, each more attractive, amusing, rich, well-connected, and in every way more acceptable than ever I could be. Mrs Lane's friendly but cool attitude did nothing to dispel these fears.

It was Christmas 1935 that altered all this. It was, and perhaps still is, the custom at Lee for the members of the Mess on leave to pay the messing and wine expenses of the officer on duty over Christmas and this included one quest on Christmas Day. Greatly daring I invited Rosemary, and to my amazement she accepted.

All through that morning I did the Christmas Day rounds, helped serve dinner in the Airmen's Mess, was entertained in the Sergeants' Mess and arrived back at Wickham Hall in time to meet the Lane family. It very rapidly became obvious that the Duty Cook and Waiter were already well aware of the importance of the occasion. The table decoration, the excellent dinner, and the overwhelming tact of the obtrusive unobtrusiveness almost posed the question for us. I cannot ever know how, but it just appeared obvious to us both simultaneously that it was essential to tell the world that we were in love and intended to get married. So, the first people to know were the Duty Cook and Waiter and the fact that they appeared with a fresh bottle of champagne at the ready suggested to us later, when we thought about it, that our engagement was expected. The news went round Lee very rapidly, and by tea time congratulations and good wishes had arrived from the Sergeants' Mess and those of my own Flight still at Lee for Christmas. Later, we remembered that we ought to tell our parents.

In January 1936, after nearly two and a half years at Lee-on-the-Solent I was posted back to sea as the RAF Engineer Officer in HMS *Furious*. I arranged to join my ship by air, because this gave me two extra days to see my Rosemary. We planned our marriage as soon as *Furious* returned home in April.

Furious was the oldest of the three sisters, the other two being *Courageous*, my first ship, and *Glorious*. She was distinctive having no funnel or superstructure. Below the flight deck she had an upper and lower hangar, and below her upper deck she remained very much as first launched. I had a comfortable single cabin right aft on the starboard side, just below the small quarter deck. A large scuttle, which generally had to be kept shut at sea looked out onto the quarter deck ladder, so that I could, had I wished, have seen everybody who came aboard that way.

When I joined, Fleet Air Arm flights had been amalgamated in pairs to become squadrons. Consequently we had 801 Squadron, now equipped with Nimrods and Ospreys in place of its earlier Flycatchers; 821 Squadron flying Blackburn Sharks; and 811 Squadron flying Fairey Swordfish. Each squadron had twelve aircraft, making thirty-six in all. As a preliminary to joining I did some refresher deck landings in an Osprey, and eventually joined that way, flying one out as spare man for 801. Thereafter 801 treated me as a sort of honorary member, and when they disembarked I was very often able to go with them.

In late January we sailed for the Mediterranean and Alexandria. During the spring in Alexandria we got on with our training, working alternate weeks at sea and weeks in harbour. The aircraft mostly flew off to Aboukir before we came in; sometimes when a spare pilot was needed, I went too. Occasionally this was followed by an early morning flight to Cairo.

Towards the end of March the ships began to leave Alexandria. *Glorious* was last but one to go and gave a cocktail party the evening before she sailed for Malta. On the way home we stopped briefly at Malta and Gibraltar, flew off our aircraft not far from Cornwall, and came up the harbour to lie alongside in Devonport on the early morning tide. Important events were at hand. The Spanish Civil War, German rearmament, the change of Government, in which Baldwin succeeded Ramsey MacDonald as Prime Minister and underground, still masked and quiet, rumblings now even in England about Edward VIII and Mrs Simpson. But all this mattered little to me, for banishing every other thought was our marriage on 10 April 1936. Our best man was Geoffrey Fairclough and 801 Squadron was there in force.

By this time *Furious* was concentrating more and more on her role as a training carrier. Each day when she was in Portsmouth I left home at 0600 and drove to the dockyard mingling with the morning rush of dockyard mateys, and leaving again for home at teatime. When she was at Spithead I came off from the Kings' Stairs with the married officers boat and when we were deck landing off the Isle of Wight, and anchoring at night off Bembridge I occupied my cabin down under the quarter deck, and schemed to find a spare aircraft to fly ashore. Occasionally I succeeded, once or twice to fetch a spare one to replace another damaged and occasionally to fetch a makee-learn (young) pilot.

After about two months of this *Furious* set sail for her summer cruise to Invergordon via the Firth of Forth. For this expedition we re-embarked our Squadrons 801, 811 and 821, now embodying those newly qualified deck landing pilots whose initial deck flying we had just completed.

We stayed in the Firth of Forth for about a month. During the week we spent days at sea flying Sharks and Swordfish, and every evening and for long weekends, returned to our anchorage just above the great Forth Railway Bridge.

After a fortnight in the Firth of Forth, *Furious* returned south and gave summer leave. She herself went into dry-dock at Devonport, during which time we stayed first in the old Royal Hotel, and later took a small house on Mutley Plain. *Furious* emerged belatedly from her dry-dock; she was at that time considered to be in poor shape, and a great deal of work had to be done on her rudder hinges, and on the A-bracket which held the aftermost bearings of her two longest propeller shafts. These had certainly suffered in the great storm that spring.

The year 1936 ended with the abdication of King Edward VIII. But *Furious* started the year with a training cruise in which we did very many deck landings, and began her part in the coronation celebrations by a ceremonial visit to Yarmouth. Because of our size we lay a mile or so out in the deep channel, and all our guests came to us in a fleet of small boats. After a Spithead review in May *Furious* returned for further dockyard repairs.

Her three squadrons were disembarked, 801 to Eastleigh, and the Sharks and Swordfish to Gosport. I was loaned to Lee-on-the-Solent where there was no engineer at the time and resumed my old duties of engineer and test pilot. By this time the land aerodrome was in crowded use having taken in the Telegraphist Air Gunner training previously at Gosport. Thus, all Fleet Air Arm aircrew training, except for pilots, was now at Lee. There were now lots more aeroplanes; these included the Seal, replacing the IIIF, and the amphibious Supermarine Walrus.

The Walrus became a special favourite. With its sturdy boat hull it was more sea-worthy than the floatplanes I had previously flown, and could land and take off in sea conditions which prohibited floatplanes. Its 775hp Bristol Pegasus engine mounted high up as a pusher, between the wings was clear of most water spray, and very reliable. Four ailerons gave good lateral response and the closed cockpit was comfortable and dry. The technique of getting off in rough water was made easier by observing the seventh wave. For some reason this is often bigger and steeper than the rest. By opening up as the seventh wave began to lift the aircraft, the Walrus would often take a harmless surge of green sea over the bows whilst still moving slowly and be off the water and flying before the next seventh wave came up. On land the Walrus waddled in somewhat ungainly fashion. The hand operated hydraulic pump which raised or lowered the wheels took a great many strokes to complete the action up, though in lowering the wheels, falling under their own weight, did most of the work.

My Walrus flying included several deliveries to ships at Plymomth when I sometimes stayed at Mount Batten with my old friend from Cambridge and CUAS days, and now an experienced flying boat captain, Bruce Cooper. During this period I was able to fly all sorts of new aeroplanes. At Airspeeds, at Portsmouth, George Errington was test pilot. George introduced me to the Airspeed Envoy, my first twin. The cockpit had room only for the pilot, like the de Havilland Rapide. The way George did it was to fly a circuit whilst I stood behind him and watched. He then stood behind me whilst he conducted me through the whole gamut of stalling, single engine performance, stalls through deliberate mishandling whilst on one engine and finally circuits and landings, including engine failure on take-off. It was a superb demonstration, not only of faith in the Envoy, but of ability as an instructor. The Envoy was the ancestor of the RAF's Oxford trainer.

Another new experience was the Percival Gull, a beautiful and fast four-seat cabin monoplane with a six-cylinder Gipsy-Queen engine. With a fast tick over the clean dragless Gull floated on and on across Portsmouth aerodrome until, with the gasworks looming up ahead, I switched off and we ended up much too close to the boundary for comfort.

Looking back I suppose 1937 was the end of an era, and the beginning of another. We lived a supremely happy and relatively carefree life. In the services, and particularly that specialised saltwater element where Fleet Air Arm, flying boats, submarines and small boat enthusiasts all met, there existed a close comradeship, which in 1937 reached its apogee. By 1938 expansion had overtaken us. From being carefree amateurs, we became professionals and our numbers increased so that, from a small family, we became members of a great team. In aeroplanes there were great changes. In 1914 it was still an achievement to fly. By 1919 the aeroplane had become a weapon of war. Until 1935 we still flew 1919 style aeroplanes with 1919 style armaments. Then, very slowly came the new high performance monoplanes with retractable undercarriages, variable pitch airscrews and higher landing speeds. By 1936 the RAF felt the first impact of these changes. For me it came in January 1938, when I was promoted to Squadron Leader and posted to Bicester to command 90 Squadron, recently formed with Hawker Harts and now the second squadron to receive the new Bristol Blenheim.

CHAPTER FOUR
RETURNING TO THE RAF

There has always been argument, much of it ill-informed, about RAF bombing policy. In its earliest days after the First World War there remained great emphasis on working as closely as had the RFC Corps Squadrons with the Army; and to continue with the Navy that close integration inherited from the RNAS. It is worth a mention the RNAS itself was the originator of what later became known as strategic bombing and, by 1917, the Navy's twin-engined Handley Page night bombers had started a bomber offensive which later caused them to become part of a mixed based around Nancy, under the command of Lord Trenchard (then General Trenchard) to attack the industrial Ruhr and Rhineland. By day the single-seat fighters to a great extent ruled the sky and Corps Squadrons and short range light day bombers worked under their protection when it could be given.

In 1925 C.R. Fairey produced the prototype Fairey Fox light bomber. Its American Curtis D12 engine and clean lines, whose ancestry was the Curtis Schneider Trophy seaplane, gave it a top speed as fast as the best contemporary fighters, and faster than most in current service. In 1926 No 12 Squadron at Andover, with its Foxes, began to show that it could evade all air defences and from this, and the subsequent development of aeroplanes such as the Hawker Hart, was born the theory that the bomber will always get through. Until the introduction of radar, complemented by new monoplane fighters, this situation remained and at the same time it was thought that the heavy bombers in large formations could develop such a concentration of fire as to repel anything but the most overwhelming fighter defences.

In parallel with this, the great theoretician of air warfare, General Douhet, developed his doctrine that any air force which devoted its every resource to bombing an enemy's means of making war could, by this single minded maintenance of a single aim, put its antagonist on the defensive and, in the end, ensure its defeat. There were many enthusiasts for air power the world over who subscribed to Douhet's ideas. Be it noted, though, that Trenchard was never one of them.

When I arrived at Bicester, Douhet's ideas were in the ascendant and the Bristol Blenheim, developed directly by Lord Rothermere could outrun most current fighters, and was the epitome of the theory that the bomber would always get through. By good fortune, I was not entirely new to the Blenheim for Harry Burke had been flying one of the prototypes at Farnborough in 1937. His advice and experience were invaluable and quite early in my time at Bicester, George Errington was sent to gain experience on the new style of aircraft coming into service. Theoretically I was to give him dual but what I actually did was to return the compliment he had paid me when I flew his Airspeed Envoy. I put him into the driving seat of my own aircraft which had no dual and I stood in the space alongside him. In the course of just over an hour I learned more about how to handle a Blenheim than ever from anybody else.

My first flight with 90 Squadron was actually as a passenger when I was taken by the senior Flight Commander, Acting Flying Officer Bock Hull, to meet the half of the squadron then at practice camp at Valley in North Wales. To find the senior Flight Commander as an Acting Flying Officer was a shock. But I very quickly found that this was the new RAF, the product of the overdue, and almost too late, expansion. My predecessor, an elderly Wing Commander dating from the First World War, had formed the squadron with Harts.

The year 1938 continued with intensive training in every aspect of making 90 Squadron into a front line fighting unit. In the late spring we all went to Northolt where under the supervision of the newly created Air Fighting Development Establishment (AFDE) under the (then) Wing Commander Tiny Vasse, we spent a month flying defensive formations whilst Hurricanes practised attacks. We all used camera guns, and every film was carefully analysed and shown to all those who took part. It was here also that we first encountered Radio Direction Finding (RDF) the first large scale and very secret experiments in the detection and fighter control and interception without which the Battle of Britain would have, without doubt, been a victory for Hitler's Luftwaffe. We found that, in the end, the AFDE fighter directors could put the Hurricanes onto us in almost any circumstances, and it was seldom that an interception failed.

It was just before this that Don Gillan had flown a Hurricane from Edinburgh to Northolt at 408mph and of course, during this month we flew each other's aeroplanes. In this way I acquired my first few hours of Hurricane. I found it a singularly tractable and delightful aeroplane. These first Hurricanes, having a fixed pitch wooden airscrew, were rather sluggish on take-off but once airborne, undercarriage up and accelerating to their best speed, they behaved like a rather more solid Hawker Fury; very manoeuvrable though somewhat more deliberate in everything and, thanks to George Bulman, very much a pilot's aeroplane. And fast, much faster than my Blenheims.

When we returned to Bicester, our first task was a great exercise in which every squadron in the newly-born Bomber Command took part. It took the form of a daylight attack on Uxbridge. Each squadron flew in formation, all at height, and were timed to arrive over the camera obscura at Uxbridge at intervals of some ten minutes. Our own route was from Bicester to the Scilly Isles, and thence to the target via Horsham. We flew throughout at 13,000 feet. Our attack was quite accurate but we were criticised for being one and a half minutes late. Looking ahead to the great raids mounted by Bomber Command only a few years later, this criticism was valid and important. For then effectiveness depended, among many other things, upon amazing accuracy of timing in conditions infinitely more difficult, not to say hazardous, than in our summer day ride round peaceful Southern England.

By this time war in Europe loomed closer and began to affect the daily lives, not merely of our hard-pressed service in the worst birth throes of a reborn RAF, but began to intrude into the daily lives of civilians. Shadow factories were being built; unprecedented sums of money were being voted to buy new aeroplanes; air raid precautions were planned; and at Bicester camouflage paint began to cover our hangars and quarters and our aeroplanes were identified, no longer by squadron colours and badges, but by code letters. We practised getting airborne in a hurry with all the station in gas masks. One day, we evacuated Bicester and took up hidden dispersals around the old First World War aerodrome nearby at Weston-on-the-Green. This we did at ten minutes notice, and for the whole day Rosemary fed the squadron on food and beer which plans had failed to provide.

When Germany effectively annexed Austria war now seemed to us, though still not to an unprepared nation, to be inevitable. Our station commander, Wing Commander Cuthbert Dearlove, who, as a Flight Lieutenant, had signed my authorisation years before to wear wings, already had our Battle Orders in his safe. Our civilian staff began to assume new, and to us, unexpected titles. The previously civilian Adjutant became a Squadron Leader; an operations room staff materialised and the education office became the OPS Room. As events led up to the now historic Munich Crisis 90 Squadron were in the front line. All leave was stopped and the squadron was brought to readiness at a few hours notice. Very silently, almost unnoticed through the country, the same thing was happening at every RAF station. At Bicester aircrew were confined to camp. In our operations room target maps were prepared and our Blenheims were standing, every one serviceable and waiting, to receive its load from the bomb dump.

Alone in our squadron I knew our target, the likely opposition, and the probable result. That evening, when Neville Chamberlain had flown to meet Hitler at Munich, all my aircrew met in our married quarter. We were cheered when Chamberlain arrived back with his piece of paper and proclaimed 'peace in our time'. Subsequently Chamberlain's arrangement has been severely criticised.

The fact is we were at that time in no position to fight anybody. Our neglected defences were minimal and, despite our few show squadrons like my own, the RAF comprised little more than a great congregation of men in training schools, and an accumulation of raw materials awaiting fabrication in shadow factories still under construction.

For the rest of 1938 90 Squadron worked hard at everything we could to become the most efficient and best. We practiced bombing at various heights on our nearby range at Otmoor. We worked out a system of low flying attacks using our own aerodrome as a target. With careful timing we were able to develop an attack by twelve aircraft, each coming in from a different direction. Looking back, I think we should have used delay action bombs, otherwise we could have blown each other up, but although we expended a fair quantity of smoke bombs, we never had the opportunity to experiment with anything larger.

By this time I had reasonable experience of the Blenheim. Ours were the short nosed Mark I with two 840hp Bristol Mercury VIII engines driving two pitch de Havilland built Hamilton propellers. One took off in fine pitch, and at the appropriate moment, which was in theory when set into climb out, pulled the two small knobs located just behind the pilot's seat, which caused the propellers to change into coarse pitch. In practice we found that an early change of pitch, preferably just as the aircraft left the ground, produced a surge of acceleration just when it was most desirable, and seemed to be a much nicer procedure. Our top speed was 260mph, and we could carry a load of four 250 pound bombs in the bomb bay. There was one pilot-operated Browning gun firing forward, and one Vickers gun in the turret. Both were 303s.

The Blenheim's handling was quite fighter like, though naturally less agile than something smaller. We used to get sunburned through the wide-visibility, Perspex nose, and I usually flew in a farmer's straw hat with headphones under it. Several years later, when I had been flying heavier aircraft, I had the chance to fly a short nosed Blenheim once more, and the comparison brought home very forcibly what a delightful, docile and well balanced aircraft those magnificent aeroplanes were and in 1938 well ahead of nearly everything else in their class.

In January 1939 I left 90 Squadron to become a student at the RAF Staff College. It was a sad parting and I would willingly have thrown away the career prospects inherent in a Staff College course, to remain with 90. I did, however, make the most of things by getting attachments, first to 19 Squadron at Duxford to do some flying on the first Spitfires to reach squadron service and later to 2 Squadron at Hawkinge to fly Lysanders.

19 Squadron was commanded by Squadron Leader H.I. Couzens. Duxford was fun, and in some ways a return to CUAS days. The Spitfire, Mark I, with fixed pitch wooden propeller, was a revelation. Strangely the hand pump operated retracting undercarriage was identical with that of the Walrus, already known to me. First solos on those Spits were always watched by the initiated, wanting to enjoy the fore and aft oscillations which attended taking off. The cause was the fact that whilst the pilot pumped away energetically with his right hand to get the wheels up, his left hand, temporarily holding the stick instead of the throttle, inevitably tended to imitate the movements of pumping. Sometimes this could be quite exciting, for the fast and responsive Spitfire required very little elevator pressure to effect big changes of altitude.

In the air the Spitfire was dramatic. I can only describe it in terms which I have used for a very few other exceptional aeroplanes. One did not precisely fly it as though it were a machine. It became, in a magical way, one's own wings. The mere thought of a manoeuvre, turn, roll, loop or whatever one intended in all its infinite variations of flight, seemed to be performed by the Spitfire. It was much in the same way as one's own limbs and hands obey the commands of the brain to which they belong. Birds must fly this way; and so did Mitchell's superb and beautiful creation, the Spitfire.

The Lysander was totally different. It was the ultimate development of the sort of Artillery Observation and Army Cooperation aircraft which had its origins in France in the First World War. With automatic slots, flaps and the Bristol Mercury engine it contrived a slow flying and short field performance scarcely bettered by the Fieseler Storch. At its high speed end it flew, with slots closed and flaps up, like a rather heavy but gentlemanly carriage, with a nice view for the pilot, perched high up ahead of the wing. As one slowed down, one waited for the automatic slots to open, and in doing so they lowered the huge flaps. When this happened with a bit of a bang, the relatively low drag high wing was transformed into a high drag, but also very high lift wing. The Lysander became a different aeroplane flying, with increased need for power on the back of its drag curve. The pilots of No 2 Squadron, many of them seconded from the Army, flew with the greatest gallantry a few months later, particularly during the last few days before the Germans took Calais. But the Lysander could not live in the same air as Me109s and they were decimated. Only later did it come into its own, in a totally unforeseen role, of flying agents by night in and out of occupied Europe.

Sadly 90 Squadron began the war by being disbanded. Together with the other first Blenheim squadron, 114 from Cranfield, it became No 17 OTU at Upwood, to produce, trained by our now experienced aircrew, more Blenheim crews to form new Blenheim squadrons. Thus, all my young pilots were, for the time being preserved, but later as they became experienced Flight Commanders and Squadron Commanders, they moved on to command and lead in the early days of 2 Group and few survived.

When I arrived at Andover the commandant was a veteran of the First World War and the RFC, and one of the founder members of the RAF, Air Vice Marshal Barratt (later Air Chief Marshal Sir Arthur Sheridan Barratt KCB, CMG, MC DL). The Staff College buildings on the south side of Andover Aerodrome were so-called temporary buildings put in the First World War. Repainted, redecorated, rebuilt and modified, they provided a splendid library, lecture rooms, syndicate rooms and mess. Because it was all rather cramped and make-do we were compressed into a close community in which a great deal of most productive work was often done by small groups working far into the night over beer and sandwiches in each other's homes.

Flying at Andover was very limited. The station flight provided an assortment of light training aircraft which we used as occasion permitted and those of us who had links with squadrons could sometimes get additional flying. In this way I was able to fly Blenheims some more and occasionally a Hurricane or Mark I Spitfire, though the latter were very scarce and closely guarded. It was during this period that I first flew a French aeroplane, a high wing very square-looking monoplane called the Farman F200. It had a radial air cooled engine, and a cabin seating six.

All I can remember distinctly is that at that time the French pushed the throttle forward to close it; the exact opposite to our own and now universal practice. The experience came in useful later when I found myself in charge of a Martin Maryland built for the French Air Force as part of an order by the French in 1938.

Increasingly we found that our exercises were concerned with the organisation and move of an expeditionary force. We studied everything from the quantity and weight of stores to keep a squadron in the field and means of keeping them supplied, to the structure of the command and communications to control them and the likely operations to be ordered. Finally the Staff College took over the whole of a hotel on the edge of Bournemouth, in which we set up an RAF Expeditionary Force Headquarters. From there we conducted an imaginary war against an enemy based in East Anglia. Our exercise port of supply was Southampton with Poole as an alternative, and our home base upon which we depended for everything, was France. One of my first tasks was to find aerodrome sites in the area.

A few days later I was summoned by telegram to report without delay to my war appointment at Abingdon. It was mid-August, and the last days of peace for six years.

CHAPTER FIVE
EARLY WAR YEARS

On 24 August 1939 the British Government ordered partial mobilisation and on 26 August I reported to my war appointment at the RAF Station Abingdon.

Plans for the war had long since been in careful preparation. The ones which affected me were those of the move of the Advanced Air Striking Force (AASF) of the RAF to France. There were two elements of the RAF to go to France. In the north, in support of the British Expeditionary Force, was the so-called Air Component. This included Army Cooperation Squadrons flying Westland Lysanders and supported by fighter squadrons on Gladiators and one on Hurricanes. The second was the Advanced Air Striking Force (AASF) which comprised all the squadrons, ten in all, of the RAF equipped with Fairey Battles. These came from the No 1 Group stations of Harwell, Benson, Boscombe Down and Hucknall. The Commander of the AASF was to be Air Vice Marshal Philip Playfair who had been my AOC when I commanded No 90 Squadron a year before at Bicester.

My immediate duty at Abingdon was to receive and allocate to their duties the vast numbers of reservists reporting on call up. They came from all walks of life; postmen, farmers, bus conductors, clerks, lawyers, signallers, engineers and drivers. One thing they all had in common was their previous experience in the RAF, and that when the call came they answered it at once.

I set up my office in the top of the Station HQ at Abingdon, in a room which had been designed for and used by the education service. The first ten men who reported I took, regardless of their trades, to man the reception. We sent them to be kitted up, fed, allocated sleeping quarters and to their war posts. The skeleton Headquarters became a fully manned organisation and the Battle Squadrons received all those additional men, which enabled them to become mobile units. They were equipped and manned to leave their home stations in England and to move as wings, each of two squadrons, to their new locations in France. The Air Officer commanding all the RAF in France was to be Air Marshal Arthur Barratt, who had been my commandant at the Staff College at Andover.

Whilst we were at Abingdon skeleton staff were already in France. Pip Playfair, his Senior Air Staff Officer (SASO) Bill Williams, his Air Officer in charge of Administration (AOA) Paddy Quinnell and a few other key people were waiting in Rheims. This was to be the HQ of the AASF in France. They lived in the Lion D'or Hotel, and wore plain clothes. The operations room was in a deep cellar under the

Chateau Pommery home of the Polignac family. Geoffrey Tuttle was also in Rheims and in his great kindness left with me his Speed Twenty Alvis so that I could grab whatever opportunity was offered to speed down to Botley to snatch some few last hours with Rosemary.

On 1 September there arrived at Abingdon a flock of requisitioned Imperial Airways and other aeroplanes. On arrival they were camouflaged in horrible drab green and brown applied by airmen with brooms and buckets. All unnecessary luxuries were removed, and all HQ were allocated to their aircraft. We stood ready, waiting, and not a little tense. Listening to the sombre news we heard of the progress of the German assault into Poland and of the frightening efficiency of the Luftwaffe's JU 87 Dive Bombers working in conjunction with Wehrmacht armour. The Luftwaffe's Me109s were wiping out the gallant but hopelessly out-matched Polish Air Force. We had all turned in early to bed but we were awakened by a top priority signal that the AASF was to move its war stations to France at first light the next morning. 2 September 1939 dawned beautiful and cloudless and so it remained that whole Sunday. When we left in our hideously daubed aircraft we were given a splendid send off and, of course, many messages and oddments for those already in Rheims. Whilst we, the future HQ left from Abingdon the ten Battle Squadrons were also departing for their bases in France. These were Rheims Champagne, Challerange, Auberive and another close to Epernay.

I was a passenger in a de Havilland Rapide belonging to Rollason Airways. We left the English coast near Shoreham and from 3,000 feet saw the sparkling blue Channel full of small boats and yachts, all of which seemed to be making their best speed towards England. We crossed the French coast near Dieppe, and saw the whole countryside below us apparently asleep, with not a movement of any sort below. The only sign of life was a huge and ugly twin-engine biplane of the French Air Force, moving so slowly that it seemed to hang in the sky. Quite what we had expected I do not really know. After the account of the German onslaughts into Poland it was difficult to think that nothing at all would be going on in France; least of all that the Luftwaffe would make no attempt to interfere with our move to aerodromes around Rheims. But so it proved and so we flew on, like holiday passengers over the sunny lovely country of France with its rolling chalky farmlands; and then in sight of the vineyards spread between Rheas and Epernay. We landed on the great grass aerodrome of Rheims Champagne, scene of the first and still one of the biggest air race meetings ever held in 1912. We disembarked, sat on our baggage, and waited. There was not a soul in sight. The hangars were all closed and within a period of about thirty minutes we had the whole of the AASF HQ sitting on its baggage on the grass.

While we waited I took the opportunity to see, as much as I could, what was in the hangars. By dint of peering through cracks and dusty windows, I found that there was what looked like a squadron of the very attractive Potez 63 twin-engine reconnaissance aircraft in our hangar. In some ways more exciting, was a single example of the little Caudron 714 single-engine lightweight fighter, developed from the earlier racing aircraft. Later, I made great efforts to be allowed to fly it, but never succeeded, but I had a sufficient look at it to discover that it had a six-cylinder in line Renault air-cooled engine and no armament. It was a monoplane with a span of about 29ft. Apart from these French aircraft, Rheims seemed to be used mainly by a flying club, some civil air transport and, until 226 Squadron arrived with its Fairey Battles that was all. It was here also that I discovered that the French Air Force, unlike ourselves and the Luftwaffe, had no Officers' Mess. There was a building called the *Popotte des Officiers*, which provided food and drinks but no living accommodation. The officers lived in lodgings in Rheims, those who were unmarried fending for themselves, and in some cases living apparently in considerable comfort.

After a long wait, some requisitioned buses arrived, and the AASF HQ moved into Rheims. Initially the officers were quartered in a huge building previously used as a school. The other ranks were housed in the Parc Pommery, adjacent to the Chateau Polignac and slept in the Champagne itself, below which were miles of caves in the deep chalk, filled with a million bottles of the famous champagne.

Our AOC, with his Senior Officers moved into the dower house of the Chateau Polignac. I became the Headquarters Camp Commandant.

In Rheims, the RAF was poised for immediate operations. France mobilised, and for several days from the time we arrived, the roads through Rheims were crowded, nose to tail, with the French Army moving up to the frontier. The main road ran right past Chateau Polignac and we spent a great deal of time talking to the halted columns of soldiers.

As the days went by it became clear that the Blitzkreig, which we had expected to burst around us was not developing. It became possible to improve our billets and several of us, including myself, moved into a small hotel. I lived in it for most of September. The RAF Police took over the Stables of the Chateau Polignac, where they lived and messed. They also requisitioned the entire stock of Peugeot motorcycles in Rheims and kept these, together with their RAF vehicles, in the stalls and stable yard. After a while, others followed their example so that by the middle of October, there were half a dozen small RAF messes set up in the town in rented houses.

It was about this time my duties as camp commandant, having become much less exacting, that I joined Harry Burke, Gil Saye and Leonard Williams as members of the AASF team to examine and report on shot-down or captured enemy aircraft. Nearly all our activity at that time went on around and over the Maginot Line and the areas around Verdun, Metz and Nancy. It was entirely reconnaissance, and the rare air fighting was when one side tried to intercept enemy reconnaissance aircraft. On our side, Battles were at first used but on 30 September five Battles of 150 Squadron were briefed to reconnoitre Saarbrucken but were set upon by eight Me109s and only one survived. This disaster made tragically clear what we had long feared; that the Battle could not live in the air against such opposition and they were withdrawn from daylight operations. Later, when the Battle of France broke, the Battles, still the main body of the AASF were thrown into the fight by day and night; again few survived.

The air fighting was not always one sided. The French were getting a few US built Curtiss Hawks, which inflicted several severe losses on the Me109s. But the Hawks were too few in number, and quite insufficient to enable the slow reconnaissance aircraft to do their work. For this reason, the RAF began to use Blenheim IVs. Aircraft of Nos 15, 57 and 114 Squadrons all took part in the flights. They were all based in UK and belonged to No 2 Group. They would fly to France, refuelling at Metz, do their task at low level and unescorted, returning to UK direct via the North Sea. They also suffered losses; one victim was Wing Commander H.M.A. Day commanding 57 Squadron then based at Upper Heyford. He was shot down near Hanover, and remained a prisoner for the rest of the war. His indomitable spirit as senior officer in his prison camp is now famous, and was rightly recognised in 1945 by the award of the DSO.

To counter the Luftwaffe, the AASF received two Hurricane squadrons; No 1, commanded by Squadron Leader Bull Halahan, based at Vassincourt; and No 73 at Etain-Rouvres. They did their best, and scored some successes, but cut off from an effective early warning system or any form of fighter direction such as existed in England, they were less effective than the home-based squadrons were to prove in 1940.

Pilot Officer Mould provided us with our first opportunity to examine a Dornier Do17. It flew directly over Vassincourt and suffered accordingly. Not much of it was left. A better specimen came into our hands at St Avold, shot down by a French Sergeant Pilot in a Curtiss Hawk. The Do17 was on the edge of a wood and not badly damaged, despite a belly landing. We had great difficulty in finding it, partly because of bad maps, but mainly because the locals refused to speak French. This floored our interpreter, and it was not until I dredged up from school recollections some German that they replied to any questions. We came to the conclusion that they were entirely pro-German, and regarded themselves as a part of the as yet unredeemed area of the Saarland. We spent a whole day with the aircraft; examined and photographed everything, and made our reports. This was the first report on the Do17 in service. It interested me particularly because it was, in effect, the opposite number to the Blenheims. It was a beautifully made aircraft, well equipped but in our view defective like our own Battles and Blenheims in rearward armament and lacking the performance to avoid attack by superior fighters. Many years later, I was privileged to sit next to Claude Dornier, son of the founder of the firm, at a Farnborough dinner at the Dorchester. We discussed this view and I was flattered to find that this eminent son of a famous father thought our assessment of the Do17 about right.

Another exciting first was an intact and flyable Me109. This was flown by an Austrian pilot who had deserted in his aircraft. Again we rushed up to Metz, and found it closely guarded on a French fighter base. With considerable diplomacy it was finally agreed that I should fly this aeroplane, after which it should go to the

French test centre at Bretigny and thence to Farnborough. It was a Me109E, (an Emil). Next day we examined everything, took photographs and sorted out controls, cockpit and, as near as we could, likely handling. The day after we were to fly it; we were pleased with ourselves, but how wrong we were. After we left the French captors, who after all owned the aerodrome, decided to fly it themselves. They detailed one of their Sergeant Pilots to do this and, on his landing he rolled the whole thing up into a ball. We were not happy.

Another of my failures was to get my hands on either a Potez 63, or the attractive little Caudron 714 I had spotted at Rheims Champagne. I did have my first experience of a Fairey Battle, and some more Hurricane flying. I found the Battle unattractive; its performance compared badly with the Blenheim, and its controls and handling seemed sluggish. The few that remained in service at the conclusion of the Battle of France were relegated to more appropriate second line jobs. Other new types to me were the variety of light civil types which, requisitioned by the RAF, became our Headquarters Communications Flight. These included the Miles Monarch, the Miles Mentor, and, of course, the Magister. A good deal of this flying was to visit our outlying squadrons and sometimes as staff pilot for our senior officers.

In November the AASF started to give routine leave home and, in due course, my ten days came up. I went by train to Le Havre in charge of an RAF party and thence by boat to Southampton, escorted across the Channel by a destroyer with depth charges at the ready, and two Coastal Command AVRO Ansons.

I flew back to Rheims in a de Havilland Rapide that needed a pilot. On return it seemed as though I had never been away. France still sheltered behind its impregnable Maginot Line, and the air war, such as it was, seemed to have subsided into occasional reconnaissance flights by both sides, and resultant fighter attempts at interception.

Shortly after Christmas I was ordered home to an appointment in the Air Ministry. I flew home in a Rapide, landing at Northolt and was told that I was to become an engineer staff officer in the organisation supporting Lord Nuffield, newly appointed to head the wartime Repair and Maintenance Organisation for the RAF. It was 1 February 1940.

Lord Nuffield's staff was housed at the end of the Strand, not far from St Clement Danes Church, and over a Short's Wine Bar. The first thing we discovered was that there was very little to do. It seemed to us that a large mob of Staff Officers and Engineers had been assembled to be used by Lord Nuffield without any clear idea of their duties. Lord Nuffield himself was provided with an office, washroom and lavatory on the main floor. Neither I nor any of my friends ever saw him, and, so far as we knew he never came there. Our frustrations were not diminished when we found that there was, assembled in requisitioned hotels and buildings in Harrogate, another staff, doing many of the things that we were eventually asked to do. Looking back, I now think that this silly situation was the result of two things. First a political decision which required the RAF to provide, without time for consultation or proper planning, a support staff which Lord Nuffield did not want. Secondly, a belated decision to create in the RAF an Engineering Branch, similar to the Royal Navy's.

By 1938 it had already become apparent that aircraft engineering was advancing at such a pace that intermittent spells of trained pilots seconded for staff duties were no longer practical. It had become a full time job; as had radio, and the new development of RDF, which was soon to expand into all the ramifications of radar and electronics. And, somewhat later the realisation that armaments had been so neglected as to have advanced little since 1919.

This period was not without its compensations. My immediate superior, Group Caption Leslie George Harvey used me as his pilot whenever he did a visit by air. We flew, usually, from Hendon, where the RAF had assembled a collection of requisitioned civil aircraft. In this way I was lucky to meet not only some old friends, but make some new ones. These included the Hendy Heck, the Heston Phoenix and the CW Cygnet. The Phoenix was a delightful four-seat tourer with retractable undercarriage. It had one snag; when the undercarriage was retracted, the compass deviated by some 30°. This we discovered after flying over cloud, as we hoped, to visit Kidlington; having descended, on elapsed time, we were disturbed to find ourselves approaching, not Kidlington, but Middle Wallop.

So continued for a few months a strange life, compounded by peacetime happiness with my Rosemary in a London rapidly resuming a peacetime gaiety and glitter; together with the infuriating frustrations. My last job with this staff was to take a series of vehicles and trailers down to the great long sandy beach which extends all around Studley Bay in Dorset. RAF vehicles were nearly all designed and bought with metalled roads in mind. So on the beaches we ploughed up and down and proved that if possible, every vehicle must have four-wheel drive; and, at the other extreme, a two-wheel drive vehicle, towing a trailer, was totally useless. I like to think that this little expedition was of some later practical use to the Desert Air Force.

Meanwhile the Battle of France developed and duties on Lord Nuffield's Staff became increasingly hard to bear. The AASF Battles were being shot out of the sky both by the Luftwaffe, and the intense and effective German flak assembled to protect all those key choke points, bridges, and defiles which were inevitably the Battles' targets. On 10 May, thirteen out of thirty-two Battles sent in at low level were lost; on 11 May out of eight Battles sent in, only one came home. In an attack on bridges at Maastricht, five Battles sent in were all lost; but one bridge was destroyed. The leader of this formation, Flying Officer D.E. Garland, and his Observer, Sergeant T. Gray, received posthumous Victoria Crosses, the first awarded to the RAF in the war. In the first three days the Battles lost sixty-three aircraft with their crews and on the fourth day of the German onslaught out of seventy-one aircraft sent into action thirty-one were lost. By the fifth day, out of the 135 Battles which the AASF had at the beginning only forty-one were left.

The French were crying out for more of the RAF based in Britain to be sent over to France. The RAF responded by sending 261 Hurricanes, of which only sixty-six ever came back. Blenheims from 2 Group were sent and Basil Embry (later Air Chief Marshal GCB, KBE, DSO and Three Bars, DFC and AFC), then a Wing Commander leading 107 Squadron, was shot down. Many of my friends in Lysanders from 2 Squadron were killed delivering much needed ammunition to the besieged garrison in Calais.

As the Battle of France came to a close, and the remnants of the Army and RAF returned from France, it was painfully obvious that not only had the Germans eliminated France, but they had inflicted on us losses so serious as to prejudice the defence of England. Had Lord Dowding and Churchill not made the decisions they did our air defences would have been fatally weakened, and the subsequent Battle of Britain would certainly have been another Luftwaffe victory.

In a broadcast to the nation on 18 June 1940, Churchill caught the mood of the people, and put into words, as he so often did, this astonishing and infectious exhilaration which seemed to inspire the whole country. He said:

'The Battle of France is over. I expect that the Battle of Britain is about to begin. Upon this battle depends the survival of Christian civilisation. Let us therefore brace ourselves to our duties, and so bear ourselves that, if the British Empire and its Commonwealth last for a thousand years, men will still say "This was their Finest Hour".'

Rosemary and I listened to this broadcast together, with our dog Blenheim, in our flat at Putney. Next morning at work, the senior officer on Lord Nuffield's staff required my presence. It was to read, and to sign as seen, an adverse report stating the 'Squadron Leader G.J.C. Paul does not seem to have his heart in Engineer duties. It is recommended that he be transferred to other duties'. I signed happily, and within five days was appointed to the Headquarters of No 1 Bomber Group at Hucknall, Nottinghamshire as a Squadron Leader Air Staff. We packed up, set off and within two days of our departure, the flat at Putney, where we had been so happy was blown sky high by Hitler's Luftwaffe. The Battle of Britain was just beginning.

Hucknall aerodrome was already well known to me. When I arrived there on 9 July 1940, there had been changes. Rolls-Royce had already taken over two hangars and adjacent buildings. They had every sort of aeroplane there that used Merlin engines. It was at Hucknall, inspired by Rolls-Royce's test pilot Ronnie Harker, that the first Merlin engine was installed in a North American Mustang, thus transforming a mediocre fighter into a war-winning aircraft, ranking second only to the Spitfire. Also on the aerodrome was a flying training school, refreshing and retraining numbers of gallant Poles who had come to England. Further down the road, some two miles away, was HQ No 12 Fighter Group commanded by Air Vice Marshal Trafford Leigh-Mallory.

At No 1 Group HQ, where we lived in temporary wooden huts, our AOC was Air Vice Marshal Bobby Breen. His task was to transform the battered remnants of the Battle Squadrons from France into a Group of Bomber Command, flying Wellingtons. What was left of the Battle Squadrons were now located at three aerodromes. At Binbrook, near the coast in north Lincolnshire were Nos 12 and 142 Squadrons, at Newton, between Nottingham and Grantham, were Nos 103 and 150. No 98 Squadron had flown, still with its Battles, to Iceland. The reforming force now included Nos 300 and 301 Polish Squadrons, already flying Wellingtons and burning with holy fire to avenge what Germany had done to Poland. Their commanding officers were two former Polish Air Force Colonels, now Wing Commanders in the RAF, Makowski and Rudkowski. All wore RAF uniforms and badges of rank, but Polish emblems.

Very soon, as the Battle of Britain developed most of us found it necessary to live on the job, and I moved into a wooden hut at Hucknall. I stood duty in the Group Operations Room, where we maintained a twenty-four hour watch. There were five of us, always two on duty, ringing the changes so that each got one day free in seven. On days off I flew to one or other of our aerodromes in the Group.

The failure of Hitler to cross the Channel and to invade England is attributed almost entirely to the fighters during the Battle of Britain, rightly accounted as one of the decisive battles of world history. But Bomber Command also played a part and No 1 Group, made its own modest contribution. To invade England, the Germans had assembled a great fleet in the Channel ports. In harbours like Boulogne and Calais they were packed side to side in their hundreds. There were nearly 2,000 barges and the whole armada amounted close to three quarters of a million tons of shipping. Bomber Command, night after night, pounded the targets. They were easily located, and not too well defended. The main brunt of this work was borne by other Groups of the Command. Our own Group did its utmost whilst it refitted and received its Wellingtons.

As the Battle faded from day into night and as invasion became less imminent, No 1 Group increasingly devoted its resources to its new Wellingtons. It was on 1 December 1940 that, with the acting rank of Wing Commander I was appointed to command No 150 Squadron at Newton.

No 150 (B) Squadron had suffered badly in France and by the time I arrived nearly all the aircrew were new arrivals, though many of the ground staff were old hands. One was the Squadron Commander who I was to succeed, a Wing Commander who had served in the First World War. He greeted me sitting cross-legged like an RAF Buddha perched in the middle of the hall table at the mess entrance. Another was the excellent Squadron Adjutant, Flying Officer Holmes, who had guided the ground staff of the squadron in their escape from France. His close associate and one of the most important men in the unit was the Squadron Warrant Officer, the imperturbable Warrant Officer Moffett. One Flight Commander was Squadron Leader Alan Frank (later Air Vice Marshal A.D. Frank, CB, CBE, DSO, DFC). The other Flight Commander was Squadron Leader R.A.C. Carter, who later took over 150 for me, and gained a well-earned DSO. Their two deputies were Hugo Beall, a Canadian, and Tony Slater, who had been ADC (Aide de Camp) to Pip Playfair.

This was a time when Bomber Command was far from being the effective force which it later became under Bert Harris (later Air Chief Marshal Sir Arthur Harris). Three factors are worth recording. First, the organisation within the squadron itself, which was still on a pre-war basis, by which I mean that each squadron was, as we had been in France, a self-contained unit in which the Squadron Commander's responsibilities included all the servicing and maintenance, its men, its transport, stores, and daily administration. It was not possible for a Squadron Commander of a night bomber unit to perform the daily administration by day, and to be an efficient captain of a crew by night. Later, Squadron Commanders were relieved of most administration other than that needed to lead their squadrons in the air. Secondly, parts of Bomber Command were still re-equipping. This imposed on the Squadron Commanders a considerable training task, only eased when the Operational Training Units (OTUs) got into their stride, and sent their products on to the front line units as complete crews, ready to start operations. Finally there was actual bombing capability. Very early on squadrons of No 3 Group had suffered such heavy losses in daylight attacks on German naval targets in the Heligoland Bight that the command policy, except for the Blenheims of No 2 Group, was night bombing. On moonlight nights against the clearly visible Channel invasion ports this had worked well. When, by the winter of 1940, Hitler had called off the invasion of Britain, it had also become plain that Bomber Command was the sole means of hitting back at Germany. So began the bomber offensive against Germany, demanding deeper and deeper penetrations of growing defences. This revealed our inability to accurately attack well-defended targets and the difficulty in finding them with existing navigation techniques.

My own preparation for this was to spend a week at Bassingbourne, just outside Royston, where the Chief Instructor Wing Commander (now Air Chief Marshal Sir) Hugh Constantine handed me over to Flight Lieutenant Sellick. He showed me a Wellington and taught me how it should be flown. I then went to Newmarket, where I met the Wing Commander of a Wellington Squadron operating from the race-course. He was in effect the Station Commander, and controlled his two flights as though they were each two half squadrons. He did not fly himself and, had not the rapid war expansion of the Service compelled it, would most likely have been long since retired as a superannuated Squadron Leader. Then followed a few days at Mildenhall, where under the enlightened leadership of Willy Merton, his Squadron Commanders were already being relieved of all administration not directly connected with flying.

When I arrived back at Newton, the grass aerodrome was boggy. In several places on the longest line of take-off springs had broken out; take-offs with full load were impracticable, and night flying distinctly dicey. Under these conditions training continued as best we could, until, shortly after Christmas, heavy falls of snow made our grass aerodrome unusable. Our neighbours on the newer aerodromes at Syerston and Swinderby had concrete runways, but were in little better state, because in 1940 the RAF had no snow clearing equipment, and little if any expertise in operating in such conditions.

About this time 150 Squadron became operational on its Wellingtons, and we were launched on our first mission. This was against the oil tanks at Rotterdam, regarded by the Command as a good training target. The oil tank farm lay on the south side of the great estuary by Schiedam and was easy to find. It was a shallow penetration, close to the coast, and strangely not heavily defended. We left Newton at dusk, following a route which took us over Cambridgeshire, and crossed the coast by Aldeburgh. There was a quarter moon and a fine night. When we arrived some oil tanks were already on fire, and the estuary and coastline around it left no doubt about the target. From 15,000 feet the curved line of the Dutch coast running north towards Den Helder was clearly visible. There were some searchlights and a little flak; all the crews from 150 and 103 returned safely to Newton.

The Newton Squadrons did the Rotterdam oil tank farm a second time, after which, considered fully blooded, they were expected to join with the other squadrons of the command in tougher targets further into Germany. It was at this time that deficiencies of the Command first became apparent. Targets at this time varied between relatively easily located places like the Naval base of Wilhelmshaven, on the edge of a visible estuary; and, a favourite at the time, the marshalling yards at Hamm, some 15 miles east of Dortmund. The German blackout was good; they were already masters in the building of decoys, located in open country, and designed to look like the target, which was in fact some miles away. At this time we had no beams to help us, such as the Luftwaffe used to devastate Coventry. We depended upon a fix, such as might be obtained by crossing a visible coastline. Thereafter accurate flying by the pilot, good dead reckoning by the navigator and visual identification of the target was required. One night, destined for Hamm we spent nearly two hours cruising, quite lost, over an area which I now think was probably the marshy north German plain to the north of Munster, and west of Osnabruck. There was fog below and cloud to obscure the stars. There was no moon and on the way home our radio packed up. This left us in the position of trying to find our way home by dead reckoning. Much fuel was wasted in our wanderings, and all we could do was to get rid of our bombs over the North Sea. After what seemed a very long night the navigator thought we were probably over Harwich but it turned out to be Mersea, near Colchester. Soon after, we saw the lighted flare path of an aerodrome close ahead. Short of fuel, and without radio, we went in, landed and were debriefed. We had actually landed at Stradishall.

It was shortly after this frustrating night out that I found myself, in the absence of the Group Captain on leave, commanding Newton. It was one night during this time that we had our first experience of a German intruder. Our flare path, which was still a line of paraffin goose-necks, was fully alight. Because it was a foul night, I ordered the street lighting on the station to be switched on to give some extra help. I was watching three aircraft circling above and a fourth coming in to land. One of the circling aircraft came in behind the approaching aircraft and opened fire. It hit the aircraft several times. Luckily no serious damage was done. I was in something of a dilemma. By extinguishing all lights and the flare path the base would be protected. But at the same time it would present a grave danger to tired crews short on fuel. In the end the decision I made was to extinguish all lights. When we turned the lights back on again the Hun had gone and we lost only one Wellington.

It was at the end of March 1941 that Bomber Command was given the battleships *Scharnhorst* and *Gneisenau* in harbour at Brest as their top priority targets. In one of the many attacks on these ships it happened again, that in the absence of the Group Captain, I found myself in command of the station. Both 103, commanded by my good friend Eric Littler, and 150 were required to take part. By this time the weight of the attack was becoming increasingly carried by the new heavy bombers; Sterlings; Manchesters; and the first of the Handley Page Halifaxes. The Lancaster was yet to come. When our orders came from Group and the operations staff set to everything in motion, it became clear to me that the bomb load ordered was too great to ensure a safe margin of fuel for our Wellingtons to return to Newton. So I queried this, suggesting either some reduction of bomb load to permit more fuel, or a diversion somewhere in the south of England for any aircraft in difficulties.

I was turned down flat. In the event my worst fears were realised; returning home poor Eric Littler force landed in the Devonshire hills, out of fuel. Worse, the dregs of fuel remaining were enough to cause an explosion and disastrous fire, in which the whole crew were consumed.

It was whilst commanding 150 that I first encountered the problem of the families of casualties. In peace time we had accidents, and sometimes mourned the loss of friends. But in war casualties are frequent. In 1940 and 1941 a great many of our aircrew were married and lived out in lodgings in the surrounding villages. Thus a pilot, home for tea, might help his wife with the washing up, after which he would have to tell her he was flying tonight, and go off to the aerodrome. It might be for practice night flying, it might be to hear that operations were cancelled due to weather. It might be never to return. One of the saddest things I remember was one of the ground crews, sitting silent on the chocks of their aircraft and its empty bomb trolleys; waiting as the sky got lighter. As the day dawned other aircraft came back, welcomed by their crews. Long after sunrise, hoping against fading hope this ground crew sat on, until they were alone on the empty tarmac, with all the camp asleep around them, gathering its strength for the next night's vigil. Then, astonishingly, they were joined by the young wives of two of the pilots, and a gunner. For some time they all waited together and then more amazing than all, it was the young girls who led the ground crew away from their vigil, and comforted them with hot tea, biscuits, and togetherness at the Salvation Army tea van which never failed us.

It was one of the tasks of the Squadron Commander to see, if possible, or at least write to the wife or family of every casualty. To the best of my ability I did this; and was constantly humbled and amazed by the greatness of character of all kinds of people, young and old, who, enduring their own great loss, found time and courage to fortify me in my own task of telling them.

On 22 June 1941 I handed over command of 150 Squadron to my senior Flight Commander, now with acting rank as Wing Commander C.R.A. Carter. On the following day I reported for duty as one of the Operations Room Wing Commanders, in the great underground dungeon at HQ Bomber Command.

When I arrived as a watch keeper at High Wycombe, Sir Arthur Harris had been Commander-in-Chief for four months. The watch keeper's day began at eight. At this time we came on duty in the deep down Operations Room to receive reports from the previous watch. We recorded results, losses, successes, and failures, and finally, by 1000 had recorded on the great board that filled all one side of the room, the squadron status of the whole Command. This displayed aircraft and crew availability.

From 0930 there would begin to assemble the more senior members of the Command Staff; signallers, navigators, engineers, meteorologists and all those whose expert and specialist opinions might be required in the decisions to be made for the next night. Finally, at 1000 Bert Harris himself appeared, and seated himself at a small desk, rather like one in a village school. It faced the great board, depicting the Command state.

First he went through the previous night's results. My impression often was that he already knew them better than those presenting them. Maybe he slept at night, but I still believe that Bert Harris, night after night, was as aware and close to every Group and Station in his command as telephones could make him. He knew what crews had said on their return, what was new about defences, and in a most extraordinary way which might have been telepathic was closer to his crews than any member of his staff.

When Bert had reviewed the previous night's results, he consulted the weather. This governed two things; first those targets in his current War Cabinet directive which would be accessible. Second the state of home bases, both for departure and return. Then would come decisions, targets, diversions, routes, bomb and incendiary loads, timings, spoofs; all these decisions carefully informed by the newest information on the probable opposition both en route, and in the target area itself. He would determine the size of the force to be launched and its coordination with any other known activities on land, sea, or in the air. Then the meeting would break up, and the duty watch would get to work sending the necessary instructions to Groups. It was a feature of these orders that they were brief, being confined to the bare minimum of words for complete clarity, yet allowing Group Commanders maximum freedom to implement them within Bert Harris's requirements.

Sometimes the weather was impossible. Cancelled days also released the watch keepers. Sometimes I was able to get some flying in the Command Communication Flight, then based at Halton. One of my favourites was a requisitioned Moth Minor monoplane in which I was able to visit friends and keep in touch. Sometimes a visit to Benson, by now HQ of the Photographic Reconnaissance Squadrons, and commanded by Geoffrey Tuttle, rewarded me with a flight in one of their Spitfires. It was here also that I was allowed to fly a Martin Maryland. It was a delight to fly, and in its time as good as a Blenheim, but by 1942 it was outdated. It was succeeded by the Martin Marauder, by comparison a pig to fly, and despite superior performance, not a success.

Occasionally I was able to snatch a night at Botley where Rosemary was looking after the house and her mother, and our first son Simon, born at Botley on 12 March 1941.

On 12 November 1941 I left Bomber Command for a posting to the Air Staff at HQ Flying Training Command at Shinfield Park, just outside Reading. Flying Training Command at that time comprised several subordinate Groups. No 54 Group, with its Headquarters in the requisitioned Golf Club House at Sunningdale, was responsible for the Initial Training Wings. These were nearly all in former seaside hotels, at places like Torquay and Bournemouth, or in holiday camps. They took in recruits destined for aircrew training. No 50 Group, with HQ in Reading, was responsible for the control of a great number of former civilian manned and operated Reserve flying schools and former civil schools. With few exceptions they all used Tiger Moths, and in 1941 were responsible for all initial Flying Training for the RAF. Typical of these elementary flying training schools were those operated by Brooklands Aviation at Sywell, where the intensity of flying by 100 Tigers had compelled the opening of Sywell's own satellite aerodrome at nearby Denton.

At this time Flying Training Command still had an emergency role as an anti-invasion force. Even our Tigers were expected to be able to put on light bomb racks, and, flown by instructors, play their part in repelling the invader, whilst former front line aircraft were expected to revert to the role for which they had been designed. Moreover all our aerodromes were expected to defend themselves against air or ground attack, or air landings.

My responsibility to our Commander-in-Chief, Air Marshal L.A. Pattison CB DSO, was the maintenance of all these defensive preparations, whilst ensuring that nothing interfered with the primary task of the Command, the production of aircrew. In this I worked closely, not only with Army units near each of our aerodromes, but in particular with the first members of the RAF Regiment; and with that splendid and gallant corps of the over-age and the too young, the Home Guard.

It was a happy accident that the Flying Training Command Communication Flight, based at Woodley, had, among its other assorted aircraft, a Hurricane. By a combination of diplomacy, cunning, and some subversion of the staff responsible, I managed to establish a sort of right of way over this Hurricane, and flew it on visits to most of the aerodromes in the Command.

Furthest north at the Air Gunnery School at Dalcross, I flew both the Defiant and the Hawker Henley, and wondered why the Defiant had been selected in 1939 as the RAF's two-seater fighter in preference to the seemingly much more pleasant Henley.

I stayed at Shinfield Park for just over one year. During this year, although I enjoyed a good deal of flying in every type that the Command used, it became increasingly clear that the purpose for which my post existed was becoming less and less important. Invasion was no longer an imminent threat. Moreover, as the Great Empire Air Training scheme took over, the role of Flying Training Command itself diminished. From being the source from which all aircrew were obtained, it became increasingly concerned with initial selection of potential aircrew for sending to schools overseas and to acclimatising them on return to flying in the clouds and mists of Europe, and the blackout at night. More and more operational aeroplanes, including those flown by Free French, Poles, Czechs and Dutch were in the sky, and more and more aerodromes needed for their use. By the beginning of 1943 the Americans were with us; and the great build up which culminated in the return to Europe in 1944 was underway. The Army especially, which unlike the RAF and the Navy had little opportunity to hit back in Europe, was engaged in an enormous programme for the officers who would comprise the junior commanders and the staff of the new Army. The training for these was at Camberley. It was to the Army Staff College at Camberley that I was posted on 1 January 1943, as the RAF member of the Directing Staff. It was odd to find the name of my uncle, Colonel Sir Harold Percival, on the board as a member of the Directing Staff in 1912/13.

When I arrived at Camberley, I reported to Major General Sir Alan Cunningham, KCB, DSO, MC, at Minley Manor, where the No 3 Senior Staff Course had assembled. The Junior Staff courses were conducted in the older building down in the grounds at Sandhurst. My fellow members of the directing staff included some particularly charming soldiers, such as Tommy Gimson, from the Irish Guards; Tommy Charles, from the Essex Regiment; Lieutenant Colonels Duncan, Daldy and Jelf, all of whom subsequently attained senior rank. The Adjutant was Lieutenant Colonel Clare, DCM, and the General's ADC, Major Keppel Palmer, of the 17/21 Lancers. My fellow instructor from the Royal Navy was Commander Ruck-Keene, OBE, DSC, who had already survived having his destroyers sunk under him twice.

Work at Minley was an endeavour to compress the main elements of the two-year peace time Camberley course into six months. No 3 was the last such course, after which Minley and Camberley worked similarly on short war courses. These were directed at producing the junior commanders and staff officers to be needed in great numbers for the invasion of Europe in 1944. On these later courses RAF students included Wing Commanders Crowley-Milling and Bob Braham. The latter by that time was one of our leading night fighter pilots.

Bob introduced me to my first Mosquito. This was when we visited Bradwell Bay together, where his old squadron was based. It was a Mk II, armed with four cannon and airborne intercept (AI) radar. Bob's final briefing was, 'forget it has two Merlins, and fly it as though it was a Spitfire'. Which is just what I did and found it one of the most delightful aeroplanes I had ever flown. Later I flew many hours on Mosquitos; but that first experience remains unforgettable. The great power of the two Merlins; an acceleration on opening up which I had never before experienced; a feel of the controls which seemed as though the aeroplane was a live thing, telling its pilot as much, or more, than the flight instruments could do. I explored all its characteristics, from stalls and single engine work, to maximum speeds, and forgot time. So that when I returned to Bradwell, as if from a private heaven, although it was still light and clear high up, it was becoming dark below, and the mists were creeping up from the creeks and saltings which surround Bradwell.

As I approached, they fired up FIDO. This I had never seen before. FIDO comprised a line of pipes, laid parallel along the whole length of each side of the runway, into which was pumped petrol. The pipes, punctured at intervals along their whole length, sprayed petrol into the air, which, being ignited, resulted in a wall of flame along either side of the runway. It was capable of clearing the whole area of the runway of fog and its use at increasing numbers of aerodromes equipped to receive aircraft coming home in bad weather saved many a crew from being lost.

During this time at the Staff College, I was able to witness exercises on the ground in which bigger and bigger army formations were involved. For this purpose I was allotted a most delightful personal aeroplane which I kept at the aerodrome at Hartford Bridge. The aeroplane was an American Vultee Vigilant. This was a high wing two-seat monoplane, powered by a 300hp Lycoming radial engine, designed for air observation, and operating from very small fields. Its performance was comparable to the Fieseler Storch, though it lacked the remarkable shock absorbing under-carriage of the Storch, and did not fly quite so slowly. But it did have a marvellously arranged cabin, in which bulged sides enabled one to look, not just vertically below, but actually past the vertical under the fuselage. The Lycoming engine, in contrast to the rough Argus of the Storch, ran as smoothly as a dynamo, and with its electric starter, the whole thing comprised a self-sufficient and very comfortable airborne Jeep, in which it was possible to go almost anywhere, and land where I liked.

Another means of escape was the fact that I was able to visit No 263 Squadron. I had first become acquainted with 263 when they were based at Matlask in Norfolk, about fifteen miles south of Sheringham. It was one of those days when the winter northeast wind brings mist and low cloud off the North Sea, and things below can suddenly disappear. In the Flying Training Command Hurricane I thankfully followed, being lost, a 263 aeroplane into Matlask, and was made welcome and warm, and their grateful guest for two nights. Nos 137 and 263 Squadrons were the only ones to fly Westland Whirlwinds; not the helicopter, but a superb twin-engine single-seat fighter, powered by two Rolls-Royce Peregrines, and armed with four 20mm Hispano cannons. The pilot's outlook was perfect, and its handling, despite the inertia of two heavy engines outboard on the wings, very agile. It was, I think, almost the best of the aircraft designed by W.E.W. Petter and a delight to fly. It excelled in low level cannon strikes. When I arrived at the Army Staff Colleqe, 263 had moved down to Warmwell, near Weymouth. They were engaged in intruder operations into the Cherbourg Peninsular. Sometimes they allowed me the privilege of flying with them.

Just before I left the Staff College, 263's aircraft were replaced by the new Hawker Typhoon IB, with the 2,200hp 24-cylinder Napier Sabre engine. By comparison to the delicate and thoroughbred beauty of the Whirlwind, the Typhoon seemed a thunderous son of Vulcan. In its rather confined cockpit I felt imprisoned by powerful machinery. But its performance was sensational. I never flew the Typhoon enough to come to terms with it. But later, in Germany, I found its ultimate development, the Hawker Tempest II, with a 2,526hp Bristol Centaurus engine, and top speed of 440mph. It was one of the best fast piston engine aircraft I have flown.

I have always believed that it was indirectly due to my link with 263 Squadron, who at that time were about to become part of the 2nd Tactical Air Force, that I was rescued from Camberley. David Atcherley, newly appointed SASO to Basil Embry as AOC2 Group, gathered me into 2 Group to become one of Basil Embry's Squadron Commanders.

On 24 February 1944 I was posted to No 13 Operational Training Unit at Finmere to train as a pilot on B25 Mitchell light bombers and to pick up my own crew, with whom I led 2 Group Squadron. On leaving the Staff College at Camberley I took my farewell of its new Commandant, General Wimberley, subsequently Commander of the 51st (Highland) Division, which I was to meet later in Normandy.

CHAPTER SIX
NO 2 GROUP

Nothing could have been more different to my arrival in 150 Squadron than my arrival in 2 Group. The Group was commanded and led by Basil Embry, then an Air Vice Marshal, already awarded the DSO and three bars. It is difficult to describe such a man. He was dark, thick-set, immensely tough, and with piercing blue eyes that spoke of Celtic ancestry. He was a brilliant pilot with an A1 Instructor category from CFS, and of absolutely uncompromising integrity. If this description makes him sound a frightening person, that is in part true, and anybody who let him down had no second chance. But anyone who did his best, even if he made mistakes would certainly get his rocket from Basil Embry, but would also be defended by him with all his great vigour against any outsider who attempted to interfere. He could, when he chose, be immensely charming, but perhaps the most decisive thing was that every aircrew in 2 Group, every Squadron Commander, and every member of his staff knew that their AOC could take over their job at any time and do it better. All this amounted to leadership of supreme quality. It was a leadership which inspired quite ordinary average men to achievements far greater than their own natural capability and, in so doing it created in No 2 Group a spirit the like of which I have not experienced before or since.

My posting to Finmere made it possible for Rosemary to join me, and we borrowed her mother's old Vauxhall and installed ourselves at the Hill House Hotel in Buckingham. Each morning I arrived at the aerodrome at 0830 and learned about the Mitchell twin-engine light bomber. For a week it was mostly book work and sitting in the cockpit until, blindfolded, I could go through any drill or any emergency by speedy touch. Then I was shown how to fly the aeroplane; not finding out for myself, but shown very carefully by a young instructor who gave me treatment no less thorough than to the pilots fresh from Flying Training School. This was followed by a month of day flying, night flying and instrument flying, until I and Bill Williams were teamed together as pilot and navigator.

Bill Williams entered the RAF as an apprentice at Halton, and spent two years becoming skilled tradesman. When Bill left Halton, he spent most of his pre-war time at the Marine Aircraft Experimental Establish (MAEE) at Felixstowe. Very often he was in charge of seaplanes embarked for catapult trials in the old HMS *Ark Royal*. Our paths must have crossed unknowingly many times, for this coincided with my time at Lee-on-the-Solent. Later he was in Singapore as aircrew, and was one of the few who, when the Japanese invaded, made their way through the Dutch East Indies to Ceylon, to return home and fight again.

With Bill we practised bombing on the range at Otmoor where, before the war, I had done the same in my 90 Squadron Blenheim. I found Bill's steady quiet voice on the run up, never hurried, never excited, easy to follow. Thus, with his skilled aptitude, we managed a consistent error of less than 100 yards from 10,000 feet, the maximum margin of error permitted for Basil Embry's lead crews.

Last of all we teamed up with our two air gunners, mid-upper and belly turret, completing the crew of four. Our two gunners were Sergeant Harris and Flying Officer Zdenek Kokes. Sergeant Harris came from the East End of London; he was small, wiry, built like a featherweight boxer and totally without fear. He demanded the belly turret because its position needed acrobatic ability to enter and to fire it. He was one of those rebels whose whole existence demands adventure and fight and whose loyalty, once given, remains unshakeable. Our mid-upper gunner, Zdenek Kokes, had already served a tour as tail gunner in the Czech-manned Wellington Squadron flying from East Wretham, near Thetford. Instructional and staff duties had not appealed to him after completion of this tour and he had persistently applied to return to active operations. He already held the Czech Military Cross. Zdenek had been an undergraduate at Cambridge when the war began. His parents and two sisters were still in Amsterdam, living in the Apollolaan only a few doors away from the local Gestapo Headquarters. Before the war his father Joseph Kokes had been the Czech Commercial Attaché to Holland. As we were later to discover, the Kokes family played a brave part in the Resistance but, at the time he joined our crew, Zdenek had had no contact with his family since the Germans overran Holland. Zdenek, with great charm and being very young and good looking, proved irresistible to the girls.

When we completed at Finmere, we were a close knit team. We knew we were competent to do whatever was required of us, and thought that we could probably do it rather better than other crews. It was a return to the kind of flying for which 90 Squadron had prepared me, that is daylight operations and formations.

Leaving Finmere had its sadness, for Rosemary and I had been singularly happy at the Hill House Hotel in Buckingham. She returned to the farmhouse at Batley, resuming care of her mother and our two sons, Simon, now three years old and his younger brother Timothy, six months.

As far as Basil Embry was concerned, completion of operational training was far from enough to reach the standards he required of anyone privileged to take command of one of his squadrons. Thus we, as a crew, were attached supernumerary to No 226 Squadron, flying Mitchells from Hartford Bridge (now known as Blackbushe) just outside Camberley. The Hartford Bridge Wing, No 137, was commanded by W.M.L. McDonald, now Group Captain and a decorated survivor from one of the Battle Squadrons. The other two squadrons there were No 88 and the French Squadron No 342, both flying Bostons.

The 2nd Tactical Air Force of which No 2 Group was the light bomber component comprised of various groups. No 83 Group were fighters, mainly Spitfires and Typhoons, working closely with the 2nd British Army Group. No 84 Group, similarly composed, worked with the 1st Canadian Army Group. No 2 Group provided the light bomber backing for both, by day mainly but sometimes at night. In addition, there were Photographic Reconnaissance Squadrons, RAF Regiment Squadrons for the close protection of aerodromes, and a great mass of supporting organisations providing facilities for airfield construction and repair, supply of fuels and ammunitions, signals, hospitals and every sort of service. The whole was commanded by Air Marshal Arthur Coningham, who had created the Desert Air Force.

We were allotted a shared room in a cold Nissen hut. Hot baths were cold showers and we washed and shaved in a sort of communal wash house where duckboards and planks covered the floor. A row of basins, served by cold taps, drained into a duct which, via the adjoining lavatories, sluiced away to the drains. On our first day at Hartford Bridge we were kitted up and taken to our temporary Flight Commander Paddy Lyall. He was a large, blonde, happy extrovert, who had already survived something like forty operations and seemed to have the conviction that, whatever might happen to other people, it would never happen to him. His crew had complete faith in his indestructibility. We were told that we would be No 4 in the box he was leading the next day.

Next morning we were briefed for an attack on the German aerodrome just outside Abbeville. It was occupied at the time by an aggressive Gruppe know as the Abbeville Boys, who flew Me109s. It was not a deep penetration and was designed not only to irritate the occupants but to entice them into the air to be met, we hoped, by a superior force of our own fighters. In the event, the nastiest thing was the moderate flak. Our position was No 4 in the box led by Paddy Lyall. The box was the standard formation used by the light bombers of 2 Group. It comprised the leader with his Nos 2 and 3 in echelon to port and starboard. No 4 flew below and astern of the leader with Nos 5 and 6 on his port and starboard. This box of six, closed up, was intended to give maximum coverage by crossfire against fighters, and to ensure that when the lead navigator called bombs away, the whole load dropped as close as possible together. A great deal depended, therefore, on the lead crew of each box.

A squadron formation comprised three such boxes. We usually operated as a wing of three squadrons tucked in tight. On this first operation we flew as part of a squadron formation in which Paddy Lyall led the first and leading box. My principal recollection of this flight is of intense concentration upon keeping my exact place astern of and below my leader. Had I considered it, I might have realised that, with over 2,000 hours of varied experience, I was the one with the most flying hours in the whole formation. But I was the least experienced in the particular job. Being shot at adds an entirely different dimension to flying, and in this dimension, Paddy Lyall was immeasurably my superior. So I stuck tight and followed him.

Flak by day is quite different to flak by night. At night, following no leader but perhaps in a stream of bombers, flak tends to come up in a sea of bright streaks, anyone of which may be the one with your own name on it. In intense flak, the sky becomes a lethal Guy Fawkes night, laced with patterns of streaming and exploding light. By day, the sky is different. The flak which hits is the one not seen. Instead there appears in front of you and in the sky all about you, sudden sooty bursts. Initially there is a little red centre which degenerates into a black, sooty and sulphurous blob, with a lingering tail. To see it is to know that it has gone off and missed. On this first expedition I had little time to realise that daytime flak, though maybe just as lethal, was not so impressive. I saw little of it.

After Abbeville we did two or more runs. One was the marshalling yards at Amiens, and the other was against a coastal battery; not a deep penetration but hotly defended and certainly one of the areas which the enemy intended to defend with the utmost vigour.

At this point, the Commander of 98 Squadron was lost with his crew, and I, with my crew, was ordered forthwith to 139 Wing at Dunsfold near Guildford to take over its command. We reported there together on 19 May 1944. On the following day I led 98 Squadron our first operation as its Squadron Commander.

Dunsfold aerodrome, situated ten miles south of Guildford, lies on the north side of the lush plain between the South Downs and the other line of hills which run from Haslemere eastward past Godalming, Reigate and on to Sevenoaks and Maidstone. It is overlooked to the north by a hill rising to 800 feet, upon which we placed a red beacon.

The aerodrome was built by Canadian engineers; the longest of its three runways was 2,000 yards. To complete the long runway, the Canadians lifted, removed intact and replaced on a mound by the south perimeter track, a charming small cottage. Named Rose Cottage, it was the 98 Squadron Headquarters. In it I had my own office and there also were all the squadron records. Round it, to the rear were the small Nissen huts housing the squadron armoury, the detonator store and the servicing equipment for our eighteen Mitchells. Nearest to Rose Cottage was our squadron briefing and ready room.

Around this little centre were our aircraft, each on its own dispersed hard standing. From my office window, formerly the dining room, I looked north. Nearest was my own Mitchell and beyond the long runway. Beyond that was the control tower and the main building of the Wing Operational Headquarters.

Because Dunsfold was a Canadian creation, the Commanding Officer and most of his staff were Canadian, wearing the insignia of the Royal Canadian Air Force. It would have been difficult to have found better people under whom to serve. Under Group Larry Dunlap, they spared themselves nothing to ensure that their three squadrons were relieved of any extraneous task which could interfere with operational efficiency. At a time when even the pubs often ran out of beer, they made sure that it did not run out at Dunsfold and the aircrew returning from night operations never failed to get two eggs and bacon, and a hot bath, before going to bed. Because the Wing was intended to move to France at the first opportunity, it was organised for complete mobility and thus we lived in tents.

Operations continued. On 20, 22 and 24 May we launched twelve aircraft against targets in France. Similar operations continued throughout the rest of May, notably against coastal gun batteries along the French coast. These operations were typical of the work of the 2 Group Light Bomber Force immediately prior to D-Day. It was part of the plan, not only to soften up the coastal defences but also to interrupt railway and other communications leading to the Channel coast. Attacks had to be as spread out to give no indication to the enemy where the impending assault would come ashore. In fact there was an elaborate deception plan already in operation to mislead the enemy and to make him believe that the attack would come in the neighbourhood of Calais or Boulogne. We know now that it was successful, for the enemy did, in fact, move some of his forces into the Pas de Calais.

The drill at Dunsfold for launching an operation was so practiced as to have become almost automatic. As soon as an operation order was received from Group, the pilots and navigators would be called in to the Wing briefing room. Here Squadron Leader John Pawson, who filled the combined post of Operations and Intelligence, would have large scale maps marked up and, having given the target, route and bomb load, would add any intelligence information. Next the flak officer briefed us. To him we attached considerable importance because of the quantity and excellence of the German 88mm gun, which was not only a fine anti-tank weapon but effective with proximity fused ammunition up to sixteen or so thousand feet. They had an awful lot of it. Because our normal operating height, for performance reasons, was not more than 15,000 and usually a good deal lower, flak mattered.

Next would come the Armaments Officer with details of bomb load and any special features such as delay fuses. Five-inch lens cameras in two aircraft in each box recorded bomb bursts and would, of course, record only those bombs with no delay. Finally came the Signals Officer with details of call signs, emergency calls and later, when we became equipped to bomb blind, the target coordinates on the G- or GH-chain which would indicate release point for bombing.

My own call sign was Fountain Two Zero. The box of Mitchells which I led was Ivory Box and the other two of 98 were Blue and Red respectively. When in formation I used the call Fountain Leader.

Whilst the main briefing was going on, the gunners were over in the squadron armoury drawing their ammunition and checking turrets. The armourers, having collected bombs from the distant dump, would be fitting fuses and loading the bombs into the belly bomb bays.

After the Wing briefing, we would hasten round the perimeter to our squadron briefing rooms and give a general briefing to the whole squadron. Then in flying clothing we would go out to our aircraft at dispersals. Here our fitter and rigger would help us in. With everybody in position and the aircraft hatches closed, the armourer would remove the bomb safety pins. Then we were free to start up.

In normal circumstances, it would be fifty-five to sixty minutes from its start. However, when necessary, we could reduce this time to thirty-five minutes. Next, aircraft would taxi out and line up in pairs on the main runway in pre-arranged order and take off in succession. As the leader of each box made a wide sweep round the aerodrome, his formation, taking shorter cuts, would rapidly join up and in turn the boxes would come together to complete the squadron formation. We reckoned to be able to set course at 2,000 feet in normal conditions in one and a half hours from the start of the first briefing and, when necessary, in around one hour.

Sometimes joining up was made less easy by low cloud base. For this we developed a technique of our own. Having taken off, each aircraft would set course towards the coast keeping accurately to one of the lattice lines on the Gee (AMES Type 7000 radio navigation system). Each aircraft was kept apart by the separation of take-off time and, when necessary, boxes were separated by using slightly offset lattice lines. It was quite an odd experience to emerge, as once happened not long after D-Day, to be the first in the sky over thousands of feet of cloud, and then suddenly to watch a succession of Mitchells emerge from below to pick up their allotted place in the formation. It required fairly accurate instrument flying by each pilot but worked very effectively.

During all this time, radio silence was obligatory and maintained until the bombing leader broadcast the order 'open bomb doors' as we neared the target. The enemy coast was the signal to secure the flak-harness. This was a garment which contained splinter-proof steel plate and was cumbersome and heavy. Bill generally used his as a mat to lie on when in his exposed bombing position right up in the nose. I sat on mine, and occasionally put on a tin hat as protection against anything that might burst just above us.

Dodging flak with a formation depended primarily on keeping away from known concentrations. Bill and I got to know Brittany, Normandy and the coastal areas up to Calais so well that we generally knew where to avoid and were able to lead our formations round such places.

When we did meet flak the formation would open up a bit. At the same time the leader, having either seen or been told where it was bursting, would have to anticipate the correction that the gunners were likely to give to bring them onto target. If it was from astern and below one would expect the guns to correct accordingly. We could defeat them by turning to the right or left. This would result in bursts appearing off to one side. Another ploy would be a turn towards the bursts causing them to come next time on the opposite side. One could also ring the changes by alterations in height. The drill when encountering enemy fighters was to close up tight, although we saw few for Allied fighters had dealt with them very effectively by D-Day and our own bombing of airfields had helped.

On the run to the target everything had to be subordinated to accurate bombing. Not only were some of our targets quite small, but on occasions they were close to French homes and no effort was spared to avoid killing French civilians. Usually Bill would open up on the W/T and call to close up when we were nearing the target. Depending upon the shape and size of it boxes would bomb in succession, each on orders from its own leader. But sometimes, when it would be more effective, the whole squadron of eighteen would let go at once on orders from Bill. By this time Bill would have moved into the nose and be busy with his bombsight. His first order to me would be to line me up on the approach run. If no more corrections were needed he would order 'bomb doors open' to the formation. As the bomb doors opened there would be a hiss of hydraulics and then the rumble of wind in and through the bomb bay. By this time I would be concentrating completely on instruments and holding speed, height and course as accurately as I could. Most of the flak would be out of sight, although a near one would make a loud bang and sometimes splinters would hit the aircraft. Throughout we would usually have had a fighter escort in the area.

On the morning of 5 June everybody was confined to camp and the camp sealed off. 139 Wing in the previous week had been visited by General Eisenhower who had addressed all the aircrew of the three squadrons. He had left none of us in any doubt of the importance of our role in the invasion and there were few of us, when the camp was sealed, who did not realise that D-Day was very close.

On the night of 5/6 June, all of 98 were out over Normandy. My own aircraft was not yet repaired after operations on 28 May and the substitute which I had used on the 29th came back with some holes in the fuselage. So again we had a strange aircraft. Our target was the road and rail running through a defile near Thury-Harcourt. At a point just south of Thury-Harcourt, both road and rail run side by side in the deep cleft of the River Orne, before it emerges into the lower land towards Caen. It would be by this route that enemy reinforcements would move from the south towards Caen. We spent a long time searching the area, which was covered by low cloud. Evidently the Pathfinder aircraft had the same problem as there were no illuminations. Our own aircraft, not having Gee-H precluded us from being one of the Pathfinders.

When it became clear that we had better go home, we left by the prescribed route which took us out to sea between France and the Channel Islands and back to England via the western end of the Isle of Wight. We had left Dunsfold at 0215 hours on the morning of 6 June. By the time we left for home, the first light was in the sky and away to the north of us the sea was visible. The whole area was a mass of distant ships and the sky full of aircraft. This was the invasion. There were numbers of explosions and some fires burning. Towards La Havre there seemed to be heavy gunfire, and around Caen a good deal of flak. It was to avoid the invasion force itself that we had been given this circuitous route home.

The next night we went back to the Thury-Harcourt defile in good weather, found it well marked with indicators, and planted four 1,000 pounds right on the dot. Later it was confirmed that the route was blocked so that on the third night, that of 7/8 June, we went to the railway at Vire. From here a branch line leaves the east-west route and goes northward through St-Lô and eventually to Cherbourg itself, whilst another line leads south to Mortain. We left Dunsfold at 0125 hours arriving at Vire about an hour later. We were still using our borrowed aircraft. It was a pleasant night and fairly light. Bill guided us down the railway line from east to west and planted our load of four 1,000 pounds nicely into the junction. The ground here rises to about 1,000 feet in places and with our altimeters set at sea level pressure, their reading of 2,000 feet meant we were a bare 1,000 feet above our bomb bursts. We felt each one and there was no question that they had all gone off. We also noted that what looked like the Town Hall was on fire, and wondered how this had come about. After that we flew low up the main road towards St-Lô, and our gunners were bitterly disappointed at finding nothing to shoot at. Returning to Vire we then completed our second task which was to drop leaflets saying 'Your Allies have arrived'.

Going past the end of Cherbourg Peninsular it was becoming light in the sky, though still dark at sea level. Perhaps foolishly, we had contented ourselves with not getting up too high for the return journey. Just to the northwest of the Cap de la Hague, there was what looked like a battle going on between German e-boats and our own light forces.

During this initial phase of Overlord the Mitchell and Mosquitos of 2 Group were ranging by night over the whole inland area of the beachhead. On the night of 7/8 June there were 122 Mosquito attacks on various targets; sixty Mitchells and twelve Bostons were also out.

It was immediately after our night out to Vire that my crew and I were sent for a week up to Swanton Morley where we were initiated into the operation of Gee-H. Gee and GEE-H deserve explanation. The Gee stations, three appropriately located in the south and west of England, transmitted continuous signals which gave readings on the Gee-box in the navigator's compartment. These signals when read off onto the chart, corresponded to the lattice lines on it and gave a very accurate fix of the aircraft's position. It gave good results up to a distance of approximately 300 miles from the ground stations, depending on the altitude of the aircraft receiving. This altitude effect is common to all VHF and UHF transmissions, and the maximum range at which our Mitchells could use Gee was governed by the height from which we bombed when using.

Gee, however, suffered from one serious disadvantage. The enemy could also hear it and found it easy to jam. Gee-H got rid of the jamming by the ground stations remaining silent until interrogated by the set in the aircraft. The ground station came to life briefly and transmitted the relevant reply. Thus the enemy never got around to jamming effectively. Using Gee-H as a blind bombing instrument we could, from 10,000 feet, place our bombs within the 100 yard circle that was the requirement. A box of six Mitchells, each releasing four bombs, produced a pattern on the ground which was almost bound to cover the target.

On 15 June we arrived back at Dunsfold in time to lead 98 on a day formation operation. The target was an ammunition dump northeast of Alencon. Taking off at 1740 hours on a lovely summer's evening, this was a good attack.

At 1840 hours on the evening of 17 June , we lead four boxes of Mitchells to attack the marshalling yards at Mezidon. The rail links out of Mezidon lead direct to Caen in the west, to Argentan in the south through Falaise, to the coast at Cabourg Plage, and to the east towards Paris. We elected to attack from the southwest, away from the setting sun and over broken cloud. The direction also coincided with a convenient Gee-H lattice. The intention was that all twenty-four aircraft should let go simultaneously, relying on the shape of the formation and Bill's accurate guidance to plaster the target, if possible without hitting the houses beyond it. The plan worked well and we were able to see through the cloud breaks some satisfactory fires and explosions in the right place. We were later told that a Panzer division had not been able to get any further.

On 18 June we went again to the ammunition dump at Alencon. We bombed by Gee-H and came home with some flak holes. It was at this time we lost Sergeant Harris, not through enemy action but a swimming accident. The replacement Air Gunner lasted only three trips. He reacted badly to flak and had to go.

The departure of our failed gunner resulted in the arrival of Mich Jansen who became a family friend and godfather to my daughter, Azalea. In 1939 he had been a Reserve Officer Pilot in the Royal Belgium Air Force flying Fairey Battles. His civilian job was as an engineer in charge of the department of power and electricity in Brussels. When war came to Belgium, Mich flew with his squadron and, when France surrendered, ended up near Bordeaux having flown and fought to the last. He made his way back to Brussels, largely by bicycle, and resumed his civilian job. At the same time he became an active member of the underground. He was caught by the Gestapo and imprisoned in the fortress prison of Breendonck and condemned to death in 1942. This death sentence was suspended because the Gestapo wanted more information about his activities and his fellow underground operators. Mich seldom spoke of this imprisonment. Mich was sprung by the Resistance, assumed a new name and continued his work with the underground. He was recaptured and imprisoned in the fortress prison of St Gilles and again sentenced to death. His brother managed to smuggle a saw into his cell. With this Mich cut through his cell bars and with three other Belgians escaped over the fortress walls to freedom. He made his way through Belgium, France, over the Pyrennees, through Spain and then to Gibraltar, where he was sent to England.

For any normal man this would have been enough, but not for Mich. At the Belgian Headquarters in London he was asked to accept a desk job, replying that he wanted to fly and kill Germans. He joined the RAF as an Air Gunner and became the fourth member of our crew.

On 20 June 1944 we attacked a NOBALL target. This was the codename used for German V1 flying bomb launch sites. The target was to the southeast of Abbeville. On the following day we tried to attack another site at Neufchatel, but were unsuccessful as the target was completely obscured by cloud.

On 22 June 139 Wing carried out what I consider to be one of their most important operations. Progress out of the beachhead had been slow and in particular around Caen the Germans were putting up very determined resistance. Just north of Caen, on the eastern side of the River Orne and the Orne canal, lies the Colombelles Iron Works. This had been converted by the enemy into what amounted to a strongly defended fortress. It had defied all efforts to take it, and had kept the 51st Highland Division pinned down on the western side of the Orne. This was our target, with the important point that it was no more than 1,000 yards from our own Highlanders. There was a good deal of flak in which the excellent 88mm guns played a large part. 98, 226 and 320 Squadrons bombed in succession from Mitchells and were followed closely by 88 and 342 with their Bostons. The results were good, for not only were the Highlanders able to cross the water line without serious opposition, but they took the iron works as well.

On 25 June we returned once more to a NOBALL target. This one was different, as it was the Chateau, just east of Beauvais, which housed Colonel Wachtel, the commander of the German Flakregiment 155 (W) and his staff. This was the unit responsible for all V1 sites and launchings in the West. Information came through the underground that the Colonel was in residence and likely to be at home between four and six in the afternoons.

Accordingly we left Dunsfold at 1440 hours leading the first box of 98 Squadron hoping to catch the Colonel. We duly dealt with the Chateau, though not all of the bombs fell on the target, and some overshot. Afterwards we heard that the Colonel had indeed been at tea, but in a summer house some way from the aiming point. He is said to have watched our performance with interest.

The V1 flying bombs affected us in several ways at Dunsfold. Our first experience of one was returning one night when the gunner reported that there seemed to be an aircraft astern and overtaking fast. It had a very noticeable exhaust flame streaming behind it. Before we could take evasive action it overtook us and, passing below and to one side, disappeared in the direction of England. It was going some 150mph more than our cruising speed home. A more apparent result was the shower of flying bombs that either failed to clear the line of hills running across just north of Dunsfold, and the concentration of anti-aircraft and barrage balloons which arrived in the area from mid-June onwards. On one occasion we sat in our aircraft, waiting on the runway, whilst an errant gas bag, adrift from its moorings, trailed across the aerodrome. After a long wait somebody in a Spitfire arrived and shot it down in flames.

On another occasion we were given a running commentary from one of the squadron members ensconced in a telephone box in Cranleigh, our nearest small town. The call was to ask for transport back to Dunsfold, and it became a description of the low approach of a flying bomb followed by the words 'The engine's stopped and now it diving!' and then came a crashing explosion.

On the night of 27/28 June we went out on an abortive night operation, when the Radar failed. I think it must have been this night that we had a brush with the balloon barrage. Nearing Dunsfold, as we thought, we were suddenly startled by the appearance ahead of a forest of searchlight beams, all pointing in the same direction. This was the agreed signal to any friendly aircraft straying into the barrage, and the lights pointed in the direction to be taken to get clear. We were very grateful and retracing our steps landed safely at Dunsfold. Thereafter we had a run of poor weather and a series of daylight operations, some successful, some not, mostly against fuel and ammunition dumps.

A change came on 24 July when we were directed late in the evening to an anti-tank concentration in La Hogue Wood, southeast of Caen, which was holding up our troops. There was intense flak and we suffered a good deal of damage and lost one aircraft.

The following day 98 was able to only muster two boxes of aircraft, pending arrival of replacements. But we went again early in the morning to La Hogue Wood. This time I took the leading box and Bill guided us so accurately that the target was thoroughly plastered. We did not have to return there again.

Replacement crews and aircraft arrived from the Group Support Unit at Swanton Morley the next day, and after that we were again up to strength and could put up three boxes of six Mitchells when required. There followed a series of attacks on fuel and ammunition dumps, and some railway yards. The sole exception was a night sortie on 28 July when we spent some time over a wood at Bourquebus, southeast of Caen, dropping target indicators and flares in order to illuminate and mark the target for the rest of the squadron. The work was hindered by low cloud, but the target indicators showed it clearly burning on the ground. We had subsequent information that the wood was being used by German armour.

After that, until 12 August, we continued again on daylight formations against supply dumps of various kinds and some troop concentrations. After the daylight sortie to a dump near Beauvais, the squadron was called out unexpectedly at night. The enemy was beginning to retreat in the British sector over the River Orne. By day the Typhoons and fighter bombers of 83 Group wreaked havoc among them. Night brought the enemy his only chance to cross the Orne in some sort of safety. We left Dunsfold just before midnight and spent most of that night marking with indicators and flares the bridges and crossings being used by the enemy. With this guidance the rest of the Squadron bombed with good effect.

On 14 August we were again out by daylight to a wood near Falaise. This was now the scene of intense fighting on the ground. Our target was an enemy strongpoint holding up our own forces. Friendly troops were very close, and displayed their positions by showing coloured flares. Bill, as always, led up accurately onto the proper aiming point. By this time, the Allies were starting to break out of the beach head, and the Falaise Gap was beginning to close around the enemy.

On 16 August we were sent to destroy a bridge over the river at Livarot, and were recalled with the news that the bridge was already blown. On 17 August we were out again at night and spent two hours making a nuisance of ourselves over four bridges across the River Risle, near Berville-sur-Mer. These were being used by the enemy as escape routes. On 18 August we came home at dawn to our eggs and bacon, and to ten days leave.

On 28 August we returned from leave. The next morning I went to see Larry Dunlap. He told me that Group had decreed that my crew had completed our tour of operations and we were to do no more operational flying. A few days after this, Bill and I were each gazetted as being awarded the DFC.

For the next month I relieved Alan Lynn as Wing Commander Operations at Dunsfold. Command of 98 was taken over by Wing Commander Hamer who, in mid-October took the squadron, accompanied by 180 and 320, to the Wing's new location at Brusselles Melsbroek. In all Bill and I had flown forty-three operations together.

Whilst I was still at Dunsfold our crew flew down to Hawkinge to thank the Belgians who had provided our escorts and protected us so well. This was No 350 (Belgian) Squadron, by now armed with Spitfire Mk XIV, which were powered by the huge Rolls-Royce Griffon engine of more than 2,000hp. 350 was commanded by Marcel (Mike) Dennet. His escape from Belgium had been aided by Mich and several others. They had hidden a light training aircraft (a Stampe). They had replaced, as best they could, all the instruments which the Germans had removed to immobilise it, obtained petrol and one night flew from near Brussels to England. Mike had been a fighter pilot in the Belgian Air Force and had been flying Spitfires ever since. This was Mike and Mich's first meeting since they had made their ways to England. We were given a great welcome and stayed the night. Next morning Mike lent me one of his Spitfire XIVs to try. It was far heavier than the Merlin Spitfires which I had flown before, but still retained that unique thoroughbred feel and control. The important thing to watch was the torque of the enormous engine which, if opened up carelessly, could make take-off tricky. In the air, any great change of power resulted in a considerable change of directional trim. But it was a beautiful aeroplane and I rated it as the best thing I had flown since the Whirlwind. Mike Donnet finished his career as Chief of the Royal Belgian Air Force, and as General of Aviation, the Baron Marcel Donnet, CVO DFC.

CHAPTER SEVEN
HQ 2 GROUP

On September 19 1944 I reported to HQ of No. 2 Group at Mongewell Park, on the east bank of the Thames, opposite Wallingford. The dining room of the grand building was the operations room. I reported to and was welcomed by David Atcherley and found myself one of Basil Embry's team of operations officers, all of whom had previously commanded one of his squadrons. My fellow operations officers included Digger Magill, Bill Edrich, Bob Iredale and Rufus Riseley. Group Captain of operations was Kipperberger. Basil Embry's navigator, Peter Clapham, acted as a sort of ADC when not flying and was generally helpful to everybody. In charge of administration, which included every sort of supply, movement, transport, getting fuel and bombs to the right places was 'Bull' Cannon.

At Mongewell we lived in a constant state of readiness to move to the continent. Basil Embry's small caravan was parked in the stable yard. I lived in a tent in the garden, as did several of us. The operations staff worked in shifts, manning the OPS room on a 24-hour rota. The usual routine was that the morning shift prepared operations orders for the day as early as possible. The afternoon shift prepared night orders and these were approved, and sometimes but not always, amended by the AOC or his SASO. All orders were of minimum length and maximum simplicity. Usually we telephoned them through to the Wing Operations Room on secure lines using a scrambler and the confirmation signal went by telex in code immediately afterwards.

Sometimes there were very special operations. Notable among these were the unique Mosquito attacks on Gestapo prisons and headquarters, one of which was in its initial planning stages whilst I was there. It later took place from Fersfield, which I was shortly to command. My knowledge of this was a most detailed and accurate model of the target and the surrounding town, which was kept under cover in the carefully guarded operations room, and used for initial planning and later for the detailed briefing of the crews who took part. On these Gestapo operations, Basil Embry took part, wearing Wing Commanders uniform and badges, and identified only as Wing Commander Smith. Peter Clapham, his navigator, went with him.

The first of these special 2 Group prison busting raids was the famous attack led by Group Captain Charles Pickard. This was in January 1944, just before I joined 2 Group. Three waves of Mosquitoes were used. The first wave (487 Squadron) breached the prison walls. The second, from 464 Squadron, attacked the German garrison billets, whilst others breached the actual walls of the prison buildings. Incarcerated in the prison were 700 prisoners, nearly all members of the French Resistance, and many awaiting execution. As a result of this operation, 258 made their escape through the breached walls. Group Captain Pickard was shot down by an FW 190 and killed. My own link with this operation was to take Dick Atcherley in our Mitchell, landing at the nearest airfield (Amiens/Glisy), as soon as it had been cleared of Germans during the advance through northern France. Our purpose was to find out exactly what had happened to Pickard and his navigator. We got hold of a Jeep from the nearest army, and in this we found the French people who had been first to reach the destroyed Mosquito. Their graphic description left no doubt that both pilot and navigator had been killed instantly and had been buried close to the prison.

The newly captured aerodrome was a huge grass field with remnants of its previous occupants still visible. The ground transport and crews of a Typhoon Wing of 83 Group was arriving as we landed, and almost at once a stream of Typhoons came in to refuel and rearm. They wasted no time, refuelling from 4 gallon jerry cans poured straight into the tanks. They rearmed with rockets and belted ammunition, and throughout the pilots and ground crews worked flat out together. It was far too early in proceedings for any organised system of guards to have been established and the aerodrome was wide open to anybody strayed onto it. The Typhoons left again quickly to pursue the enemy still close at hand, whilst we left the Mitchell guarded by Bill and a gunner amongst the Typhoon ground.

We brought back with us a Squadron Leader from Tangmere who had been shot down near Amiens earlier. He was a French Canadian and had been able to assume the appearance and speech of the locals. Sheltered by the underground, he soon established himself with such good effect that he obtained a job as a civilian carpenter building lavatories on a German flying bomb site. He told us that after launching, the flying bombs often turned back onto the launching site and occasionally blew up on the launch rails. Eventually we landed him back at Tangmere, where he greeted an astonished commanding officer by identifying himself with the pass issued to him by the Germans to go in and out of the site where he worked.

The 2 Group communications flight was based at Benson a few miles away to the north of Dunsfold and home base of the Photographic Reconnaissance Squadrons of the RAF. They flew specially cleaned up high altitude Spitfires, and Mosquitoes.

It was from Benson that they left each morning to photograph the results of Bomber Command's work on the previous night. They also carried out reconnaissance missions of Peenemunde on the Baltic coast. This was the German V-weapon experimental establishment. There were several pilots I knew at Benson, some from the days when the PRU had first formed at Heston under Geoffrey Tuttle. Geoffrey Tuttle, by now an Air Commodore, was the AOC and mastermind behind PR operations. Through him I was privileged once or twice to fly their special Spitfires. The most dramatic of these was the special PR Mark XIX. It had a pressure cabin, no armament and a Griffon 65 or 66 engine with a five-bladed Rotol airscrew. There were extra fuel tanks to give it the extreme ranges that PR work required. The tail wheel, as well as the main wheels, retracted. The engine cowling over the Griffon engine was longer and more pointed than earlier marks and resembled the Mk XIV, from which it was developed. Its maximum all up weight was 9,050 pounds compared with the 6,250 pounds of the 1939 Mk I. Its maximum speed was 450mph at 19,000 feet, and its ceiling 43,500 feet. It was marginally faster than the Mk XIV but heavier so that the Mk XIV could get a little higher, having a service ceiling of 45,000 feet. It is interesting to compare these figures again with the Mk I, which had a maximum speed of 362mph at 16,000 feet, and a ceiling of 32,000 feet. The PR XIX, in its sky blue colour and smoothed, like the finish of a Rolls-Royce car was in my opinion the best looking of all the many marks of Spitfire. Though for sheer enjoyment I thought the Mk XII with Griffon engine and clipped wings excelled all.

On 19 October, Basil Embry told me that I was to take over command of his No 2 Group support unit at Swanton Morley with effect from 20 October. This meant promotion with the rank of Acting Group Captain. After some frantic telephoning to give the news to Rosemary, and to ask her to stand by to come up to Swanton Morley as soon as I could find somewhere to live, I set forth. I had the complicated ranks of Substantive Squadron Leader, War Substantive Wing Commander, and Acting Group Captain.

The Group Support Unit had been formed at Swanton Morley on 1 April 1944. Its purpose was to hold at readiness complete crews and aircraft, so that losses in squadrons or crews could be replaced immediately. As CO of 98 Squadron, I had already experienced the value of the GSU. When I took over in October 1944, the GSU had expanded considerably, and now aimed to hold at immediate readiness, five spare crews and aircraft for each front line squadron in the Group. It also had a stock of thirteen Squadron Leaders and five Wing Commanders. In addition, we had our own permanent staff, all of whom had operational experience in the Group. My Wing Commander Flying was the redoubtable Paddy Maher, who later lost his life commanding 107 Squadron and Gunnery Leader, Teddy Frayn. We had several of all the types of aircraft used in the Group: Mosquitoes, Mitchells and Bostons, as well as sundry communications aircraft, including the Ansons, based at Benson. My first job was to become familiar with all the types as well as the Mitchell, and I did as much flying as possible in both Bostons and Mosquitoes.

Swanton Morley was a pre-war station, with a mess and quarters almost identical to those at Bicester. It was a historic 2 Group station, and it was from here that Hughie Edwards had led 105 Squadron in the raid which resulted in his VC award (awarded for an attack he led on Bremen on 4 July 1941).

Swanton Morley had been constantly in the front line during 1941 and 1942. When I arrived the station was in war time drab; camouflaged paint disguised all buildings, aircraft lived for the most part on dispersals and all married quarters had, since 1939, became overflow barrack blocks for the enormously increased population. On the station were the RAF Regiment, ground gunners manning anti-aircraft defences, men and women to keep the unit working twenty-four hours day and night and staff to supply, feed, and provide medical and fire fighting. Initially I lodged in the Mess, which was the best way of getting to know everybody. I was able to take over the Swanton Morley Rectory which had been requisitioned earlier in the war as the station commander's house. I took twenty-four hours off to collect Rosemary to come back with me to our first married quarter since 1939. The children we left in the care of Rosemary's mother.

We had one glorious month at Swanton Morley, and then the GSU was ordered to move to a new and totally uncivilised aerodrome at Fersfield near Diss. It came about because the AOC of 100 Group, Air Vice Marshal Addison, requested the use of Swanton Morley for his very specialised intruders. Part of his group comprised signal jammers and flew Mosquitoes nightly into Germany. They were key factors in preventing the increasingly active Luftwaffe night fighter force from taking greater toll on Bomber Command.

On 14 December we moved the GSU to Fersfield, Rosemary returned to Botley and I moved into a hut surrounded by mud. Fersfield had not long been built and was used by the US Army Air Force as a holding unit for reserve crews for the 9th Air Force, which flew mainly Marauders and Thunderbolts. On my arrival there the USAF were still there in force. The site had originally been well wooded and had been cleared by bulldozers. There were the usual three hard runways and perimeter track, dispersals and one hangar for the more serious maintenance work. Living accommodation was entirely in unlined Nissen huts, with the exception of the sick quarters and the one small brick hut adjacent to the Mess. This provided me with the luxury of a bedroom, sitting room, bath and lavatory, and two adjoining rooms kept for senior visitors such as our AOC. The main Mess building was the biggest Nissen hut I have ever seen. By mid-December the east winds of the North Sea had already resulted in the whole place being chill and damp and as the winter developed into one of the coldest for several years the cavernous Mess Nissen became quite awful. The only heating was provided by a pair of 50-gallon drums, pierced with holes and standing on flagstones at opposite ends of the hut.

I found among our crews a man who had been an architect and some bricklayers. Within a week they had designed and constructed the biggest fireplace I have ever seen. It stood in the middle of the hut, and its size matched its surroundings. In each of its four faces was a huge open grate, and in these we burned the unlimited supplies of wood resulting from the clearance of the aerodrome. These fires never went out and transformed life. Similar constructions served to warm the smaller huts in which everybody lived.

It was during this time that we introduced a scheme intended to 'blood' new crews in the way that my own crew had been 'blooded' with 226 Squadron. During their retreat through France and Belgium, the Germans had left garrisons in several of the Channel ports. 2 GSU was authorised to carry on a sort of private war against some of these garrisons, who could be relied upon to put up a fair show of flak. This would provide our crews with the kind of experience that no amount of simulation can give. When we had a suitable number of crews ready we would mount our own attack, going through all the procedures with the same care that crews would find when they went to their front line units. One such operation took place on 27 December. A force of nine Mitchells attacked Fort Ouvrage Ouest at Dunkirk. The attack clobbered the fort to such good effect as to lead to its surrender.

It was from Fersfield that 2 Group mounted what is now perhaps its best known Gestapo prison busting raid. It took place on 21 March 1944, and its purpose was to release from the Shell House in Copenhagen, members of the Danish Resistance being held in Gestapo HQ. The prisoners were mainly held in the storeys of the building, whilst the Gestapo staff were mainly in the lower parts of the Shell House. The building was in a built up area. The plan was to launch bombs into the basements. 2 Group Mosquitoes were capable of this due to the extraordinary standards demanded by Basil Embry. The attack was led by Wing Commander (later Air Vice Marshal) Bob Bateson, and his navigator Squadron Leader Sismore. Basil Embry, with his navigator Peter Clapham, also took part. My part in this epic and very daring raid was to act as host at Fersfield to all the 2 Group crews on the night before. Basil Embry and Bob Bateson stayed in my two spare rooms in my brick hut and we did our poor best to provide comfort for all the others. The fighter escort was provided by the Mustang Wing at Bentwaters, near Woodbridge, commanded by our old friend from Hawkinge, Mike Donnet. Bob Iredale led the Mosquitoes from 464 Squadron, and Wing Commander Denton.

The Danish Resistance reported 150 Gestapo men killed and thirty Danish prisoners freed (the codename was Operation Carthage. Tragically the Jeanne D'Arc School was also accidentally destroyed. Eighty-six children were killed and sixty-seven injured).

Shortly after the raid Basil Embry told me that he had selected me to take over command of the new OTU. Consequently, on 30 March, I moved to Harwell to take command.

Until March 1944 the operational training of crews for 2 Group had been undertaken by two Operational Training Units, neither under 2 Group control. The first OTU was No 60, based at Hawarden, where it trained Mosquito Intruder crews, and came under the control of 12 Group in Fighter Command. The second was No 13, based at Bicester and Finmere, and controlled by the training group of Bomber Command, whose front line squadrons no longer used any of the type of aircraft on which 13 OTU trained. This was clearly unsatisfactory and the two were combined under the name of 13 OTU.

We were given three aerodromes, Harwell, Finmere and Hampstead Norreys to house the OTU, each commanded by a Wing Commander. At Finmere we assembled the initial training squadrons for Mosquito pilots and navigators. Two of these squadrons concentrated on the initial conversion of pilots and navigators to the Mosquito. In the third squadron the crews joined up and completed their initial training. The Commanding Officer at Finmere was Wing Commander I.S. Smith DFC, an experienced 2 Group operational pilot and a New Zealander. From Finmere, Mosquito crews moved to Hampstead Norreys, commanded by Wing Commander Teddy Frayn. His Chief Instructor was Squadron Leader Murray DFC. At Harwell we concentrated the Mitchell and Boston training. Here was also based the Fighter Affiliation Flight, equipped with the very exciting Spitfire Mk XII. The pilots of these had the task of behaving like FW 190s attacking our formations, and provided realistic training for the gunners using camera guns. There was also the repair and maintenance unit, commanded by my engineer, Wing Commander Williams, and a large equipment section holding the stores needed to keep 103 Mosquitoes, Mitchells, Bostons, Spitfires and Ansons flying.

The whole of this organisation was designed on the back of a Gee-chart, which I still have. It gives the established posts, and the names of those filling them when first completed. The principal architect on behalf of Basil Embry was Group Captain Wykeham Barnes, DSO, DFC (later Air Marshal Sir Peter Wykeham, RCB, DSC, OBE, DFC, AFC, Retired). He paid frequent visits from the 2 Group HQ, by now at the Cavallerie Barracks in Brussels, arriving by Mosquito and being always a welcome and helpful guest. In this work we were greatly helped by Wing Commander Robinson, a banker in peacetime, and one of Basil Embry's top administrators. He became my Station Commander at Harwell and was a tower of strength. My Chief Instructor for Mitchells and Bostons was Wing Commander Adams, formerly commanding 226 Squadron, who had led us on operations with 2 Group from Hartford Bridge. Finally I controlled the whole of the OTU from a small HQ at Harwell located in the offices of one of the hangars looking out over the aerodrome. To complete the HQ I was allowed to bring Bill Williams as my Adjutant, and Koky-Joe as Assistant Adjutant.

Mich had remained with 98 Squadron and later moved with 139 Wing to Melsbroek, where he was once more invaluable to the Wing in all its dealings with the Belgian authorities.

I commuted between my three aerodromes and the 2 Group HQ in Brussels in a Mitchell allotted for the purpose. Visits to Brussels were always a special treat and I enjoyed a return with champagne and perhaps scent for Rosemary. The source of the champagne was the German Luftwaffe. When they left their big area HQ in Brussels, they left their wine and spirit stocks, carefully accumulated over the war years.

One of the joys of Harwell was that Rosemary was able to rejoin me. Early one morning, I rushed Rosemary to the nursing home in Oxford where our daughter Azalea was born.

When we had got settled at 13 OTU Basil Embry flew over to have a look at us. He arrived in his Mosquito from Brussels with Peter Clapham and, in formation with him, Peter Wykham in another. It was an inspiring visit, partly because that was the effect Basil Embry had on all those he commanded, but also because he knew personally, and usually by Christian name, all the staff who had been so carefully selected to help me. Having toured Harwell and met everybody there we went on to Finmere. I joined the tour flying my Mitchell. It was a slower aeroplane than the Mosquito and it was typical of Basil Embry that, having seen him depart from Harwell, he then detoured from the direct route thus allowing me to arrive at Finmere in time to greet him on his arrived there.

After Finmere, we went on to Hampstead Norreys, where he did the same. He seemed pleased with what he saw, and not least I think the fact that 13 OTU was now a completely 2 Group organisation. It was producing crews trained to meet the very high standard that he required. It was this trip that persuaded me that the time had come to swap my Mitchell for a Mosquito. I took over a brand new Mark VI on which I had painted by broomstick, a relic of 98 Squadron days, and marked with 13 OTU and my own letter A. I kept this particular Mosquito for over a year and did more than 300 hours flying in it. It never let me down during all this time except once when the port engine failed just before reaching take-off speed. Luckily there was enough runway and overshoot to abandon take-off. The subsequent examination showed that the Merlin engine had shed an inlet valve head, thus allowing an explosive blow back into the induction system. It made quite a bang!

As a side effect of this incident, we reviewed the single-engine practices which we taught at 13 OTU and, under Wing Commander Smith's direction, all pupils were taught single-engine flying, including single-engine landing with the dead engine. Provided that the pilot never selected undercarriage down and full flap until he was certain of getting nicely onto the runway there was no problem. In the nineteen months that I commanded 13 OTU we never had any accident due to our methods of teaching single-engine flying.

It was at Harwell that we celebrated VE Day. First, however, there was the German surrender and the cessation of hostilities. We knew this was about to come and a day before, Bill Williams, Koky-Joe and I flew to Brussels. There we borrowed a Jeep and, armed with a special pass, waited for the news of ceasefire, to set out to Amsterdam to find Koky-Joe's family. He had not seen them or had contact since 1939. We loaded the Jeep with every sort of necessity that we could cram into it. We wore khaki battle dress with RAF badges of rank as we had done all through the invasion period. This was for the good reason that faded and well used RAF blue battle dress, our more accustomed wear, was almost indistinguishable from German field grey. We had no wish to be mistaken for Germans.

Our pass, signed by the Dutch Air Force at Eindhoven, and countersigned by Supreme HQ Allied Expeditionary Forces Security (SHAU) authorised us to proceed on or about 26 May and to return to Eindhoven on completion of duty. The duty was not specified. We carried our pistols and ammunition.

Leaving Brussels before dawn, we passed through Eindhoven and then through S'Hertogenbosch to Nijmegen, where we crossed the great steel bridge over the Waal branch of the Rhine. This had been the front line when fighting ceased, and had been captured the previous September during the courageous and frustrated airborne attempt to capture both the Rhine bridges and to sweep into Holland through Arnhem. Between Nijmegen and Arnhem the road runs on an embankment, some 15 to 20 feet above the surrounding level and soft ground that lies between the rivers at Nijmegen and Arnhem. The distance between them is a bare ten miles. All around, on either side of the raised road, were the untouched remains of the tremendous battle which had raged there. Burned out tanks, wrecked vehicles and discarded equipment. Just to the east of the road was a wrecked farmhouse, projecting vertically upwards through the shattered roof was the fuselage and tail of the Spitfire. It must have been totally impossible for any armour or men to have got along that road. Silhouetted against the sky, the target they presented to the enemy flanking them must have been impossible to miss. The wreckage of tanks and men on either side of the raised road still bore evidence of this and to the incredible bravery of those who had attempted against all the odds to join up with the airborne forces already waiting at Arnhem.

Over the still intact Arnhem Bridge we found a wrecked town in which nearly every house had been a strongpoint occupied by one side or the other. In the town, the main road had been cleared of possible mines and traps, and the safe route was marked by white tapes. Following the road towards Barneveld, we passed the scene of the airborne landings where gliders and their wreckage still strewed the area. Barneveld was, at least outwardly, untouched by fighting.

The small town was full of German soldiers. Among them, for they were still fully armed and moving around as though nothing had changed, we felt rather conspicuous. So far as we knew, we were the first RAF to be there, and probably the first British. However, they merely ignored us, as did the inhabitants, who were conspicuous mainly by their absence from the streets, and the fact that the small shops all seemed to be closed.

From there our route took us through Amersfoort, whose railway junction had recently been a 2 Group target and then through Baarn and Bussum to Amsterdam. For the last few miles we found ourselves engulfed in a lengthy convoy of German Army lorries, all crammed with fully-armed Wehrmacht. Leading the convoy were the officers in their staff cars. At a railway crossing a few miles from Amsterdam the whole convoy was halted, where the barriers were down awaiting a passing train. In the middle of this convoy was us in our Jeep. The astonishing thing was that nobody at all took the slightest notice of us. Even when we overhauled the leading staff cars we got no more attention than if we had been their own service police. And so we arrived in Amsterdam.

Here Koky-Joe navigated us to his parents home in the Appollolaan. This was a wide avenue in a pleasant residential part of the town and had been lined with trees. The trees were stripped and many quite gone. In the roadway, the wooden playing blocks had in many places disappeared. We learned presently they had been taken to provide fuel for the tiny wood burning stoves that were the sole means of heating and cooking in the houses which lined the Appollolaan.

We got the impression that nobody could really believe that the war, and the occupation, were over. The Germans were still there, they were moving about very much as they always had, still fully armed and with no apparent difference in their routine. Leaving Koky-Joe, we had a quick look at Schiphol airport. The aerodrome had been thoroughly bombed, all the hangars were in ruins. When we returned to the house we found a joyous family, father, mother, son and two sisters, in a state of still unbelieving happiness which defies description. It embraced us all. We unloaded the Jeep, and for his part, Josef Kokes, Zdenek's father, went down into his cellar where he chipped away part of the wall. This revealed some hollow bricks, in each one was concealed a bottle of pre-war Bols Gin.

During the evening we learned some amazing things. The Kokes family showed us the little wood stove upon which they had depended. In the hard cold winters it had been very cold and warmth depended upon wrapping up and blankets. It had been normal for the house to be below freezing and the water frozen. A few doors away was the local Gestapo HQ. Despite this, Josef Kokes had listened nightly to the BBC from London. His aerial was strung up inside the chimney and the set hidden beneath the floor. With this he had disseminated news to his friends. Without it, he said, they could not have continued. His two daughters had been couriers for the underground. After three days in Amsterdam we returned by the same route to Brussels, but took with us a Dutch friend of the Kokes family whose home was in Arnhem.

Shortly afterwards, VE Day was celebrated. At Harwell, as at all RAF aerodromes throughout England, all aircraft were immobilised and, if hangars were available, the aircraft were put in them and locked up. At Harwell, we turned one of the large hangars into the biggest bar I have even seen. The only duty that day was a single, and very informal, parade of the whole station. It was held in the hangar and I read out the messages from the Air Council, from Field Marshal Montgomery to the RAF, and the reply to him from the Chief of the Air Staff. Montgomery's message, beginning with the words 'We have no Germans left to fight in Western Europe', was greeted with tremendous cheers. When I toured Harwell, at 2100 that evening, the hangar bar was deserted and every barrel and keg empty.

There was one more, perhaps more exclusive, celebration. Basil Embry summoned all his commanding officers to a party in Brussels. We arrived by air to Melsbroek and were driven to the cavalry barracks, the 2 Group HQ. The occasion was marked by the award to our AOC of the DFC. He already had the DSO with three bars, but this award of the DFC, which he happily referred to as his 'boys medal' seemed to give him more pleasure than all.

I returned to Harwell to find that 2 Group days were soon to be over. The RAF in England was reverting to its earlier organisation. The Tactical Air Force which, with Montgomery's 21st Army Group, had fought their way from Normandy to the centre of Germany, were to become the forces of occupation. 21 Army Group's new name was to be The British Army of the Rhine (BAOR), and the 2nd Tactical Air Force, slimmed down by the return of some of its fighter squadrons to England, The British Air Forces of Occupation (BAFO). Fighter Command in England resumed its old name, and with it, my 13 OTU left the command of 2 Group and became a part of Fighter Command, under the control of 12 Group whose HQ was at Hucknall.

Our role was to train crews for the Pacific war. We kept our Mosquitoes but lost our Mitchells and Bostons and, oddly, our Mosquito trained crews were intended to fly Beaufighters when they reached the Far East. Finally, we were required to move the whole OTU from our three aerodromes in southern England and to plant it at two aerodromes just south of Darlington. The HQ was to be at Middleton St George and our second aerodrome, Croft, a few miles to the west. This move took place in July 1945.

When we first heard that we were to move up to the north, Wing Commander Smith and I flew up together in a pair of Mosquitoes to have a look at our new home. Black was flying a strange looking Mk VI which had come our way to test out a new camouflage colour scheme. Its purpose was to conceal a low flying aircraft in poor visibility from any attacker who might try to find it from above. It was a rather dingy pink with odd shadows.

At Middleton we were greeted by a French Canadian Wing Commander. Until recently the base had been occupied by two squadrons of the Royal Canadian Air Force, flying Lancasters in Bomber Command. A third squadron occupied Croft, the satellite. The aircraft and crews had flown home to Canada a few days before; those remaining were ground crew, French Canadians, all impatient to get home fast.

We found the base to be one of those begun in the final pre-war expansion of the RAF. But the war had overtaken its completion; the Officers Mess was, outwardly, a standard pre-war pattern for a two-squadron station. Inside none of the furnishing had been provided and the place was fitted out with stark simplicity The airmen's barrack blocks had been completed and were in good shape, except for being very dirty and in need of paint and cleaning. There were no permanent hangars and only T type hangars for work which could not be done in the open. All aircraft lived in the open on dispersals and all the other buildings except the sick bay were temporary wartime huts. It was a bit of a come clown after our much loved Harwell, but better than it might have been. The satellite Croft was a standard wartime aerodrome where everything was temporary and very like Fersfield.

The move itself took four days. First a small advance party. Next the air party in which numbers from Harwell, Finmere and Hampstead Norrey flew up on the second day, taking with them as much as could be carried by air. A second party, who left on the third day travelled by road, packed into all our vehicles and finally a rear party left by a special train. It was the rear party that led to a most extraordinary local war.

When we left, Harwell was handed back to No 38 Group, which had been responsible for command of the air element of the airborne forces during the invasion of Europe. It was from them we had taken over Harwell on the formation of 13 OTU within 2 Group. When the train party arrived at Darlington incomplete,

Bill and I flew down to Harwell to investigate. There we found that the incoming unit of 38 Group had refused to let our cooks, butchers and mess staff depart. They were held, as one indignant WAAF who loved 13 QTU described it, as prisoners. Our representations to the incoming commanding officer met with no response, so Bill and I flew back to Middleton, consumed with fury, and planning revenge. At Middleton we held a council of war; it seemed ridiculous, having been fighting the enemy, suddenly to find ourselves embroiled in a fight with one of our own service. We solved the problem by issuing orders signed by myself, to the senior NCO detained at Harwell to have all members of 13 OTU remaining there, on parade, bags packed, and ready to move in transport, which would be lined up on the parade ground early one morning. Bill and I flew down very early to take command of the parade. I never did discover whether or not my senior NCOs revealed this plan to the enemy, but they were all there, ready and waiting, and so was my transport from 13 OTU. We departed on time.

At Middleton St George we settled down to our task of training, on our Mk VI Mosquitoes, crews intended for Beaufighters in the Far East. I found myself the senior RAF Officer in the local area, with responsibilities to the Mayor of Darlington, and the Councils of our local villages.

It was on 14 August 1945 that the Japanese surrendered. We had a parade in one of the big hangars at which I stood up in front of everybody to read out the messages from the Air council. It was rather an emotional occasion, because we had become something of a close and happy family and none of us were sure what might happen next to us all.

What actually happened was completely unexpected. We acquired three new tasks and one new problem. The new tasks were to train a Czechoslovak unit as a Mosquito squadron. The second was a conversion of our old friends 320 Squadron (the Dutch squadron from Dunsfold) to Mosquitoes. Thirdly, and in some ways the most difficult of all, was to become a station from which a great horde of wartime-only servicemen were released into civilian life.

Again Bill Williams came to the rescue. During a period of forty-eight hours, during which neither we nor Harry Chambers (our chief administration officer) slept, we devised a control room in the old operations room for processing every man and woman that came through our station. Later, when it was found to be working well, our system was copied by a number of other units who had the same problem.

Despite all the hard work I still managed to get in a fair amount of flying. Our Spitfire XIIs, which we had used at Harwell, were replaced at Middleton by Hawker Tempest IIs. In my opinion, this was the ultimate in piston-engine propeller-driven fighters. It had a wing of elliptical shape in plan view not unlike the Spitfire. It had a Laminar flow section, four 20mm cannons mounted in the wings and was powered by a 2526hp Bristol Centaurus engine. The aircraft had a range of 1,640 miles, much more than the contemporary fighters without drop tanks and a top speed of 440mph. Its climb was sensational. The official figures were four and a half minutes to 15,000 feet. The Tempest II had been designed for war in the Pacific. A variant of it became the very fast and successful Sea Fury, which the Fleet Air Arm used to great effect during the Korean War. It came too late for the Second World War, but it later equipped our fighter squadrons in Germany. Its delightful handling and superb performance made it the only other aeroplane except the Spitfire XII that had tempted me to adopt it in place of my much-loved Mosquito.

Another new flying experience was the de Haviland Hornet. It too had been intended as a long-range fighter for the Pacific. It was an aircraft of quite outstanding performance, with a top speed of 472mph and a range of 3,000 miles. In effect it was a scaled-down single-seat Mosquito, highly manoeuvrable and a delight to fly. The Hornet saw service in Malaya and was the fastest single-seat fighter with piston engines that the RAF ever used.

We had other de Haviland aeroplanes at Middleton; our Ansons had been replaced by the Dominie, which we used for navigational training. Dominie was the RAF name for the better know civilian, Rapide. They were a good gentleman's carriage; the pilot sat alone in the narrow nose in front, with a perfect outlook in all directions. Provided one remembered that it was really nothing more than a large twin-engine Tiger Moth and treated the Dominie accordingly, it handled perfectly. Like the Mosquito, as soon as the pilot began to get funny ideas about twin engines and swing problems, it could play up, with bent wing tips as the result. Finally, when we arrived at Middleton all alone in the hangar, was a Tiger Moth.

The Tiger became my early morning jaunt; before breakfast on a fine summer's morning, the open cockpit and the sheer delight of the little Tiger was a perfect start to any day. Some slight aerobatics in the clear cool morning air, or perhaps a low chase among the slopes and valleys of the Cleveland Hills. The Tiger also caused me trouble, and the fault, I think, was entirely mine. It was my custom, after my morning half hour, to land it on the small patch of usable grass outside the hangar in which it was kept. When the SW wind was right this could be done neatly, so that a slight swerve at the end of its minuscule landing run and cutting the engine just before finish, resulted in its arrival neatly, with engine stopped just inside the hangar doors. It was, of course, sheer showing off, but the crew enjoyed it, and I was not above the belief that a little showmanship of the right kind can sometimes help in a service which likes to see its commanding officers flying and enjoying it. This arrival at the hangar doors required a nicely judged approach over the roof of the hut in which the radar operators did their ground training. This produced no problems until one day they had erected a co-axial cable suspended between two low masts along the whole length of the buildings. As I found afterwards, it ran about 3 feet above the top pitch of the roof. I found it by hitting the cable in such a way that it slid over the top of the Tiger Moth landing wheels, and acted as a splendidly efficient arrester cable. The only trouble was that it brought the Tiger to a standstill about 20 feet up, from which height it descended, nose first. The immediate results were dramatic. The crash alarm went, the ambulance, fire crews and rescue teams sprang into lightning action and the senior air traffic controller in the tower immediately rang Rosemary. I, having descended with a bump, had only one thought, which was to get out of the cockpit fast in case anything caught fire. I was able to watch from a comfortable distance, the very efficient operation of the fire and rescue services which we took great pains to keep at concert pitch.

The most serious immediate effect was that, by some means which only an electronic genius could explain, the radar people's co-axial cable had become tied up with the perimeter telephone circuit which went all around the airfield. It was in some way linked up to the station Tannoy system. We all became aware of this when the Tannoy began to recount to us, all over Middleton, in clear female voices, the conversation of two young women describing in uncensored detail, the previous night out in Darlington. Everybody was held spellbound whilst the two girls continued to talk. Nobody knew how to stop it. Two days later there were some very hurried postings. At the time, on 11 March 1946, all I had to show for the incident were two most impressive black eyes. Later, however, my left eye went blind as a result.

In the spring of 1946 I had my first experience of flying a jet, about which the following article was published in *Esso Air World*, Vol 26, No. 4, July 1974:

Imagine, please, a beautiful morning in May. The early mist has gone and the sun is shining from a bright blue sky. No wind has yet arisen to clear away the haze and it is difficult to see far up sun. What makes this morning even more beautiful, however, is that I am about to have my first ride in a jet.

It was 1946, and although the first Gloster Meteors had been in action with 616 Squadron and were just in time to do some useful work before the end of the war, very few pilots had actually flown them. They were therefore something of far more than ordinary interest and competition to get a place on the jet familiarisation course at Molesworth was intense. Sitting in the cockpit of a Meteor Mk I at the take-off end of the runway, I reflected on all this; it was to be the biggest event, so far, in my flying career. In another ten minutes, I would know what the new flying was all about.

It had, of course, taken some time to work up to this supreme moment; first, the application to attend the course; furious envy of those who got in first and then came back with tales of this superb new wonder-plane; then at last, instruction to report to the Conversion Unit at Molesworth, where we received two day's instruction on the airframe and engine and indoctrination into the mysteries of jet propulsion. Some of this, by great good fortune, was not entirely new to me; not many pilots can have been taught the first principles by Sir Frank Whittle himself, and the recollection of Frank, then Flight Lieutenant Whittle, using his finger to draw explanatory diagrams in the sand on the foundry floor of the Engineering Course School at RAF

Henlow, is one that his brother officers who were there will treasure all our lives.

The favourite question in those days was 'When the whole turbine is revolving, why should the products of combustion prefer to squirt out at the back, instead of taking the shorter course to the front of the engine and so stopping the whole process?' This question always produced furious arguments and was, I suppose, typical of the many put to Frank Whittle, whose determination and faith, in the face of every sort of difficultly, won through and resulted in one of the most important developments in power production yet seen in the world; and the result of whose efforts I was about to fly.

The ground instruction had been thorough. There were no such things as dual Meteors in those days. Some people queried their necessity at all and used to make snide comments about the introduction of the dual Mosquito, saying that it was not until that training aircraft enabled the instructors to teach students how to mismanage the beautiful aircraft that accidents with it began in training schools. However, as far as the Meteor was concerned, this was quite academic and, having satisfied the ground instructors that I was a fit and proper person to trust with jet power, the next step was to go out and fly a Meteor Mk I. The early models of this make had the reverse-flow Rolls-Royce Westland engine, giving, if my memory is correct, a maximum thrust of 1,700 pounds. It was also distinguished from later marks of Meteors by having a sideways-opening canopy, like an Me 109. One taxied out, or at least I did, with this canopy open, and my first and lasting impression of this wonder-plane is of being followed by a smell which reminded me of nothing so much as with a Primus stove on a pre-war holiday in a small boat which had run aground on a mud-bank in the HAMBLE River. I hoped that this was not an ill omen but on such a beautiful morning, after delicious bacon and eggs, such thought could hardly last. I closed and locked the canopy.

Ground instruction, including specification of engine performance, had by no means prepared me for what happened on opening the throttles. The recommended technique was to open up slowly, on the brakes; early jet engines were allergic to too sudden throttle opening and response could vary from a relatively mild reluctance to produce the required thrust, to an enormous hiccup which put out the flame, a humiliation that was, of course, to be avoided at all costs. So, with due care, and brakes locked on, the throttles – or power levers, to describe them more accurately – were pushed forward. The result, seen on the rev counters was, to one accustomed to Merlins, quite astonishing. The two hands on each counter, an 'hour hand' registering thousands and a 'minute hand' reading hundreds, flew round the clock like a demented stop-watch whilst the corresponding noise from outside increased, not to the accustomed heavy growl of piston engines, but to something like the howl of distant banshees. There was no vibration at all, and the only response from the aircraft itself was to lean forward slightly as the nose-wheel oleo leg compressed.

At some 13,000rpm. . . yes, 13,000rpm, the brakes were released. Braced against the back of the seat, just as I had done years before when being launched by a ship's catapult, I waited for the expected dramatic launch down the runway and into the air.

Nothing happened.

Or so it seemed then, rather like a large and sleepy dog, roused after a good lunch, the aircraft got, so to speak, on to its feet, and started to rumble along the runway. Power levers on the stops? Yes! Maximum revs? Yes! Everything as it should be, by the book; and yet there was this apparently slow and dignified progress along the runway; almost I looked for the police out-riders, the crowds lining the side of the street and, if I had found them there, lifting my hat to right and to left as I moved on like a Lord Mayor's coach.

All designed to deceive, for still at the same apparently ambling gait, both ASI and elevator response indicated beyond doubt that the aircraft was soon travelling at a very high speed indeed and the end of the runway was approaching with a rapidity which made the accustomed take-off in a Mosquito seem like a slow motion film. Airborne and over the threshold of 120 knots, wheels up, and with speed now increasing fast, up and into that lovely morning sky.

The next half hour was a never-to-be-forgotten experience. There are three others which I remember with equal delight; one, my first solo; two, my second first solo yes, one can first solo twice, for this was in a helicopter, and a very useful and humbling reminder of what it is to be once again a complete novice; three, the first soaring flight, when my glider shared a thermal with a bird – and out-climbed him (I did not realise that he, practical chap, was intent only on his dinner, and did not want to climb).

And now this! At cruising power, in the quietest cockpit that I had ever known in a powered aircraft, the Meteor reminded me of nothing so much as a very fast sailplane; no noise; no vibrations; and a feeling of speed and soaring power that was without parallel. All commonplace stuff now, I dare say, and my Westland Meteor would today be a museum piece. On that day in 1946 it was a delight beyond description. So much so that I got completely lost.

Up sun, no view. Down sun, nothing recognisable. Radio, damn bad. Luckily one can't go far in middle England without seeing something well known, especially on such a day as this, and just at the safe limit of endurance, there was Molesworth placed in position by that benign Providence that moves airfields to the aid of idiot pilots who have ventured too close to Heaven.

I got a well-deserved rocket for being late, and for all the other things which I did wrong. But nobody can ever take away the memory of my first ride in a jet!"

It was at Middleton that I first became seriously involved with gliding. The interest in gliding began with a visit to the small grass aerodrome at West Hartlepool, which had previously been a fighter satellite. Its facilities were minimal, comprising only some temporary wooden huts, and one Bessoneau hangar, which was in very bad shape. It was from West Hartlepool that the local squadron of the Air Training Corps (ATC) operated, and the dilapidated hangar housed their primary training gliders. They asked if we could repair their hangar for them, and this we were very glad be able to do. This led to a flight in one of their Kirby Cadet trainers, launched by a converted balloon winch and in turn led to an invitation to fly at Sutton Bank. At that time it was used by the ATC, and also the site of the post-war revival of the Yorkshire Gliding Club. The ATC gliding instructors in Yorkshire were mostly members of the Club, and their functions were interlocking.

At Sutton Bank I had my first experience of soaring, flying one of the gliders. It seemed to me a very bumpy sort of performance and the lateral control of the Cadet glider heavy and ineffective. Half an hour's juggling with the turbulent slope lift, never much higher than two or three hundred feet, secured me the British Gliding Association's A, B and C certificates.

It was in 1945 that I think the whole technique of teaching and flying gliders had diverged furthest from powered flying. The ATC still introduced pilots under instruction to the Kirby Cadet by putting them into this single-seater, and dragging them along the level grass aerodrome at a speed calculated to give aileron control, rudder control, and some elevator feel. But they were not fast enough to become airborne until it was judged that the pupil had mastered the control sufficiently to undertake what was termed a low hop. If all went well, the hops became higher and longer. Later small turns were introduced, and finally a complete circuit. The system was more reminiscent of the pre-1914 style of instruction. The handling characteristics of the Kirby Cadet were not such as to encourage good flying techniques. The poor response of ailerons and the excessive aileron drag inevitably resulted in the need for coarse application of rudder. This tended to produce heavy footed pilots.

At one meeting of ATC instructors which I was invited to attend, I listened, astonished, to one of them propounding his theory that all turns should be initiated by firm use of rudder, followed as necessary by corrections with what he termed the secondary controls, namely ailerons and elevator. Actually, the theory was by no means as bad as it sounded, given the type of aircraft in mind. It was based on the idea that the cadet glider would normally be launched into wind and subsequent soaring flight would also be into wind, over a cliff face. In these circumstances forward speed in relation to the ground would be small, in fact sometimes zero. In these circumstances, it was argued, there was no need to bank the aircraft when making changes of heading, because bank is necessary only when

Christopher Paul with his father in the summer of 1925.

Christopher Paul at Filton airfield, beside a Bristol Jupiter, in June 1927.

No 14 AB Initio Flight Training Course at Netheravon 1929.

Christopher Paul on his FAA conversion course in July 1930.

Hawker Hart J9937 at Brooklands in 1930.

A Hawker Horsley J8615 in June 1932.

Christopher Paul in his office in December 1938.

Fairey Battles of RAF 12 Squadron over Douai in Northern France in December 1939.

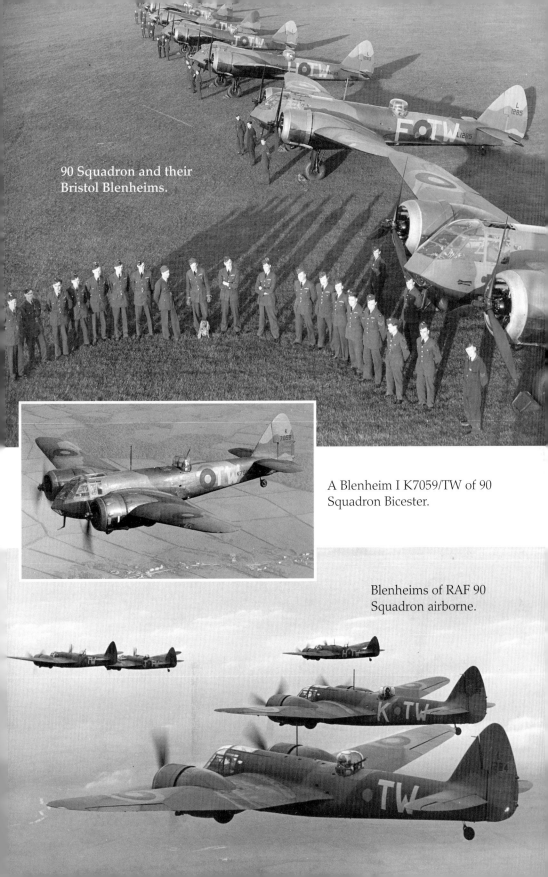

90 Squadron and their Bristol Blenheims.

A Blenheim I K7059/TW of 90 Squadron Bicester.

Blenheims of RAF 90 Squadron airborne.

Six pilots of RAF 90 Squadron in front of their Blenheims.

RAF Bicester from the air. It is now Bicester aerodrome, after the RAF left in 2004.

The Commanding Officer of RAF 105 Squadron's Wellington at RAF Newton, near Nottingham, in 1941.

Christopher Paul and his crew of their North American Mitchell at Dunsfold in 1944.

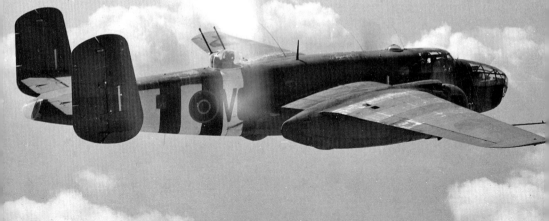

Christopher Paul's Mitchell VOA
of RAF 98 Squadron in 1944.

Rose Cottage, Dunsfold
which served as 98
Squadron HQ in 1944.

Mitchell EV of 180 Squadron.

Christopher Paul and his crew of the de Havilland Mosquito FBVI TA476 of 13 OTU.

Aircraft ready to take part in the 1945 Battle of Britain Day fly past over London on September 15.

Christopher Paul with Lady Teddar and Captain Peter Whitfield with a DFS Kranich in March 1948.

Christopher Paul as a Senior Air Staff Officer in Aden.

Flying a Weihe glider in Germany in the summer of 1948.

A unit of the Aden Protectorate Levy at Ataq Fort in the 1950s.

AHQ Aden with a new top storey on the main building.

Refuelling a Vickers Valetta in Southern Sudan at Malakal in August 1953.

Christopher Paul inspecting a US Marine Corps Guard of Honour in the summer of 1955.

Rigging a DFS 108 Weihe at Central Flying School 1954.

Christopher Paul in a Weihe glider at St Auban, France.

Turbulent G-AJCP, taken in England. This aircraft was built in 1959.

Christopher Paul in a Druine D31 Turbulent G-AJCP
at Fairbrooks September 16 1961.

Christopher and Rosemary at Steamer Point (Tawahi) on their last night before leaving Aden.

Christopher Paul with his Tipsy Nipper G-AVXC.

Her Majesty The Queen Mother with the CFS Associaton June 4 1992.

needed to counter centrifugal forces set up in a turn. At zero ground speed, there could be no centrifugal force and no need to use ailerons in making a change of heading. The result of this teaching appeared in some startling accidents when pilots brought up on it flying fast over the ground, down wind but with insufficient airspeed, using the rudder turn technique with too heavy a foot.

By 1945 there were few powered aircraft with aileron control as poor as the training gliders from which the ATC suffered. Even the old techniques of holding off bank in an established turn, necessary on such old timers as the Avro 504, was a forgotten subject. So the Cadet was a fascinating glimpse of what it must have been like learning in 1914 and something of a revelation of at least one likely reason for many accidents resulting from spins or turns whilst approaching to land.

Later on we established our own gliding club at 13 OTU, which was certainly the first post-war RAF Gliding Club in England, and can fairly claim to be the ancestor of today's RAF Gliding and Soaring Association. We had accidents using the ground slide training technique, and very soon abandoned it, making use of our Tiger Moth to give students an elementary grounding in the use of flying controls before they approached the Cadet. Sadly one of the accidents was to Rosemary, who spent a month in plaster with a damaged back, and continued to suffer from this injury for many years.

Later the 13 OTU Gliding Club conducted several successful hill soaring camps up in the Cleveland Hills. Our favourite was on top of the escarpment at Ingleby Greenhow where there is a steep rise from the lowlands of the southern Teeside up to heights of 1,400 feet or more. At Ingleby Greenhow there is a bowl facing northwest, such that the wind blowing into it produces vigorous lift up to considerable heights. Our camp was based on the station at the top of the incline of what had once been an old cable railway bringing ironstone down from the hills to the furnaces of Middlesbrough. Mostly we used the Kirby Cadet and in these our pilots, initiated on the Tiger, made many very good flights and many obtained their BGA A, B and C certificates.

We also obtained the loan of some other interesting sailplanes which had been in storage during the war. One such was the Kirby King Kite, three of which were built by Slingsbys for use by the British Gliding Team which competed at the Wasserkuppe in the 1937 International contests. The King Kite was a development of the original design in collaboration with Slingsby and in some ways resembled the German Minimoa which followed in later years. I flew it a number of times, launched by winch from Middleton. It was pleasant enough to handle, despite heavy ailerons, but with its span of 51 feet, and operating speed of 40mph, it circled well once established in a turn and at about 30 degrees of bank and required no aileron forces to hold it there. In consequence of this, there was no aileron drag in such a turn, and therefore, little need to use rudder. In such a turn it was nearly as efficient as in straight glider flight, when it had a sinking speed of less than 3 feet per second and could therefore circle and gain height in quite moderate thermals. For the provision of thermals we were fortunate in the presence, close to the eastern end of Middleton, of a large aluminium smelting plant known as Eaglescliffe.

The oddest thing we got from the ATC was the Hillson Praga. Hillsons were a firm of furniture makers in Manchester who, before the war, became interested in light powered aircraft. The Hillson Praga was a high wing cantilever monoplane of about 40 feet span. It had two seats side by side close in front of the leading edge. In the nose was an air-cooled flat twin Czechoslovak engine, the 45hp Praga. The ATC acquired it for ground instruction, and it was in a somewhat battered state. Our woodworkers repaired it for them but we never dared fly it, though we ran the engine, and did some very noisy taxi tests before returning it to the ATC.

Our nearest neighbour in the RAF was Thornaby, where George Ward commanded the station which was at that time, in Coastal Command and principally concerned with Air Sea Rescue. There were two squadrons there, one equipped with the Vickers Warwick, and the other with the Supermarine Sea Otter amphibian. The Warwick was a bomber design to replace the Wellington, and had been overtaken by the superior Lancasters and other four-engine types before it could get into bomber service. However, with two Bristol Centaurus engines it performed well in its Air Sea Rescue role, being able to carry and drop the Lindholme dinghy and associated apparatus to crews in the sea. It seemed to fly and behave like a larger and statelier Wellington, and was pleasant without being remarkable. The same applied to the Sea Otter, which was an enlarged Walrus, with a tractor engine installation. It lacked the very individual sort of charm that I remembered of the Walrus, but perhaps that was merely because I had so little experience of it.

The final peculiarity of Middleton was our German prisoner of war detachment. The war being over, they awaited repatriation working on farms, and some on other jobs. Some wished to stay in England. They lived under their own NCOs and discipline on a dispersed site surrounded by a high mesh wire fence. It was originally put up, not to keep the inmates in, but to protect the WAAFs who formerly lived there from unwanted intruders from outside. All their problems were handled by our ever efficient Administrative Squadron Leader, Harry Chambers. In theory, I was their Camp Commandant, and paid a weekly visit there with Harry. All the 150 or so were from the Wehrmacht, with none from the Luftwaffe.

The oddest thing that happened to me whilst at Middleton was to be detailed to lead the Fighter Command contingent in the Victory March through London on 8 June 1946. Never having been in Fighter Command throughout the whole of the war it seemed to me to be a curious assignment. However, it was a historic occasion, and something to be remembered. My part in this began by flying down to Hornchurch in my Mosquito, with Corporal Johnson to look after it, a fortnight before the event. Here were assembled the twenty-four officers and· 120 other ranks gathered from the whole command who were to represent it on the day. The official programme lists the groups of Fighter Command which my contingent represented as Nos 9, 10, 11, 12, 13, 14, 38, 60, 70, 81, 82 and 88; and, in addition, the four Balloon Groups, Nos 31, 32, 33 and 43. It is an astonishing roll call of the size of the RAF at its greatest and includes the sixteen groups, no less, of the Mediterranean and Middle East Commands, another fourteen of South East Asia, to say nothing of the home-based commands, and contingents of the Iraq Levies, the Royal Observer Corps, and the WAAF. In the Air Forces' column were included contingents of all our wartime Allies; France, Belgium, Czechoslovakia, Greece, Holland, Norway, Poland, Yugoslavia and the USA. The Navy, as Senior Service, led the Armed Forces and had about the same sized column as the RAF; the Army in the centre were the most numerous, with representatives from every Regiment in the Commonwealth. The whole of this marching column contained just over 2,000 officers and nearly 19,000 other ranks. When marching eight abreast, with its numerous bands, it was over two miles of road.

At Hornchurch, our Fighter Command contingent drilled and drilled and marched and marched, and practised the awkward eyes left march past. For some reason it is much more difficult than the less contorting eyes right. But it was imposed upon us that we were to enter the Mall through the Admiralty Arch, and the Sovereign would be at the saluting base on the south side of the route. As the time the King and Queen would be on the dais taking the salute was likely to be two hours, it was essential to ensure that at least they would be spared the discomfort of facing into the sun had they taken the salute from the other side. Following a longer route, which converged with ours at Parliament Square, was the mechanised column. This included every sort of vehicle that the armed forces, the fire brigades and the rescue services had used. For the RAF these ranged from motorcycle dispatch riders to ambulances, crash tenders and snow ploughs, right up to the biggest of all 2,500 gallon refuelling tankers. There were also representatives of every sort of civil defence organisation, and, leading the entire parade, the senior commanders of all the services, and our Allies. Finally, when all had marched past, there was a fly-past by the Royal Air Force and the Fleet Air Arm.

We left Hornchurch three days before the great march and went into tented camp in Hyde Park, all 21,000 of us. The RAF section of this astonishing camp was under the command of Group Captain Dawes, formerly the senior Personnel Officer at Bomber Command. The commander of the whole parade was Field Marshal, the Viscount Alanbrooke, GCB, DSO, ADC.

The route followed on the day led us out of Hyde Park via Marble Arch, and down Oxford Street. At Charing Cross Road we turned right emerging into Trafalgar Square. We passed through the eastern side of the Square, down Northumberland Avenue and along the Embankment to Westminster Bridge to Parliament Square. Here we had a thirty minute pause whilst the mechanised column preceded us up Whitehall. We then followed it back to Trafalgar Square and through the Admiralty Arch into the Mall. All along our route, every window of every building had become a decorated box crowded with people watching the march. Most were making a day's picnic of it and the celebrations were obvious, not only from the cheers and streamers thrown as well as flags and bunting, but in raised glasses, and, not infrequently, drinks offered during some of our many pauses. All along the route pavements were packed and many of the crowd had camped out all night to be sure of a good place.

When we paused in Parliament square, this was the moment for tidying up. When we moved off again, 1155, exactly as on the programme, it was nearly two hours since we had first moved off from Hyde Park. As we moved into Whitehall the march began to assume a more formal performance than its previously jubilant and noisy progress. When we came to the Cenotaph there was a hush. The Cenotaph bore the standards of the services and there were wreaths too, not only the imposing ones of organised remembrance, but an amazing number of tiny tributes placed, I have no doubt, by parents, widows, sons and daughters to whom this day was perhaps not a celebration but one of proud remembrance.

The Cenotaph was the point at which I had to give my first command of importance; Fighter Command! Eyes Right! This was the moment, more than any other, when I thought how completely inappropriate, even unworthy, I was to give such a command. I wished it could have been somebody more appropriate; at least a pilot who had fought in the Battle of Britain, and then inevitably, of my friends who might have been there. Up through Whitehall and into the western side of Trafalgar Square there were checks, because the column moving down the Mall and past the saluting base had to be evened out. It was here that we met difficulties with the bands which were in the column. Our contingent was almost equidistant between two bands that were inevitably unsynchronised, so that when the breeze blew we heard one more clearly and marched to it. Clearly this could not continue as we approached the saluting base. For Fighter Command to shuffle past the King and Queen out of step would have involved me, its temporary and unworthy representative, in a fate worse than death. We solved the problem by deciding which band was dominant at the moment, and passed the word for every NCO inside the lines to call the time. This established a sort of rhythm and we arrived at the saluting base in the Mall in creditably good order, and all, I believe, in step.

Here I had to order again; Fighter Command!, Eyes Left! Strangely I recollect only one thing; an unforgettable memory of the Queen, our beloved Queen Mum as she now is, very close to the King, and I could be totally mistaken, but it seemed to me that her lovely smile was very close to tears.

The Fighter Command contingent went past the saluting base in impeccable order, accurately dressed by the left, and exactly as the most ambitious could have hoped. Up Constitution Hill we became an out of step rabble, parched, hungry and longing for a drink. However, we preserved some sort of order to get us back into Hyde Park, where we quickly dismissed, and moved rapidly into the generous canteens.

Miraculously, Mich and Koky-Joe had contrived to be in London. We met up, and via the RAF Club, joined later in the summer's evening, with the tumultuous packed crowd which surged around the Albert Memorial, and the Mall, hoping for a Royal appearance on the balcony of Buckingham Palace. We were not disappointed.

First, a chink of light showed between the drawn curtains behind the great balcony window. The crowd saw it, and became tense and quiet. Then the curtains were drawn, and then opened, and we saw the King, in full Naval uniform, as he had been on the dais that morning, followed by the Queen. The cheer that greeted them was unforgettable. It began among those nearest the Palace and around the memorial. It grew into a roar that seemed to fill one's head and reverberate through the earth itself; and it was taken up by the crowd all down the Mall, on Constitution Hill and into the parks. It swelled and continued, and swelled again until it seemed the fill the whole earth and sky. After quite a long time, the royal party went back inside, but the crowd would not let them go. I forget how many times they came back, but each time they were greeted again in the same tremendous explosion of affection and loyalty. Queen Alexandra was there too, and other members of the royal family, and there were many of us who remembered Prince George who lost his life whilst serving in the RAF, in a Sunderland flying boat. We remembered those pictures of the King inspecting the bomb damage to his own home in London, the Palace itself, where he had remained throughout the bombing; no evacuation for him. And the Princess, now our Queen, in uniform and going through the same training as any other young woman joining the women's section of the armed forces. We knew also that in the Royal household, they had imposed upon themselves, exactly the same strict rationing as their subjects so that, as many of her subjects discovered, the Queen understood just as they did the problems of making half an ounce of butter and next to no meat and sugar, go twenty times as far as it had ever done before. All this and a hundred other things, the great crowd acknowledged that evening of the June 1946. For me that evening outside the palace was a fitting climax to a day which I shall remember, and treasure that memory, as long as I live.

During the late autumn of 1946 I was confirmed in the substantive rank of Group Captain. I learned that my time at Middleton was to end and that in early November I was to be posted to the headquarters of the British Air Forces of Occupation in Germany (BAFO).

We left Middleton with every sort of regret. We had been very happy there and the kindness of the many friends we made all around is something that I will always treasure. It is not possible to describe one's feelings on an occasion such as this. For me it was a final parting from 2 Group and though we did not know it at the time, the beginning of a period of several years before Rosemary and I could be together again in our own home.

CHAPTER EIGHT
GERMANY

From my home in Botley I went once more to Henlow where Angus Horne, who was to be my Wing Commander Training in Germany, had thoughtfully left a Mosquito for me to make my journey. It was another Mk VI. The two Merlins had short stub exhausts, and the twenty-four cylinders of the pair produced the same resounding crackle at low speeds and the Merlin noise under power, that one expected from two Spitfires. It was a well kept and particularly nice aeroplane, with only a few hours from new. I was privileged to use it as my own for the whole of my time in Germany. Its number was TA 591 and having inspected and approved what I saw, I loaded my luggage into the bomb bay and flew solo to Manston.

Over the Thames the weather became increasingly foul, and after a short ride of twenty-five minutes I landed at Manston to clear customs. Customs was one of the first signs of encroaching peace. In the old days at Harwell I had been accustomed to shuttle between 13 OTU and 2 Group Headquarters in Brussels direct. Manston was covered in low cloud and a nasty drizzle which limited visibility to a little over a mile. After consulting the meteorological forecaster, I found that this was the western edge of a complicated occlusion whose eastern front already extended well into Holland and towards the Rhine. Prudence, I suppose, would have suggested waiting till it had blown away.

There were no landing or navigation aids at my destination. The aerodrome at Bucheburg, close to the HQ of the RAF in Germany at Bad Oeynhausen had numbers of transport aircraft whose pilots had already made this sensible decision. I met a disconsolate old 2 Group navigator impatiently waiting to get back to his squadron in Germany. We teamed up and set off into the murk. Going high, we agreed, was pointless. This was 2 Group weather so we stuck, never above 300 feet, across the unobstructed sea to Flushing, south of Rotterdam. Then over Dordrecht, and up the Rhine lowlands, towards Nijmegen and to the south of Arnhem, hoping to run into clearer weather. Instead, the gradually higher ground merged increasingly often here and there with dragging wet cloud steamers. Reluctantly we went up a little way into it. We had never flown together before, but I had utter confidence and to my great regret, his name, recorded in my pilot's log book with gratitude, have been lost with many other things I wish I still had.

So we continued, until he suggested that we might ease down. Carefully we did, slowing down to a rather rumbling 150 knots, probably too fast. Just short of Gutersloh we emerged from the muck, where we fastened on to the autobahn which led us towards Bielefeld, Herford and Bad Oeynhausen and to our destination at Buckeburg aerodrome, exactly one and half hours from Manston.

Near Bielefeld I had my first sight of the massive destruction wrought by Bomber Command. Here the main arterial rail route between the Rhineland and Berlin passes over a long viaduct. The viaduct was in ruins, and the whole of the area around it for a distance of about a mile in diameter, was pitted with water-filled bomb craters. The whole area looked like the pictures one remembered of the trench battle areas of the First World War, a desolated swamp of wet mud and wreckage. The Germans had not repaired the viaduct but had built a winding single track line bypassing the whole viaduct and along this uneven and temporary track, a goods train was plodding. At Buckeburg our arrival was greeted with some surprise, and we discovered that no other aircraft had got through that day.

On arrival at Buckeburg, having seen my TA 591 stowed away and covered up, and met her crew, a staff car took my navigator to the club in Buckeburg and myself to the Senior Officers' Mess in Bad Eilsen, the headquarters of the British Air Forces of Occupation (BAFO).

BAFO was the diminished remnants of 2 Tactical Air Force. In Bad Eilsen the headquarters occupied the largest and formerly most luxurious hotel in this pre-war spa. Before the RAF moved in it had been the design headquarters of the Focke-Wulf aircraft concern under the direction of its brilliant leader Kurt Tank. Even when I arrived, some time after the ending of the war, we were still finding in our formerly Focke-Wulf offices all kinds of aircraft drawings and designs, some modifications of the current and successful FW 190, and others of extraordinary futuristic appearance. Kurt Tank had made an amazing exit from Germany with the most important of his forthcoming jet fighter designs.

One of the first transport services to be restored was a refrigerated road lorry service bringing frozen meat from Denmark into hungry Germany. The Allied Control Commission did its utmost to help, realising that the renewed supply of food by road was a top priority. The refrigerated lorries returned north empty, and in one of them travelled Kurt Tank, a few key members of his staff, and his designs. From Denmark, by means still unknown, he travelled to Argentina and, welcomed there and sheltered by the strong German colony, continued his work as an aircraft designer. The result was one of the first post-war jet fighters, the Pulqui, built in the Argentinean government aircraft factory. It was tested and demonstrated by Kurt Tank.

My own office was formerly a luxurious bedroom, surrounded on three of its sides by built-in polished wood cupboards and hanging wardrobes, all with similar doors. Exit into the outside corridor was another identical door, which caused constant laughter when my visitors let themselves out into a cupboard, and had to be rescued from a place that could not be opened from inside. We were also greatly intrigued by the system by which each bedroom was discreetly connected, usually through a disguised wardrobe, to the bedroom next door.

Two other Luftwaffe stations which I came to know well were Sylt and Lubeck.

Both these were interesting for we had found the Luftwaffe organisation and methods so similar to our own. At Sylt, for example, an RAF Air Traffic Controller presided over the former enemy air traffic control personnel, still doing for us the same work that they had done before. At Lubeck, the Mess Staff were nearly all ex-Luftwaffe. One remarkable person was the barman, who turned out to be an ex-night fighter pilot who claimed a good many Lancasters as his victims. He made no secret of this and was a very likeable person who had done his job as efficiently and courageously for his country as our own crews had done for us. Later, he was able to provide a good deal of valuable information for researchers writing the history of the bombing campaign against Germany and his claims were proved to be factual and exact.

All over Schleswig and northeastern Germany there were still a multitude of aircraft and aircrew who had made their escape from the Russians advancing from the east. I talked to many of the aircrew, including one remarkable young man who had piloted an FW 190 with his friend sitting on his lap, in order make his surrender to the RAF rather than be captured by the Russians.

At Sylt was established an armaments practice camp, and also a holiday resort. On the aerodrome were still, untouched, some forty or more of the German's final night fighter. This was the Heinkel He 219 (Owl). It had a tricycle undercarriage, a four-aerial centimetric array protruding from its small nose, and twin tails. The power plant, almost dwarfing the slim fuselage between the engines, was a pair of BMW 603 air-cooled radials, which gave it a top speed of 370mph. Its armament was five cannon. It was ready for service at the beginning of 1943, and the Luftwaffe's best night-fighter pilots were enthusiastic about it. These included Prince Lippe-Weissenfeld and Lieutenants Streib and Lent.

At Fassberg the widespread dispersals were still crowded with another Heinkel aeroplane, the four-engine He 177. The prototype of this heavy bomber had first flown at the Luftwaffe test centre at Rechlin in November 1939. Thereafter mismanagement had held up its development and production so that by the time it was ready, as the much revised He 277, it was too late. The He 277s at Fassberg were twin-propeller aircraft in which each propeller was driven by a pair of coupled Daimler-Benz water-cooled engines. Its designed performance was to give it a cruising speed of 335mph, a range of 3,730 miles, and space for up to 3 tons of bombs. Daimler-Benz never succeeded in making the coupled engine design work. It was subject to disastrous fires and many failures.

There were many other relics of the Luftwaffe scattered at occupied and abandoned airfields all over the country. Among these were the former seaplane and flying boat stations on Sylt. They had remained untouched since the final destructive attacks in the closing stages of the war. Sylt is an island separated from the mainland by some six miles of shallow open water, spanned only at that time by a railway bridge constructed on piles above the water. Road vehicles, in order to reach the island, had to embark on the railway flats, and go by train.

In the town in the centre of the island was the Westerland Hotel, formerly a

Luftwaffe Mess and now the RAF Officers' Mess for the aerodrome at Sylt. At the north and south extremities of the island were the two great German naval flying boat and seaplane bases. List, in the north, had been an important naval seaplane station in the First World War. Hornum, in the south, seemed to have been more recently built. Each was similar, with concrete slipways for launching into the sheltered waters lying between the island and the mainland. It was from List and Hornum, and other seaplane bases in Schleswig, that a fleet of 150 flying boats and seaplanes were launched to supplement the more numerous landplane transports that ferried German troops during the invasion of Norway.

In shattering contrast to the relative peace of the island of Sylt and Fehmarn (to the south of the Danish island of Laaland) were the big cities. On my visit to the aerodrome at Wahn, where 98 Squadron was now based and equipped with Mosquitoes, I was taken to see Cologne. My most vivid recollection is of streets in the centre of the city, along which it was only possible to walk along a narrow winding path from which the worst of the rubble from destroyed buildings had been cleared. There were great areas of destruction, and here and there, from among the ruins protruded a stove pipe chimney with a little smoke coming from it. This showed that in the basement, somebody was still living. Gangs of homeless children roamed parts of the city, existing by what they could find or steal.

It was the first and greatest task of the Allied Civilian Control Commission to rebuild the civilian administration which in the last days of the war, had not just broken down but entirely disappeared. Large parts of Germany were without any of the services which keep the water supply going, the drains working, the trains running, food, heat, light, or law and order. One of the greatest problems was to recreate the native German organisation to take over again. One of the major challenges was that anyone with sufficient knowledge or experience were tainted by their associations with the Nazi Party. Slowly but surely a new administration was created by the return of exiles and de-Nazification.

In the small country towns, the problem was less acute. The beautiful little town of Hamelin had survived untouched. It was well supplied with food from the surrounding lush farming country. There were many other similar smaller and lovely old towns. But if the destruction of Cologne had been by contrast shattering, that was nothing to what I saw in Hamburg.

Hamburg had been attacked in 1943 on the nights of 24 and 25 July, and again on 2 and 3 August, and received over 8,000 tons of bombs, a high proportion of which were incendiaries. Hamburg had received other visits after this in 1943. When I walked through the devastated remains of the city, and viewed it from low level from the air, it was black and scorched, with tumbled rubble blocking streets and, on a still day, what seemed the terrible smell of death pervading the air. Rescue work had been largely impossible, so that the city became its own tomb. Only in the outer areas were buildings of any substance habitable and in use. Beyond Hamburg, down the Elbe estuary, the big shipyards were a mass of tangled wreckage. In marshalling yards tracks and rolling stock still lay around, rusting, rotting and untouched.

Berlin, oddly, seemed less terrifying than Hamburg. It had been badly wrecked not only by bombing, but by the fighting which had taken place there in the last stages of the war. The city was already divided into four sectors: the British, the American, the French and the Russian. At that time, there was no great difficulty in moving from one to the other, at least in daytime. The British sector was served by the airfield of Gatow, where the station commander was an old friend, Brian Yarde. The owner of Brian's house was said to have been the personal physician to Frau Emmy Goering, wife of Goering, at that time held prisoner at Nuremburg, and on trial for war crimes.

By 1947, when I visited Gatow for the first time, the journey from the airfield at Buckeburg, still known as B.151 took forty-five minutes by Mosquito. By road, which I never attempted, it took a great deal longer. Travellers had to negotiate checkpoints on entering and leaving Russian-controlled territory. Later this developed into the famous Berlin blockade, defeated by the Air Lift, but that was after my time in Germany was over.

In Berlin, one essential visit was to the burned out Reich's Chancellery, in the grounds of which one was shown the site of the bonfire on which the body of Hitler and his mistress, Eva Braun, were burned. All this was in the Russian Zone. To reach it, one passed the Russian War Memorial, with its permanently mounted guard of Russian soldiers. The memorial had few names inscribed upon it. It was supposed to commemorate all those Russian soldiers who had lost their lives in the assault on Germany, and the campaign leading up to the capture of Berlin.

The Reich's Chancellery was one of the most imposing of Hitler's Berlin buildings. Even in ruin it remained vastly impressive. Behind it, in a former garden, lay the entrance to the bunker in which Hitler had committed suicide. By 1947 the bunker had been picked over by many visitors. It was unwatched, unguarded, and open to anyone who wished to enter. Few, any longer, did, and scattered bits of paper, charred remains of documents, and oddments too unimportant to interest anybody, littered the floors of the once tidy underground rooms.

In Germany in 1947 the RAF had two major problems. The first arose from the transformation of the Service from its former war footing to a peace time establishment. Large numbers of experienced ground crew were being demobilised and returned to civilian life, and this caused great difficulties in the maintenance of aircraft in the squadrons. In my capacity as Group Captain Training I was particularly concerned with the state of the Tempest squadrons. The monthly flying time for each pilot had been severely rationed. The result was that accidents increased, and it became apparent that pilots were simply not getting enough flying practice to maintain that razor sharp efficiency which the squadrons had attained by the end of the war. Investigations with the help of the Squadron Commanders and Wing Leaders led to the conclusion that anything less than sixteen hours per month for each pilot was insufficient. We accordingly devoted great efforts to ensure at least this minimum, and if possible more. Accidents thereafter declined. The other problem was the provision of spare time facilities for people who, until recently, had been used to having little or no spare time from the war. To this end, various kinds of clubs were established, most notably the Malcolm Clubs, which proved their value over and over again. In Buckeburg, the RAF established an Officers Club in the former castle of the Prince of Schaumberg-Lippe. This was run, and run very well, by the NAAFI.

But best of all were the sailing clubs and Gliding Club. Most of these were based on former Luftwaffe facilities, and had been lavishly equipped. I found myself officially placed in charge of all RAF gliding clubs in the zone.

Nearly all the gliding clubs were based on former Luftwaffe schools. Before the war Germany had pioneered soaring flight on a national scale. Germany was forbidden powered aircraft and gliding had continued to be the main source of Luftwaffe aircrew. It was, in effect, the basic stage of military flying training. In consequence, vast state subsidies had been put into schools, buildings and aircraft, with impressive results. One of the best of these was the ridge soaring site at Scharfoldendorf, southeast of Hamelin. The ridge itself rises abruptly from the plains of the River Weser to the west of it, and the River Leine further from it to the east. To the east there was a secondary, and somewhat lower ridge which, in the right conditions boosted the Scharfoldendorf Ridge lift to make gains of height greater than 2,000 metres possible. The soarable length of the ridge was some fifteen miles. The camp site itself on the highest part comprised a large main building, which had housed the German student glider pilots in three huge dormitories, running the whole length of the building. Each dormitory on a separate storey looked out to the west over the Weser Valley at the bottom of the steep slope 500 feet below. The bottom storey of the castle-like building contained kitchens and dining halls. Below it, in a little hollow to the east, was a flat concrete paved parade ground, which also served as a tarmac for the aircraft from the hangar and workshops on the side of it away from the castle. Next to the hangar was a pleasant open air swimming pool, and beyond it the Officers' Mess. Scharfoldendorf, in its busiest days, had a pupil population of between 150 and 200. Flying training continued all the year round. Courses lasted between three and four months, depending upon the weather, which was normally good, thus the school must have been turning out around 600 gliding pilots a year, each trained to something like Silver C standard. Successful pupils then went on to the Luftwaffe training schools equipped with powered aircraft.

All flying training started with ground slides on the SG.38: the simplest possible glider, nicknamed the Broomstick. As soon as he was judged competent, the pupil was taken to the steep slope near the castle, and catapulted by means of lengths of bungee stretched by fellow students over the edge. He was required at first to perform only a straight glide, and land in the flat field at the bottom of the hill. Turns came later and, as his proficiency increased, he was allowed to fly an SG.38

onto which very lightweight wood and fabric panels were fitted to give some semblance of fairing around the pilot. The SG.38, thus fitted, was nicknamed the Boat. Gliders which had landed at the bottom were brought back to the launch point at the top on a railed carriage and track, which ran straight up the slope. However, in the winter, the instructors improved on this by skiing down the slope after their descending pupils. Then, launched by a winch in the field at the bottom, flew the glider back to the top.

From the Boat, the pupils advanced to the Grunau Baby, and to winch launching. At this stage of training he was aided by the use of the dual two-seater, the Kranich. He would also be initiated into ridge soaring. Finally, if his progress justified it, and conditions permitted, he would progress to one of the more advanced sailplanes such as the Meise and the Mu13. The latter, with its large span and low wing loading could stay aloft when lift was too weak for any other of the types then available. The Meise, later somewhat modified and heavier, was built in England after the war as the Olympia and was widely used in the early post-war days of competitive flying. The highest performance sailplanes were the Weihe's, normally kept for the instructors. At Scharfoldendorf we found six of these beautiful aircraft.

Under the RAF we retained, at Scharfoldendorf, the former Commandant and Chief Instructor, Sepp Niederstadt. In theory he was forbidden like all Germans to fly. This was a rule we did not observe, requiring him to do all test flights after repairs and maintenance by the German staff. This was probably completely unnecessary, because they worked most loyally and well, and took great pride in their wood working and fabric skills.

There were two other similar schools in the British zone, one at Salzgitter, between Hildesheim and Goslar, and another at Oerlinghausen, about half way between Gutersloh and Paderborn. The Salzgitter site was too close to the border with the Russian zone for comfort. In addition to these three main sites, there were many smaller ones which were made to serve the Army and Air Force units closer to them. Their equipment was less extensive and few of them possessed living accommodation. The lesser sites included the little aerodrome at Minderheide, close to Minden, another at Detmold, which we closed, and two operated mainly by the Army, one at Soltau and one near Hamelin. We also put numbers of gliders on aerodromes occupied by the RAF. But it was at the three big schools that most gliding took place. Each of them was nominated as a Rest Centre and an RAF Officer, usually a Flight Lieutenant, with a small RAF staff put in charge. To these rest centres went not only those interested in gliding, but many others and often this became their introduction to gliding and they became enthusiasts. It was all free, with the whole organisation, like sailing, riding, skiing, and other things regarded as one of the essential amenities to keep the personnel of the occupying forces happy.

It was in mid-winter that I had my first introduction to the SG.38 Broomstick. I was winch launched to 250 metres and, although its gliding angle of barely one in ten ensured a speedy return to earth, the flight was quite long enough to freeze the tears from my frozen eyes, and to land with frost on my eyebrows. This, together with the sight of nothing between myself and the earth below, except my boots, did not endear the SG.38 to me, and I never flew one again.

At Scharfoldendorf we had use of a Minimoa (the Schemp-Hirth GO-3), a Schleicher Rhonbussard, a DFS Habicht and a Rhonsperber. The latter was a small single-seater designed by Hans Jacobs. The DFS Habicht, with a span of only 13 metres was interesting because it had been used in the training of pilots who were to fly the Me 163 Rocket Fighter.

At Oerlinghausen there was a DFS Reiher, a 19 metre span design by Hans Jacobs, with a best gliding angle of one in thirty-three, and a minimum rate of sink of half a metre per second. The Reiher I liked; it flew nicely. It gave me the impression that its long wings not only flexed, but twisted slightly under the influence of the aileron loads, thus making lateral control inefficient. It was the first sailplane which I encountered with something like the modern cockpit, where the pilot lies nearly on his back. In the Mosquito I was accustomed to sitting bolt upright, and in the Weihe I found an upright seating position which I was used to, and liked.

Another one off at Oerlinghausen was the Achen Technical High School built FVA 10b, the Rheinland. This, with a span of 16 metres, and a cockpit enclosure rather like a Heinkel 111 had a retractable undercarriage with a single wheel. It had been designed, built and flown by the students as a technical training exercise. It handled quite nicely.

Two other oddities were the side by side two-seater GO-4 Goevier, which was used by the Army Club at Soltau, and the favourite mount of Jumbo Roberts, its Chief Instructor. It became the prime mover in the foundation of the Army Gliding Association in England, and the Dittmar designed Condor HD-1, a strutted design of similar performance to the Meise, which was at Minderheide.

A memorable occasion at Scharfoldendorf was the visit of Lord and Lady Tedder. Lord Tedder (then Chief of the Air Staff) was visiting the Air Forces in Germany and came to Scharfoldendorf so that Lady Tedder, who was the head of the Malcolm Clubs, could examine the rest centre. They were accompanied by our Commander-in-Chief Air Marshall Sir Arthur Sanders, who, as Group Captain Sanders, had been one of the instructors, and Deputy Commandant of the Staff College at Andover when we were there just before the war.

One of our visitors to Fassberg was Hanna Reitsch. She was quite small; rather grey looking in complexion and greying hair scraped back and tied in a bun. She was dressed entirely in black and, at that time, must have been about forty-five years in age. She looked a good deal more. The last that any of us knew about her was that she had flown a Fieseler Storch into Berlin, landing it under fire on the wide avenue close to the Reich's Chancellory in May 1945. She went into the bunker and made a last endeavour to persuade Hitler to go with her to the Storch. It was a hazardous and brave act. The black she continued to wear was for Hitler.

Before the war she had become a skilled sailplane pilot and during the war played a considerable part in the test flying of the Me 163 Rocket powered Interceptor. She had also test flown a V1 flying bomb, fitted with a small cockpit just large enough to hold her and so solved some of its difficult control problems.

I have devoted much of this part of my story to gliding. This is because at this time I became an addict to a sport that I have loved ever since. But there were lots of other things going on and other aircraft to enjoy. One such was another go at flying Meteors. This was at Lubeck, at time commanded by the charming and hospitable Group Captain Micky Dwyer. I visited him by Mosquito, and stayed for a week flying the Meteor Mk IIIs of a visiting squadron from England. The Mark III differed from the Mk I, which I had first experienced in 1946. It had a sliding canopy, similar to the Spitfire, and somewhat extended engine nacelles. These improved its longitudinal stability, particularly in a dive. It had the same armament as the Mk I, namely four 20mm Hispano cannons, which the squadron used on the armament practice ranges at Lubeck, on the Baltic coast. I could never claim to have become an accurate shot but the resulting fusillade when the firing button was pressed was both satisfying and impressive. It was also interesting to note that, in level flight, a two-second burst with all four guns slowed down the Meteor by a perceptible amount.

Another delight was to renew my acquaintance with the Hawker Tempest Mk II and its Bristol Centaurus engine. This I was able to do during the summer exercises in 1948 when we dispersed our squadrons from the permanent bases to other German airfields abandoned since the war. It was an essential part of my responsibility for training to be in on this, so that I was able to fly some sorties with the Tempests at the old airfield at Ahlhorn, and later some even more exciting ones with a Photographic Reece Spitfire XIX.

In the autumn of 1947, I was granted a spell of ten days at Bentwaters in Suffolk to fly the newly introduced de Havilland Vampire. Ten hours Vampire flying spread out over ten days enabled me to explore this new type to the point of reasonable competence. I never really came to terms with the little Vampire. I did with it everything that I could; climbed it till it ran out of breath; did aerobatics which I enjoyed; explored its low speed flying with stall, clean, dirty and level, and in turns and throughout it behaved faultlessly.

My last days with BAFO were spent in what amounted to a farewell tour. The immediate reason was the detachment of a Tempest Wing in Austria, where it was based on the former Luftwaffe aerodrome at Zeltweg. The reason for this move was tension between Czechoslovakia and Austria, when it was thought possible that the former country might profit by the presence of strong Russian forces not far away in Vienna to make an attempt to extend its northern boundaries, towards Graz and into Styria. We travelled in some style in the Commander-in-Chief (Sir Arthur Sanders) VIP Dakota, flying via Munich and Salzburg to Vienna. The flight provided my first sight of the Danube, which really was blue.

Vienna, at that time was occupied, not unlike Berlin, by all the Allies, though the

French presence was minimal. The Russians occupied the city north of the Danube and that part of Austria north of it, and through Hungary and Czechoslovakia. Sachers Hotel in Vienna was used as the British Mess and transit hotel. After two days in Vienna and various meetings, as well as some exploring, we took off from the aerodrome at Schwechat just to the east of the city, and flew, on a brilliant clear day, southwest and over the Alps to Udine in northern Italy. One of the most astonishing views I remember is coming suddenly to the southern edge of the mountain chain, which descends steeply to the broad level plains of northern Italy. We landed at Udine aerodrome and were whisked off to the castle at Duino, just outside of Trieste. The castle stood on a rocky promontory overlooking the Adriatic. After a night at the castle, and meetings with the Commander-in-Chief and his staff, we returned to Udine, and back over the Alps to Zeltweg.

At Zeltweg we dealt with the orders for the Tempest Wing, and how, if the need arose, they were to work with the ground forces whose headquarters we had just visited. I was able to do a little local flying and see something of the lovely Austrian country. In the hangar there were still a few German bits and pieces, including one complete and apparently fully serviceable two-seater Klemm light monoplane. Nobody seemed to know what to do with it, which was a pity because it was a very nice little aeroplane.

On the morning we intended to leave on our return to Bad Eilsen, it snowed a blizzard. By midday there was thick snow and low cloud everywhere and air movement was out of the question. Our Commander-in-Chief Sir Arthur Sanders borrowed two Army staff cars, one of which he drove himself very fast and well despite having no right arm. In the other Peter Anson, his ADC, and I shared the driving. We set off to enjoy a return by road, and to see the country. We arranged that most of our meals en route should be roadside picnics, and to this end, the mess at Zeltweg treated us to a good deal of luxury. I also took the opportunity to buy from the equipment section, a number of khaki shirts and slacks. These had their own interest because they had come in the RAF stores all the way with the Desert Air Force from Africa, through Italy, and finally arrived in Austria. The shirts cost me nine pence each and the slacks were free.

Our drive took us west through country roads, through Steinach, Hallstadt and Hallein. From Austria we entered Germany at Salzburg. From Munich we continued through Nurnberg and by Eisenach to Hildesheim, and finally Bad Eilsen. A few days later I packed my bags and, after a last flight in my Mosquito, was flown home to England in an Anson to take some leave, and to prepare for my departure to the United States on an exchange posting with the United States Air Force. My TA 591 was faithful to the last. There had been a good deal of muttering about my refusal to let anybody else fly her, and I heard later that the chief mutterer had hardly waited until I was out of sight before having a go. But TA 591 never got off the ground. In strange hands she rebelled, and half way through take-off produced a monumental swing, ending up in a rubbish dump. I was both sad and glad. I loved that Mosquito and she never once let me down, carrying me to and fro, often to England in most weathers, and at high speed. I never flew a Mosquito again. I have more hours, over 600, on Mosquitoes than on any other type, and if asked what aeroplane I liked best of all that I have flown, I think it would have to be the de Havilland Mk VI Mosquito.

CHAPTER NINE
THE USA

When I left Germany on 13 June 1948 the war had been over for three years. It was already very apparent that the country, although in some respects still seemingly stunned from its final and disastrous collapse, was making progress towards recovery. The railways ran to time, the farms were fat with produce and industry was again taking shape. Foremost among industrial enterprises was the revival of the Volkswagen plant, working full time to produce the first runs of the famous Beetle. These were bought by the Forces of Occupation in enormous numbers as their principal small transport vehicle. Credit for this must go to a team of British Royal Engineers, headed by Tony Rolt, well known before the war in competition motoring, and in 1945 given the task of getting the VW factory at Wolfsbuttel going again to produce in quantity the vehicles which the services wanted.

There were many similar examples on a smaller scale. British Trade Unions played a notable part in creating a German trade union structure which snuffed out the remnants of Nazi doctrine in industry. The Allied Control Commission worked wonders in rebuilding the civil organisation to administer the lands, and restore native control of law and order.

My first move on leaving Germany was, of course, some leave with my family. This we spent, for the most part, at Botley but with visits elsewhere, including to my own parents at Nottingham. But the fifty days before leaving for the United States was interrupted by a whole round of visits, not only to RAF units in England and briefings at Air Ministry, but also by a series of visits to the aircraft industry. Fascinating though all this was, for I was made aware of all kinds of future plans such as those which were to lead to the production of English Electric Lightning, I resented the time away form my family.

There was some compensation, however. At Hatfield, John Cunningham showed me the first Chipmunk to arrive in England. It was built in Canada. He said to have a test flight and then meet him for lunch in an hour and tell him about the experience. This was my first experience of the Chipmunk and in one hour I explored it as far as possible. After deep thought, mostly between zero and five thousand feet, I came to the conclusion that it was a beautiful basic trainer, with just one shortcoming. It could not do the same job quite so well as the Tiger Moth. My reasons were these. First, the Tiger, whilst being capable of forgiving serious mishandling, always makes it abundantly clear to the pilot that he has failed. The Chipmunk forgives but does not explain, and this allows the pilot to think he has done alright. Subsequent hours in this aeroplane have convinced me that my first assessment was right, and that the Tiger Moth is, to this day, the only trainer which can lay substantial claim to be heir to the old Avro 504.

The other memorable visit was to Bristol where I had been taught to fly. This was totally enjoyable, and included the brief loan of one the most charming small sports cars, the little Bristol Coupe. It had a two litre engine based on the pre-war BMW engine, and its compact shape and road holding ability was remarkable. Once more I met Cyril Unwins, Cy Holmes, and my old instructor who taught me to fly, Jock Campbell. It was a very happy visit.

On 30 July I left Southampton in Cunard's the *Queen Mary*. I was one of 2,000 passengers, sharing a four-berth cabin with three of my brother officers, all of whom were destined to become students of the Air War College of the United States Air Force at Maxwell Field, Alabama.

As Air Ministry policy at that time was for overseas posting of only one year families were not sent as well. After Germany I had hoped for a home station where we could be together again. Later on, Rosemary did come out to America and joined me, but that came towards the end of our posting there. However as a result of our representations it was agreed that all subsequent RAF students to the USAF Air War College would be able to take their families as family life is an integral part of social affairs on any USAF Base.

The family saw me off at Southampton and thereafter we slipped into a routine for four days. The great ship, still not fully refurbished after her wartime use as a troopship, was luxurious in parts, and dinner was an experience; no rationing whilst rationing in England was as strict as ever. Our four-berth cabin in the middle of the ship, several decks down, was uncomfortable and stuffy, and the fresh air system inefficient. The *Queen Mary* was a vast ship and impressive for her sheer size. To travel in her, regardless of expense, was no doubt the height of luxury; but to travel in 1948 as cheaply as the Air Ministry could arrange, was far from it.

Arrival in New York, however, was unforgettable. Arrival in the *Queen Mary* was a stately affair, which permits each new spectacle to be examined and remembered. The low-lying coast is not easily visible at first, so that the high skyscrapers of New York itself appear on the horizon almost as soon. Then the coastline on each side closes in as the ship enters the Narrows. Staten Island is to port, and to starboard, Coney Island and Brooklyn. After the Narrows, the water opens out again into the Upper Bay, in which lies Ellis Island, Governors Island and the whole dominated by the vast Statue of Liberty. Quickly then comes New York itself where, at the Battery, the waters divide, becoming to starboard the East River, and to port the wide Hudson River. Very slowly now, accompanied by tugs and overlooked by skyscrapers, the *Queen Mary* is edged into New York's Ocean Terminal. Highest of all the skyscrapers and overlooking the dock is the Empire State Building.

Ashore, there is enormous activity so that we were off the ship, surrounded by our bags and heavier luggage, and in front of the immigration officers in thirty minutes flat. We were asked to sign documents promising to make no attempt to overthrow the Government of the United States by force, our racial origins were noted and finally we were asked why we had come to the United States. To this I replied, perhaps without too much tact, that I personally did not want to come; that I had been sent. This was totally unprecedented and stopped the swift routine flow dead. For one moment I had the wild hope that I would be put back on board the *Queen Mary* and returned as quickly as possible to Southampton. No such luck, for at that point the uniformed RAF port detachment still functioning in New York arrived in the person of a small corporal. He immediately took charge of us and the situation and swept us off in large cars to our hotel.

We were allowed two days in New York. With my brother officers, Guy Bolland also a Group Captain, and Wing Commanders Alan Saw and Headley Blasberry, we explored New York. After two days the RAF corporal arrived, paid our hotel bills, and put us onto the train for Washington, which we took from the New York Central Station. The line passes under the Hudson River and Hoboken and only emerges into the open air well clear of New York. It passes through Trenton and Philadelphia and within sight of the shore of the Delaware River. Then, just before crossing the big bridge over the Susquehanna River at the top of Chesapeake Bay, the line enters the State of Maryland. Maryland is as beautiful as its name, and the railway runs through the shore side of villages and farms and settlements along the edge of Chesapeake Bay to Baltimore. Thereafter it cuts inland, and to Washington DC at the head of the Potomac River.

In Washington we were met by representative of the British Joint Services Staff Mission. We were to stay for six days to be briefed by the RAF Element of the Mission, and to pay our duty calls to the Embassy in Massachusetts Avenue. We lived in Erskine's Hotel, on a quiet street not far from the Embassy, and in easy walking distance of the centre of the city. The owner/manager, Mr Erskine, was a former First World War fighter pilot who had flown with the Royal Flying Corps and later with the US Army Air Corps. His hotel in Washington had become a sort of unofficial RAF Mess where nearly everybody stayed when passing through. Unlike nearly every other hotel there was no form of air conditioning, which was why it was cheaper than most. On the other hand, all the windows opened, there was a pleasant garden, and Erskine's bacon and scrambled eggs for breakfast were the best. I liked it.

In Washington our guide and mentor was Flight Lieutenant Reg Vincent, whose task it was to look after the pay, allowances and welfare of all 100 RAF officers on exchange duties with the USAF. He could not have been more helpful, and among his parting words, when we left for Maxwell Field, was the reminder that we would find it expensive to return the hospitality which we would experience from our hosts. Therefore arrangements had been made for us to have a routine supply of 'diplomatic whisky' at half price. This was a great blessing and this not only proved very popular and enabled us to return hospitality, but also to avoid appearing as poor cousins.

By August 1948, having travelled overnight on a train whose wheels must have been square, such was the discomfort of the sleeper, we arrived at the Central Railroad station in Montgomery, Alabama. Boards and notices proclaimed it to be The Cradle of the Confederacy.

We were met at the station by Group Captain Leslie Bower, the resident RAF Staff Officer at the Air War College. Leslie Bower was an old friend from 2 Group days, where he had commanded No 138 Mosquito Wing at Lasham and later in France. We were taken to the Bachelor Officers Quarters assigned to us, which were in two-storey wooden wartime huts. We were accommodated two to a room. Washing facilities were in a communal bathroom, and the place was overrun with cockroaches. After a few days, it was realised that we had been put into quarters not intended for the Air War College students and we were moved into very nice single rooms, each with its own shower and refrigerator, and being stone built, much cooler and almost roach-free. They were in a long row, along the outside of which ran a stone corridor, the outer side of which was screened with mosquito proof wire mesh, as were the windows of our cabins. These were pre-war buildings and very pleasant places in which to live and study. Outside was grass and trees and they were within easy walking distance of the Officers Club.

The Officers Club is an institution peculiar to the United States Service, and in fact is an Officers Families Club in which wives and children are likely to be found at any time. At Maxwell Field, the Club was a large and delightful pre-war building such as might be found at the most expensive and exclusive sailing or golf clubs. The bars, dining room, ballroom and changing rooms were first class and the patio outside, shaded by trees and flood lit at night by hundreds of fairy lights. The swimming pool had a full time guard, and everybody using it was required to shower before going into the pool. It was inspected daily by the medical staff, and if considered in any way unclean, was immediately drained, cleaned and refilled in time for use again that afternoon. Adjoining the Club were the married quarters, in one of which lived Leslie Bower and his wife. Nearer the airfield was the enlisted men's pool, once again of full Olympic size, and used by all their families. The same strict clinical supervision prevailed there also.

Finally one came to the College itself, composed of three main sets of slightly Spanish style buildings. First was the College Administrative HQ in which was General Kenny, formerly USAF Commander in the Pacific and now commanding General of the College. Then there was the Command and Staff School which had up to 300 students. Finally the Air War College which we were to attend, presided over by General Orvil Anderson, former Second-in-Command of the USAF Bomber Forces in England. We were the senior school, intended for Officers of the rank of Lieutenant Colonel or full Colonel which most were, and we numbered 140. The RAF were treated in all respects, except one, exactly as though we were American officers. The one exception was the result of a congressional decision taken shortly after the war ended, that nuclear information would no longer be fully shared with any foreigners. In practise, the result was that we were excluded during our year's stay, from three lectures on this subject.

The normal routine was to attend lectures starting at 0830 each morning. A mid-morning coffee break would be followed by work in syndicates or seminars, in which students were divided up into groups of six or seven under their seminar leader. We each stood our turn as leaders, and as such were required to present to the assembled students and staff, the solution to the problem worked out by our particular group. In the afternoon there was a nine-hole golf course on the far side of the aerodrome, swimming and, when necessary, work in one's cabin.

Once a week every pilot spent an afternoon flying, and for this purpose Maxwell Field housed a practice flight comprising over 100 aircraft. These were my old friend, the Mitchell, the B.25 as it was known by the USAF, Mustangs, mainly the P51H model; the Beech C.45 Expeditor, which was a light twin, some Harvards and some C.47s (Douglas Dakota).

My first task was to obtain the full USAF instrument rating, which was awarded to me on 17 November 1948. This entitled me to fly when and where I liked, by day or by night, in whatever weather conditions were acceptable. Its effect was to give me a valuable freedom of the airways, by which most navigation was then done. The airways, marked by radio beacons, covered the whole of the United States. In the absence of many aerodromes equipped with landing aids such as Ground Control Approach (GCA), the approach was entirely pilot-controlled by locating oneself over the appropriate marker beacon, usually right on the aerodrome. Flying a set pattern at exactly regulated speeds and heights and timed by stop watch, one arrives on the approach at the outer marker beacon at the right speed and height. One is also within the glide path pattern whose centre was indicated by the merging of the Morse dots heard on one side and the Morse dashes heard on the other. This merged into a steady note which indicated that one was in position on the centre line.

On Friday evenings, large numbers of the Air War College would leave Maxwell Field for destinations all over the United States, to return late into Sunday night, in time for the first lecture on Monday morning. Ivan McElroy went off regularly with friends up into the wilds of South Dakota or Nebraska, for duck shooting.The Navy were apt to disappear to Jacksonville or Pensacola; and I, escorted by Harold Bundy, enjoyed some wonderful visits to San Antonio and beyond to the Mexican border and the Rio Grande. There was also a little opportunity for civil flying, and two interesting aircraft which I was allowed to fly after obtaining a Civil Pilot's Licence, were the Piper Cruiser and a civilian version of the PT Cornell.

The first term at Maxwell Field was mainly devoted to bringing everybody up to date with administrative duties learning about the United States Air Force, its organisation, planes, management and future intentions. We also had outside speakers of great emminence, for example, the President of General Motors, and from Government Departments such as the Treasury, and from the aircraft industry. In the second term, the scope of this exploration of knowledge was extended to the Army, the Navy, and to the State Department itself. We were extensively instructed in the workings of Congress and its committees, and how to behave. Any serving officer could have been called to give evidence before the Committee of the Budget, for example.

In the third and final term the course concentrated in applying its accumulated knowledge and experience, aided by up-to-date intelligence lectures to the solution of problems relating to the world as it seemed in 1948. Some problems were set by higher authority and the results used in higher planning. Naturally, a great deal of our work was concerned with the Russians, Communism and the Russian Armed Forces. They were at that time building up the first of their long range heavy bomber force, based on copying a captured Boeing B-29, and known in Russia as the Tupolev TU-4. Russia had not yet exploded its first nuclear weapon, but had numbers of the Rolls-Royce Nene turbo jet, at that time the most advanced jet engine in the world. This again was promptly copied in Russia, and these copies enabled Russia to design and build, in quantity, their first successful jet fighter, the MiG-15.

My visits to San Antonio and El Paso were another unique experience. They came about through the kindness of Colonel Hal Bundy in whose seminar I had been at the beginning of the course. Hal Bundy had been the Commanding Officer of a basic flying training school at Eagle Pass, on the Mexican border, south of Del Rio. His friends at Del Rio invited him to bring me down for a weekend visit and, it being a special occasion, we were allowed a long weekend. We took off from Maxwell Field on a Thursday evening, about an hour before dark, with the intention of staying the night at San Antonio where Hal Bundy had business on the Friday. Our route, in our comfortable B.25 Mitchell, took us towards New Orleans. From Maxwell Field we passed just north of New Orleans, using the beacon at Moissant Field and from there to the Ellington Air Force Base beacon at Houston in Texas. By this time it was dark, and I remember my astonishment at the lights all over the country. Each town was a blaze of light; not just from the non-curtained windows of houses and street lighting, but from a blaze of neon-signed advertisements in red, green, blue and white. Houston was visible for fifty miles. This was the first time I had flown at night since the blackout in England and it was something of a shock. From Houston we went across the endless State of Texas, over Luling and south of Austin to land, after a three hour ride, at Kelly Field just outside San Antonio. We took a taxi into town, and booked into a hotel in time to change, wash and dress before dinner.

On Saturday morning, Hal Bundy and I flew on to Eagle Pass, going via Laredo in order to have a better look at the Rio Grande tumbling through its ravines and rapids, up to Eagle Pass some 100 miles further north. There we were met by Hal's friend with an enormous station wagon, and in it were driven another forty or so miles further north along the border to Del Rio, where they lived on what they described as a small farm. The small farm took in about 10,000 acres, extending north along the border to the junction of the Rio Grande and the Pecos River.

On Monday evening we flew back to Maxwell Field, stopping once more at Kelly Field to refuel. The weather forecast was not nice. It foretold of what is locally known as a Norther, which indicates a burst of cold northern air breaking through into the warm, moist air of the south. It creates much turbulence and thunderstorms, with all the accompanying rain and low cloud beneath. It is a particularly vigorous and large cold front. This one stretched almost along our flight path through Louisiana, Mississippi and Alabama, and we ran into it just before Baton Rouge on the Mississippi River. From then on we flew in it, being considerably bounced about, and finding several of our beacons blotted out by electrical storms. However, at Birmingham, some way north of Montgomery, is, or was, a big and powerful broadcast station. This continued to come through on our Direction Finding loop, and using this we navigated past Meridian, and towards Birmingham until we could get the Maxwell Field signal. After that there were no further problems, and we landed in pelting rain and got to bed at about 0300. I would just mention that as Hal Bundy had flown down, I drew the short straw and flew this trip.

Another memorable trip with Hal Bundy was also in a Mitchell to Fort Worth. Here we landed at a huge Naval Air Base, most efficiently run, and some 300 miles from the nearest saltwater at Galveston. We stayed in Dallas and toured the fabulous city which, even then, seemed to be populated solely by millionaires.

Another, and shorter, visit was to the civil airport at Birmingham, again with Hal Bundy, and this time flying a Beech C.45. The purpose was to visit the Federal Aviation Office there in order to obtain my civil (FAA) pilots licence, and thus qualify legally to fly civil aircraft. The licence was no trouble, but again on the return trip, we plunged into the nastiest thunder weather I remember. Because there is high ground up to several thousand feet south of Birmingham, there was no question of getting under it, and we had to plunge through or go back. By this time, the thunder weather developed behind us, leaving no escape route. So we went in, at around 8,000 feet, both of us holding the controls. The little Beech was tossed about like a leaf. We concentrated entirely on altitude; there was little possibility of maintaining a constant height. During the passage through the front, we experienced height changes of plus and minus 1,000 or more feet, with great rapidity. During these moments of extreme turbulence, the air speed fluctuated violently, and to add to problems, we had a certain amount of icing. Then, quite suddenly, we emerged into a beautiful cloudless sunlit day. It was exactly like flying out of the side of a mountain. When we turned to examine what we had come from, we saw the whole mountain, snowy white in the sunlight, yellowy brown in its sulphurous unlit caverns, and black below, boiling like a witches' cauldron. Just ahead of us was Maxwell Field and we landed and taxied up to the apron, just in time to get soaking wet as the storm burst with tropical ferocity on the airfield. The apron was quickly inches deep in water and the gutters and drains roared and overflowed.

Some of the most interesting flying was during the ten day Christmas break. I was attached to No 79 Squadron of the 20th Pursuit Group of the USAF at Shaw Field in South Carolina. They flew the Republic F-84S, powered with an Allison jet engine. The evening I arrived coincided with their Christmas party in the Officers Club.

The F-84 was the first aircraft I ever flew with powered control. The system applied power only to the ailerons and could be adjusted by the pilot, quickly and easily, by rotating a knob by his knees, graduated from zero to ten. Zero was without power assist, when the ailerons were very heavy at low speeds and going fast in a dive, almost rock solid. Ten was maximum power, when there was very little feel at all and one felt to be balanced on a pinpoint, ready to topple suddenly either way. With ten, the rate of roll was phenomenal, making the F-84 the first aircraft in my experience capable of what has now been named the twinkle roll (flying in formation with all aircraft rolling simultaneously).

In all I flew ten hours on the F-84, starting with general familiarisation and exploring all its characteristics as my experience of it increased. It was very comfortable and quiet. The pressurised and air-conditioned cabin ensured a pleasant climate in the cockpit, whatever was going on outside. It did fail me once, filling the cockpit with a dense fog so that even the instrument panel was momentarily invisible. The effect was exactly as in the white out which comes before the blackout. As I was in the circuit at the time I knew it could not be a white out, and before I had much time to think about it, it cleared sufficiently to pull off an emergency landing, accompanied by a Mayday call. I thought I was on fire and said so to Air Traffic. The result was a rush of fire engines and ambulances, and a great deal of spectacular effects. As I came to a standstill on the runway, the engine seized solid. Later I learned that the Allison jet of those days, one of the first, had a life expectancy of only 100 hours. Mine had done 101. Next day I took an F-84 to 20,000 feet in ten minutes, which seemed a fine rate of climb, and completed my attachment with a trip to Maxwell Field and back to collect mail. Cruising in comfort at 15,000 feet, the 360 miles took exactly forty-five minutes, that is a speed of 480mph, quite good for 1948.

During the four days of Christmas I went to Washington to see Zdenek Kokes. This came about by sheer chance. Zdenek came down to Shaw Field in his car and I was given permission to put him up in the Bachelor Officers' Quarters. On our first evening we were the only inhabitants of the Club and, without thinking much about it, I slipped a nickel into one of the one-arm bandits as I passed it on the way to the bar. Suddenly there was a ringing of bells, and a jingle jangle of coins as the jackpot came out. It came out in an endless stream until the surrounding floor was covered in coins; and still it went on and on and on. It must have been the first time that machine had paid out for months and the total was an amazing 200 or so dollars. There and then we packed our bags and set off for Washington, staying the night near Fayetville in North Carolina and arriving on Christmas Eve at the Universities Club in Washington.

The Universities Club is, in the USA, a unique institution, for it admitted no women. I am an honorary member by virtue of my Cambridge degree. Zdenek was a member and there we stayed for Christmas Day, having the place almost to ourselves and making every use of the swimming pool, the bar, and the superb food and service. On Boxing Day, we moved on to Virginia to visit friends of Zdenek's parents in the foothills of the Blue Mountains. There was snow and ice, and the old stone farmhouse in which they lived had been fortified when it was built back in pioneer days. It had its own well inside the house so that, when besieged, there was always water.

In the spring, Rosemary came out to join me. This was an epic in its own right, for the difficulties which she overcame in order to achieve the journey were very great indeed. At that time there was very little transatlantic air travel and was mainly prohibitive by cost. Sea transport was almost impossible to book, and money exchange controls made it impossible for ordinary people to get dollars. There was no help from the service for any families to join their husbands in the USA, unless they were expected to be there for more than twelve months.

Rosemary finally embarked at Southampton in the *America,* a pre-war ship belonging to the United States Lines, used during the war as a troopship and now, without much change, used to convey immigrants to New York. She shared a cabin in the depths of the ship with four Irish women who, embarking at Cork, were on their way to join sons and daughters already in the USA. The weather was appalling, the food foul, and Rosemary's cabin mates were constantly ill.

By now problems at Maxwell Field had been overcome largely by the generosity of our American friends. As Rosemary was there, as it were, unofficially, we had no allowances to cover anything but my own living costs, and no entitlement either to quarters or lodging allowance, which in any case would have required the unobtainable dollars. The Air University and the Base Commander swept all these problems aside by allocating us a small quarter reserved for visitors to the University.

After Rosemary's arrival I did fewer long trips by Mitchell and most of my flying was in one of the Mustang P 51-H8s. One of these burnt off my shoe. I wore a pair of thick soled shoes for flying and this saved my foot. It occurred at some 15,000 feet or so over the forested country between Mobile and Montgomery. The P51 has a great deal of heavy electrical bonding and, if I remember rightly, the negative side of nearly every circuit is through the metal airframe. In this case, a section of braided copper bonding by my right rudder bar came adrift. In the process it produced a great deal of smoke, some flame, and a particularly nasty smell. It quickly burned itself out and I continued my journey back to Maxwell without the aid of anything electrical. Apart from that, I found the P51-H a very comfortable high speed tourer. It lacked the sweet handling of a Spitfire, particularly near the ground, tending to run out of lift suddenly, rather than more gently like the non-laminar flow wing of the Spitfire. The Packard-built Merlin engine was faultless.

Our final week at Maxwell Field was taken up with farewells and the christening of my godson, William Christopher, son of Marion and Jock Wilson. There was also the Graduation Exercises, which took place in the biggest hall on the base. It was opened by General George Kenny, the Commanding General, who welcomed

Mr Stuart Symington, the United States Secretary of the Air Force who made the main speech. After this, each student in turn, from both the Command and Staff School and the Air War College, went up to receive his diploma and to be shaken by the hand by the Secretary of the Air Force and General Kenny.

At the end of the course, Rosemary and I had a month's leave in the United States, before returning to Washington and on to England via New York. This came about partly because the USAF had requested my attachment on exchange, for a further two years as a Staff Officer at the Flying Training Command Headquarters. However we opted for home and the month's leave resulted. After a thoroughly enjoyable holiday touring America we returned to Washington and to Erskine's Hotel. We had a brief stay and visited the Embassy then finally we went onto New York, where we spent the last of our dollars on presents for the children and a visit to the top of the Empire State Building. Penniless, we embarked on the Royal Mail vessel *Britannic* the next day and sailed for Liverpool. We arrived in England on 22 July 1949. The first thing we had to do was to cash a cheque with the RAF Port Officer in order to pay our ship's bar bill.

CHAPTER TEN
LONDON TO ADEN

Almost as soon as we had returned to England, the news came that I was to be posted to the Air Ministry for duties in the Intelligence Branch. At that time it was still in its wartime London building in Monck Street, close to Lambeth Bridge. This required something of a family upheaval for we had no house of our own, and service in the Air Ministry was not given the benefit of married quarters. I went to see my old friend, Dicky Drew, at that time in charge of Group Captain's postings, and asked for time to solve the housing problem. He solved the problem in five minutes flat, by offering to sell us his own house in Fleet in which he had lived whilst working in London, having just heard of his own imminent posting back to aeroplanes and wanting to sell it as soon as possible. This was an astounding piece of luck for in 1949 there was a serious housing shortage everywhere and building restrictions were still severe. In due course Dicky Drew's house became ours and we moved in. The house, named Green Hayes, was in Pondtail Road, which is down at the eastern end of Fleet, close to the bridge over the old canal which runs between Odiham and the River Wey near Woking.

I bicycled to the station, and fitted my machine with a special stand to carry my London umbrella. Bowler hat and umbrella being essential items of Air Ministry uniform, for in London one worked in plain clothes. There is an interesting reason for this. The Air Ministry and War Office were civilian departments of State, controlled by their respective Ministers. Serving officers were seconded to these civil departments of State, and each appointment had to be approved by the Minister concerned. Unlike some foreign countries, the Chief of the Air Staff, for example, was not the Commander-in-Chief of the RAF. His actual position was that of Principal RAF Adviser to the Minister.

In the Department of Intelligence in Monck Street, serving RAF officers outnumbered civil servants in the ratio of about two to one. The head of the department, the Assistant Chief of Staff for Intelligence (ACAS(I)) presided over and controlled our affairs. This was Air Vice Marshal Pendred, and I could not have had a better or more considerate boss. We worked hard, for this was the time when it was becoming apparent that the Armed Forces of the USSR were being built up and modernised in a big way. They were busy, amongst other things, building up a vast long-range, bomber force, armed at that time with the four-engine TU4.

In 1949, the Intelligence Organisation was similar to that which had the Luftwaffe as its main target. Now this organisation was building up its information concerning Russia. There was much hard work, and I seldom returned home before eight in the evening, and sometimes much later.

I still managed to get some flying. At first I used the former Reserve Flying School at Fairoaks, presided over by the genial and greatly respected Wing Commander Arthur. It was equipped with Chipmunks, and in addition to providing Reserve training, produced aircraft for such as myself, posted to Air Ministry. Later I found friends at Odiham, and they generously allowed me to fly their Vampires. However, the most interesting new type that came my way resulted from our interest in the MiG-15. The significance of this was that the Supemarine Attacker, built to comply with Air Ministry specifications, also had a Rolls-Royce Nene engine. I had no doubt that experience of the engine on which the MiG-15 was based would give me improved insight into one of the important spheres of my current studies. It was arranged that I should visit Chilbolton, then the Supermarine test base, and have a go at the Attacker.

At that time there had been the prototype, which first flew in 1946, and this had been followed by a second prototype, which was a deck landing version of the first. This aircraft was lost in an accident. A third Attacker then joined the first prototype, and included further modifications to improve its deck landing qualities. In the meantime, aircraft No 4, the first production aircraft, serialled WA 469, had gone to Boscombe Down. This was in the RAF specification as an Attacker F Mk I, and was the aircraft to which I was introduced by Lieutenant Commander Mike Lithgow, then Supermarine's Chief Test Pilot, when I arrived at Chilbolton.

The Attacker was based on the laminar flow wing used in the Supermarine Spiteful, itself a Spitfire fuselage, married to a wing very similar in some respects and in general appearance to the Mustangs. The Spiteful achieved a top speed of 494mph, the highest recorded for a British piston engine fighter. The Attacker married the Spiteful wing to a new fuselage holding the Nene engine and was, in some ways unique, for it defied the new tricycle fashion by retaining a conventional tail wheel undercarriage. Its maximum level speed, with full military equipment but without external stores, was 508mph at sea level. Its rate of climb at sea level was 6,350 feet per minute, making it the highest performance aircraft that I had yet flown. It was a fascinating aircraft to fly for a number of reasons, quite apart from my particular interest in the Nene engine. On my first take-off, I was alarmed by the noise of a singularly rude raspberry sounding just behind me, audible through my helmet and above all the other noises in progress. However, nothing seemed wrong and I was later told, with apologies, that they forgot to warn me about this little joke. It was, in fact, the pressure relief valve blowing off as the undercarriage retraction completed. The handling characteristics, no doubt due to the somewhat similar wing, seemed to me to be not unlike the Mustang. In particular, the suddenness with which the laminar flow wing seemed to run out of lift at touchdown was familiar. In the air it was delightful. It was certainly very fast. I enjoyed myself moving round Hampshire faster than I had ever done before. At low level, it was fun when going fast, to point the nose at the sky and, aided by this rocket, climbed to be at 12,000 feet or more above the cloud layer in less than two minutes. I recollect the Attacker seemed to have less than desirable directional stability when going fast, and often wondered if that might have been the Boscombe Down verdict on this delightful aeroplane. As regards the Nene, I found it a far more responsive engine than that in the Republic F-84, especially when increasing power quickly. I learned later that the Nene was found to be unduly sensitive above 35,000 feet. Altogether I learned a great deal, and when we were able to examine the performance of the MiG-15 against other aircraft, the knowledge became very useful.

The hard work of Intelligence was rewarding. The dedicated staff accumulated a vast store of practical experience. On occasion we would be required to pass judgement and provide analysis late on a Friday evening, just as we were about to leave. This often meant that we had to work through the night and I would catch the early morning train from Waterloo on a Saturday morning.

During my time in Intelligence, we moved from Monck Street to Whitehall, and adjacent to the War Office and Admiralty. Besides my work on the Attacker there were other interesting experiences whilst I was in the Air Ministry.

As well as the Vampires and later, Meteors at Odiham where I was allocated the personal and appropriate call sign Madhouse Two, there was some fun flying for a week at Dyce in the summer of 1952. This was at an Air Training Corps Air Experience camp, where a number of pilots from Air Ministry went to fly Tiger Moths in which we flew the cadets around that part of Scotland. I flew some thirty cadets.

During the same August I took both my sons for their first flights at Lasham, in a Slingsby T-21 two-seater glider. I also spent a week at Bourn airfield, where Hiller helicopters were being used for crop spraying. I was given a week there to learn all I could about helicopters, and found the Hiller a fascinating and enjoyable experience.

Perhaps the most far reaching event whilst I was at Air Ministry as far as my flying was concerned was the formation of the Royal Air Force Gliding and Soaring Association. By the time I returned from the United States there were already back in England, scattered around various stations, a good many of us who had become devoted to the kind of soaring flight we had enjoyed in Germany. From this, there grew the determination to create in England, opportunities for us to continue to enjoy the sport. It was from this definition of soaring as a sport that our first difficulties began. The Sports Board, then headed by that veteran of RAF Sport, Jimmy Lawson, would not accept that it was a sport. We had some splendid rows but always ended up friends and eventually Jimmy Lawson became a good friend of the newly emerging RAFGSA. Officially the association was formed on 15 December 1949. Our gliding site was Detling and when, in early 1950, Jimmy Lawson persuaded the Sports Board to grant us a small sum of money, we bought a Slingsby Prefect. I made the first flight in a truly RAFGSA glider from Detling in the Prefect on 27 May 1950. One of my passengers was Philip Wills who invited me to become a member of the British Gliding Association Council, with the particular responsibility of accidents analysis, an invitation I gladly accepted.

The RAFGSA progressed at first very slowly and there were constant difficulties to overcome. The first, of course, was lack of funds. Not unreasonably, the Sports Board took the view that they should spend their limited grants where the effects would benefit the greatest numbers. We gliding enthusiasts were still quite small in numbers, however we managed to put together an RAF Team to fly in the British National Championships.

In its first few years, we suffered many changes. Some of the old hands like Prosser Hanks developed other interests, key people were posted abroad and, more than once when we had established a new club at some outlying station, the removal of its most important people caused it to collapse. In 1951, the Vice Chief of the Air Staff, Air Marshal Sir Ronald Ivelaw-Chapman, agreed to become our first President and gave wonderful backing to us. At the same time, Paddy Kearon, another stalwart from Germany returned to England and became Senior Equipment Staff Officer. He was able to acquire for us many former balloon winches and cables and all kinds of important equipment.

In early 1951 we managed to persuade the Meteorological Office to underwrite an RAFGSA visit to the French Gliding School in the French Maritime Alps. It had come at a good time, as a Dakota had flown into a mountain in North Wales as a result of turbulence and down draught. We undertook to take our Weihe glider to explore waves and turbulence. Flight Lieutenant Williams, the secretary of the association and I departed by cross-channel ferry in March 1951, towing the Weihe in its trailer. We travelled via Paris, arriving in the middle of a metro and bus strike, and chaotic traffic. Through this, and via the maelstrom of La Place de la Concorde, we made our way to an astounded British Embassy, to whom we must have appeared like part of a new kind of travelling circus. However, they received us kindly and having taken us out to a very good lunch, launched us back into the maelstrom and on our way down south through the Rhone Valley.

It was a very delightful journey. Finally, in Lyon, the Packard, which had for some time displayed an alarming tendency to get into two gears at once, thus locking the back wheels, gave up entirely and remained fixed in all gears at once. Thankfully we managed to secure the services of a garage which undertook to house our circus whilst helping us do the necessary repairs. They towed us in for the last ten miles, sweeping through Lyon in our elongated three-vehicle train with a verve which terrified everybody except the driver of the tug. The climax came when rounding a right angle bend in narrow streets. The tail of the Weihe's trailer swept from the pavement, the entire stock of an ironmonger's store. We got clean away and into a cavernous hangar-like garage where the doors were promptly closed, hiding us from pursuing vengeance. The garage occupants then took us to lunch in their bistro on the other side of the narrow street. On advice from the garage, we removed the gearbox from a wartime MC truck, found that it fitted the Packard perfectly though the gear ratios resulting were lower, and reassembled our vehicle, setting off again for St Auban.

We continued our journey down the Rhone Valley through Vienne, Valence and Montelimar. Eventually we arrived at our destination, the State Gliding School of St Auban. Here we were welcomed by the Commandant, his chief instructor, Rousillon who had flown Spitfires with the Free French, and we were fed, wined and allotted our one room for the three of us.

The French Gliding Schools at this time were largely State organised and controlled. There were three main types of school. Big ones like St Auban, Montauban in the Garonne, and five or six others in which all aircraft were supplied by the State. At these schools, courses ran continuously, teaching pupils to bring them mostly up to the point of obtaining a Silver C. Any student over the age of sixteen, at school or university, was eligible to apply for these courses. The only charge was the equivalent of three shillings and sixpence a day for food. All else was free. The second grade schools were about forty in number and had their equipment and senior staff supplied by the State. In the third grade were numerous smaller schools and clubs, which received financial help in varying degrees and, like all the rest, rent-free airfields and buildings.

The Gliding Schools were part of a national aviation scheme which included similar facilities for model flying, parachuting and power flying. The total cost must have been enormous. The origins of this national scheme are interesting. During the war, most of the French aircraft industry was destroyed. What remained was under German control and used for the construction of some German types, notably large numbers of Fieseler Storch by Morane, and repairs. No Frenchmen were able to fly in France, or to develop their engineering and design skills in an industry in which they had once led the world. After the liberation there was a determined effort to rebuild France's aviation reputation.

The school aircraft comprised a fleet of two-seat training gliders, corresponding single-seaters, a more advanced sailplane corresponding to the Olympia, and the high performance Arsenal Air 100. In all there was something over 100 gliders.

All except occasional launches were by aerotow. For this purpose they used the Morane built Fieseler Storch, or the two seat Morane trainer with a 230hp Salamon air-cooled radial engine. Also among the twenty or so powered aircraft was a two seat side by side Nord NC.859 with a four-cylinder Walter engine of 105hp. This, the Commandant's personal runabout and he lent it to us freely.

We had a fortnight at St Auban and were not favoured by good weather. The March air was cold but when the wind blew it was not from the direction which produced the famed St Auban standing waves. However, on still days, the midday and afternoon sun, beating strongly onto the steep cliff sides of the Durance valley, resulted in quite nice thermals. These were aided very often by the sulphur plant near Sisteron. On our final day, the wind did oblige, blowing strongly from the southeast. I was towed off in our Weihe behind the Morane, and its pilot took me at a cracking pace into the area in the lee of the mountains where the wave was supposed to operate. On arrival there, at some 4,000 feet above aerodrome level, we encountered some of the nastiest turbulence and startling down draughts which I recollect except in powered aircraft in thunderstorm conditions.

Nose up, at full power, the Morane staggered along, losing height, with myself in the Weihe wedged tightly into my straps. The Weihe's great 60 feet span wings were flexing like fishing rods, and lateral control was quite inadequate on ailerons alone. Rudder and skidding were required, which of course added greatly to the drag of the tow, and made matters worse for the tug. All this was in clear dry air, and the area was the downward side of the rotor wave system which was known to form in the immediate lee of the wave forming mountains. It is formed by the air curling over the steep top and hurtling downwards. As the air reaches lower levels, heating and drying out as it descends, it curls round in a horizontal direction, away from the lee of the slope. Rounding up it begins to ascend, eventually returning nearly to its original height and curling over through a full 180 degrees back towards the obstructing mountains which first deflected it course. This rotation is continuous whilst the conditions are right. Meanwhile the higher air flowing over the mountains is pushed higher still when it meets the opposing flow of the top of the rotor. This is the initial push which sends it higher still into the undulating waves. We never reached the rising side of the rotor. When I could stand it no longer, I released, and flew towards where I hoped I might meet the rising air I needed on the up going side of the rotor. But being too low, I never met much except odd traces of turbulent lift, so close to what I wanted but never enough to make it. That was our last flight at St Auban because on return to England we found a foot long crack in the ply web of one main wing spars, and the wing had to be stripped and rebuilt.

We were sorry to leave St Auban, but despite our disappointment with the wave producing weather, were able to bring back enough good information. Much of it had been culled from the local experience of the very competent and helpful meteorologist appointed to St Auban, and more from the facts given to us by local pilots.

My tour of duty in the Air Ministry ended on 31 December 1952, and on 1 January 1953 I became a student at the College of Imperial Defence (the IDC). The College of Imperial Defence, now the Royal College of Defence Studies (RCDS), is located at the western corner of Belgrave Square, in the angle made by the junction of Chapel Street with Upper Belgrave Square. This is Seaford House, a singularly beautiful mansion dating from Regency London. One enters into a large hall from which open the principal reception rooms of the ground floor. Opposite the front door are the two arms of an impressive staircase, each of which, turning inwards, joins at the half landing and then, turning again, complete the ascent left and right, to the first floor. Here were the vast drawing rooms and family dining room. Higher still are the principal bedrooms and, above again, the smaller bedrooms and what were once the servants' quarters. At the back, between Chapel Street and Chester Street, are the mews, some converted into small and attractive town dwellings. On either side are various Embassy buildings, the nearest, on the other side of Upper Belgrave Street, being the Belgian Embassy.

The IDC was created after the First World War and was the brainchild of Winston Churchill. Its purpose was the study of the higher conduct of war, and to examine and report on particular problems of imperial defence which might, from time to time, be submitted to it by the Prime Minister or the Service Ministries. This latter function, which was originally considered to be of the greatest importance, seemed to have been relegated to second place. Neither the Prime Minister nor any of the ministers appeared to take cognisance of the carefully selected members of the Services all gathered there for one year. The Commandant was from each of the three services in turn. During my year the commandant was General Sir Frank Simpson, GBE, KCB, DSO. He was fond of referring to himself as 'a good old-fashioned red-faced soldier'. He could have fitted perfectly into the role of landed gentleman farmer of East Anglia. Anyone who accepted Sir Frank's description of himself would have been totally deceived, as indeed I suspect many were, including his opponents in war. He could see further through brick walls than most, and had the ability to reduce complicated problems to such simple components that even the dimmest could see clearly the best solution. He was liked and respected by us all, and in a very short time had welded us students from all kinds of diverse services and countries into a happy and united family. He was a Royal Engineer, product of Bedford School, the Royal Military Academy Woolwich and Trinity College, Cambridge. He was a brilliant example of those soldier-engineers who can not only fight but also tackle the problems of restoring a broken nation.

Sir Frank was supported by a handpicked directing staff, two from each of the three services and two from the Foreign Office. From the Royal Air Force there was Air Vice Marshall Claude Pelly, CB, CBE, MC, assisted by Wing Commander Paddy Menaul, DFC, AFC. Claude Pelly, who retired in 1959 as Air Chief Marshal Sir Claude, left the IDC to become Commander-in-Chief of the Middle East Air Force. He, like the commandant, concealed an unassuming and charming exterior, a shrewd and swift capability to sum up a situation, and drive to the heart of any matter. He had that valuable and rare gift of making you think that the views you reached were quite your own; and rejoiced when he found that they coincided with his own. Paddy Menaul was a member of the Pathfinder Force of Bomber Command from 1943 to 1945. He became Air Vice Marshall Menaul, CB, CBE, DFC, AFC and the Director and frequent spokesperson on defence affairs for the Royal United Services Institute in Whitehall. The Army was represented by Major General CB Fairbanks, CB, CBE, an old Sherwood Forester, supported by Lieutenant Colonel Pat Man, OBE, MC, and old friend of mine when we were fellow instructors at the Army Staff College, Camberley in 1943. Pat Man retired as a Major General in 1968. The Royal Navy had Rear Admiral Carlill, DSO. Carlill was typical of the singular breed in the Royal Navy who have spent nearly all their lives in destroyers. Before he came to the IDC, Admiral Carlill commanded the aircraft carrier *Illustrious* and it must have been a splendid period in the life of that great ship. He was supported by Commander IE Steel, MVO. The Foreign Office Director was PH Dean, later Sir Patrick Dean, KCMG, supported by Mr. GRR East,

The students came from the RAF, the Army and the Navy, and from the Foreign Office and the Dominions, including India and Pakistan. From the United States we had representatives of the Army, Navy, Air Force and State Department. In all, we students numbered around forty, all of at least Group Captain or equivalent. Without exception, all the students from the armed forces had taken part in the war and seen fighting either in Western Europe, the Pacific or the Far or Middle East. The normal routine was for a lecture in the morning and for syndicate work in the afternoons. The lectures were nearly all given by such eminent people as the Head of the Foreign Office, various ministers, the Ambassador of the United States, the heads of our own and other armed forces. There were experts on economics, on Communism and on particular aspects of different countries or areas in which our studies were concerned. The general idea behind all this was that the students were supposed to know how our own particular forces operated in war. What we were now being taught were the policies, stresses and strains which pushed the peoples of different parts of the world in varying directions.   There is, in popular imagination, the belief, and often conviction, that career officers of the armed forces are dedicated to war. The truth is that most of them, especially those who have been at war, are dedicated to the preservation of peace. They know a great deal more, not only of the horrors of war but about the severely practical means of avoiding it. Foremost amongst these is to understand the dangers and how to guard against them. A large proportion of our studies were taken up with such examinations.

The year's course included several visits. We spent several days in the Liverpool area, seeing shipyards and docks and local industry. We spent a fascinating evening in the offices of the local newspaper; at Cammel Laird's we explored the *Ark Royal*, launched in 1950 and still, three years later, fitting out, little knowing at that time that she would be the last of the Royal Navy's big carriers. Captain Charles Evans (later Vice Admiral Sir Charles Evans, KCB, CBE, DSO, DSC) who had been shipmates with me in *Courageous* and *Furious* was vastly interested. There was a time, I recollect, when Charles, who in those days flew Flycatchers and Nimrods, had more flyinq time than myself, but I actually had more sea time. The IDC was therefore a happy reunion and we enjoyed our visits together. There were a whole variety of other visits at home, but the highlight of the whole year was undoubtedly the foreign tour.

There were, in fact, three foreign tours; one around Western Europe, one to the United States and Canada, and one through the Middle East and Africa. My choice was naturally for the Middle East and Africa, having already spent a year in the United States and before that I had been in Germany.

We went on the Middle East tour in some style. We were allotted our own RAF Transport aircraft and crew, a Valetta, captained by Flying Officer Blackburn. Being qualified on Valettas, I was able to constitute myself as an occasional second pilot, and managed a nice bit of interesting and unexpected flying time as an additional bonus on a fascinating trip. We left from Heathrow on 1 August and lunched at Nice, then over Corsica to Malta, where we stayed the night. Next day we flew to El Adem, close to Tobruk in Cyrenaica, where we lunched in the RAF Mess. It was a hot day, and at intervals throughout lunch there were loud explosions in the desert. There were old mines going off in the heat and sometimes when they were disturbed by humans. The whole desert round El Adem was still strewn with war debris, much of it in dangerous conditions. Despite this, the local population was conducting a steady trade by bringing in salvage to an Italian firm operating in Tobruk. Salvage could be anything portable and metal, such as bits of guns and tanks and parts of aircraft. In the process of getting it, there were numerous casualties. In Tobruk it was common to see Arabs with limbs missing as a result of the forays for salvage into the desert.

From El Adem we continued in the cooler evening over the places made famous by the fighting in the Western Desert. Bardia, Sollum, Halfaya, Sidi Barrani, Mersa Matruh, Alamein and over Alexandria to the RAF base at Fayid on the Suez Canal. We spent several busy days in the Canal Zone, visiting nearly every one of the numerous bases, both RAF and Army. There were enormous stocks of war materials transport, armoured vehicles, ammunition, bombs, clothing and everything needed to support the kind of fighting which had ended in 1945. The newest was eight years old and, like the bombs that were exploding in the desert round El Adem, the bombs still stored in the RAF explosives depot, were becoming increasingly dangerous and difficult to handle.

Egypt was still the main British centre of power in the Middle East. Its most important role was, since the Canal was built, the security of the vital waterway through which almost the whole of British trade to the Far East and oil for home was carried.

From the Canal Zone we went to Cyprus, landing at Nicosia and staying in an attractive hotel in its centre. We looked at the military area at Dhakalia with its new buildings. At Famagusta we swam as well as making visits to farms, villages and vineyards. We met great numbers of the Greek-Cypriots and Turkish-Cypriots. We found them charming and hospitable people and the village elders men of great dignity and often commanding presence. The British government was doing a great deal to encourage farming and I remember that we were particularly impressed, as were our hosts who accompanied us, with the work of the government stock farm at Alhalassa. But we were all terrified by the Cypriot drivers of our cars. The mountain roads, especially those we followed up to Government House at the top of the Troodos mountains, are narrow and winding and, in places, hair pin bends wind dangerously on the edge of a rocky precipice. They were approached as fast as possible, braking viciously at the last possible moment. Loose gravel from the slipping wheel would go rattling down into the gorge below whilst the driver now accelerating towards the next hairpin, would drive one handed, gesticulating with the other towards some distance eminence which seemed to occupy more of his attention than the down hill track back towards Nicosia.

We entered Turkey by way of the Gulf of Anatolia, going direct to Yesilkoy Airfield outside Istanbul. We were driven into the city in a fleet of Mercedes cars and parked in various hotels all near to the waterfront. I was delighted to find that one of our hosts during this visit was Commander Beard, know to all his friends from Fleet Air Arm days as Bog Beard. At this time he was on loan to the Turkish Navy engaged, he alleged, in bringing them up to date. Under his guidance we visited the Turkish Naval School on the island called Marmara, in the sea of Marmara. It was a delightful outing in a Turkish naval launch, on a sunlit day with a warm scented wind from the Dardanelles. The journey from the waterfront in Istanbul, through the busy Golden Horn shipping, past buildings new, through age old slums, palaces and ruins and into the open sea, was beautiful. The Naval School was not. It seemed small and neglected and gave the impression that, despite Bog Beard's best efforts, the Turkish navy was never likely to become a force of any significance.

At Balinkesir aerodrome we found a somewhat similar outlook. Here the United States had set up what was almost a replica of the USAF base where I had flown Republic F-84 fighters in South Carolina. The Turkish sergeants were wearing American type caps, with the long peaks turned upwards, United States fashion. In the men's messes, food from the modern kitchens was collected on trays, sliding on rails in front of help yourself counters. Even the food itself was American. On the concrete ramp were lined up spotless rows of F-84 jet fighters, of which we found only one third were serviceable. In the operations room, two officers presided over a beautifully arranged schedule of training exercises, but most of the schedules were blank, and indirect questioning extracted the information that most pilots enjoyed aerobatics and chasing round the countryside very fast at low level. They added that it was not easy to persuade them to come in for careful briefing for those less interesting things like ground controlled interceptions or instrument work. Only one of the three Squadron Commanders was an active pilot.

From here we went on to Ankara, which was a strange city. Ankara is dominated by the memorial tomb of the Kamal Attaturk, the founder of modern Turkey. At the time of our visit, it was in its final stages of completion. It stands on higher ground about a mile from the centre of Ankara, and is a vast and imposing structure as would have delighted a pharaoh of Egypt. It is intended to be as enduring as the Pyramids. Built from reddish granite its cost has been vast. After a very happy and informal visit to the British Embassy where we were most hospitably entertained, and a final meeting with the Turkish Chiefs of Staff at the War Ministry in Ankara we flew on to Iraq.

The route from Ankara to Iraq lies mostly over mountainous country split by deep craggy ravines. Here and there are areas of dusty plains, un-watered, and for the most part sparsely inhabited. Our route over eastern Turkey and the edge of Kurdistan led to the Tigris, whose course we joined at Mosul and followed down to the RAF base at Habbaniya, some distance from Baghdad and close to the great

River Euphrates. This area is historically known as Mesopotamia. From the air it is possible to see in the sand, the shadowy outlines of former canals, irrigation channels and towns and buildings.

We landed at Habbaniya during the afternoon, having had a pleasant and cool journey and as we taxied in the Valetta cabin still contained the chill air from 10,000 feet. As we came to a halt and the fuselage rear doors were opened wide the blast of hot air was like the opening of an oven door.

Habbaniya has a history going back to the First World War, after which it was the principal RAF base in Mesopotamia. It was from here that the RAF established air control of the country, which was proved to be possible at a fraction of the cost of the same task formerly undertaken by ground forces. To guard Habbaniya, and other aerodromes such as Mosul and Shaibah, the RAF recruited locally a force who became famous as the Iraq Levies. It was here that we were shown something of their recruitment and training. They were commanded by British officers and were an extremely loyal and efficient force. In 1943 Habbaniya housed the Middle East Flying Training School, evacuated from its former home at Abu Sueir in Egypt. When, under German persuasion and with German help, the Iraqis from Baghdad marched out to capture Habbaniya, the Levies helped to defend the besieged perimeter. The Flying Training School, fitting whatever armament they could improvise to their training aircraft, mostly Hawker Hart biplanes, bombed their besiegers. The aircraft had to take off from between the shelter of the hangars, since the whole aerodrome was under fire. They landed back over the heads of the enemy round the perimeter which they had just bombed and strafed. Habbaniya held out, and finally the Iraqis gave in.

Next day we flew into the airfield at Baghdad and went into the city where we stayed either with British residents or in the Embassy itself. The Embassy had a fine swimming pool which we enjoyed to the full. Its origin is interesting. When Prime Minister Churchill went to the Conference at Teheran (28 November-1 December 1943, a meeting between Churchill, Roosevelt and Stalin), he stayed at the Embassy in Baghdad. History relates that before setting out, he enquired if there was a swimming pool there and was told no. His brief reply was, 'When I arrive, there will be'. And sure enough, there was. It is said to have been built in four days.

From Baghdad we flew back to Habbaniya, and I see from my log book that I was in the pilot's seat for both these thirty minute flights. We flew low and observed the shadows in the sand, the modern villages and cultivation, and the great and majestic rivers which gave Mesopotamia its ancient name. Next day we continued southeast, over the marshy areas towards Basrah, the old RAF flying boat base, over the refinery at Korramsha and briefly to Kuwait. Here we exchanged civilities with the Ruler.

We continued the same day to the island of Bahrain and were given a thorough two day course of instruction in the oil industry as it affected Bahrain and the neighbouring territories. It was in Bahrain that I saw for the first time airborne pilgrims for Mecca. On the aerodrome was a wire-enclosed compound, not unlike a prisoner of war cage. Inside were a horde of pilgrims from every land east of Arabia. Whilst we watched, a large British civil transport aircraft (Avro Tudors owned and operated by Don Bennett, formerly Air Vice Marshal Bennett, commander of Bomber Command's Pathfinder course) drew up alongside the cage. The doors were then opened, and a mass of pilgrims rushed out, fighting for a place. When the aircraft captain judged the aircraft to be fully loaded, the doors were closed and the aircraft took off for Medina. The aircraft was said to contain far more passengers than the design had intended. There were no such comforts as seats, and the pilgrims who had paid in cash for the ride to Medina, had to pay again to get back.

From Bahrain we followed the coast observing Abu Dhabi and continued to Masirah Island, some ten miles off the coast of Oman on the Indian Ocean. There was nothing there except a long concrete runway, twenty airmen of the RAF regiment and twenty airmen to service itinerant aircraft such as ours. The normal tour of duty on Masirah was six months, but as there was absolutely nothing there on which it was possible to spend money, it was a popular place for men saving up and many applied for an extension. There being no harbour or jetty, aircraft fuel and heavy supplies unsuitable for flying in were brought up by coastal steamer, tipped overboard just off the island, and brought ashore by the wind and waves. Recovering these supplies was a busy task, combined with fishing and trying to catch sharks. They were numerous and active, making bathing impossible. Our Valetta was refuelled from supplies floated ashore in fifty gallon drums. From Masirah, we continued to Salala on the coast in Dhofar. This was another of the concrete strips which had been built during the war to provide for aircraft flying anti-submarine patrols in the Arabian Sea and Gulf of Aden. A third, which I did not see until three years later, was on Socotra.

At Salala we were greeted by the Sultan, the British resident and an astonishing guard of honour composed of fifty members of the sultan's personal bodyguard. Having emerged from our Valetta, the guard fired a salute. The noise and black smoke were most impressive and so was the discovery that the guns were using live ammunition. It seemed to be the custom to aim as close as possible to those thus being honoured without actually hitting them. The salute was not fired in unison, but in a sort of ripple fire, which permitted those who had a spare round to reload and fire again. Salala seemed a little cooler than the Gulf, probably because we were getting used to it and the air blowing in from the ocean was cooler. By the time we got to Aden that evening, it was quite a cool dusk and the ride in from the aerodrome at Khormaksar was relatively comfortable.

In Aden we stayed with various hospitable families. My host and hostess were Wing Commander and Mrs Robert Radley. Robert, only a few months later, became the Commander of my Examining Wing at the RAF Central Flying School. Also there were my old friends Giles and Sylvia Gilson from Fleet Air Arm days when we served together in HMS *Furious*. We were there for several days and given very thorough instruction in all that pertained to the Colony of Aden and the surround

Protectorate from the Governor, Sir Tom Higginbottom. He had served many years in the Middle East and spoke fluent and perfect classical Arabic. We also heard from the AOC, Air Vice Marshal MacFayden, from the Chief Justice, from the Commander of the Aden Protectorate Levies and from the manager of the newly constructed BP Oil Refinery. On the way there we viewed the old wartime aerodromes at Sheik Othman and its satellite a little further round the bay. All these had been active in the campaign which threw the Italians out of Abyssinia. Two and a half years later all this experience came in most useful when I was posted to Aden as the Senior Air Staff Officer, but in 1953 Aden was a peaceful colony. Certainly there was sporadic trouble far off in the Protectorate but by the time of my posting there, things were beginning to change.

From Aden we flew over Berbera and British Somaliland. We crossed the Ogaden Province of Abyssinia, entered the former Italian Somaliland and landed at Mogadishu. The whole of this area, where it is impossible to find any distinctive landmarks to delineate the boundaries which separate the Somaililands from Abyssinia, are the traditional grazing grounds for Somali tribesmen. They are constantly on the move to wherever there is feed and water for their animals. Mogadishu seemed, in 1953, to have stood still since the Italians departed. The town had clearly begun to take on Mussolini Empire design streets and buildings and, if well looked after, the Italian part of the town could have looked attractive with its wide streets, planted along each side with trees, and lined with pleasant buildings. But it was not well cared for. In the hangars at the aerodrome, we saw the remains of the once proud Regia Aeronautica; notices on office doors, discarded stores, and the skeletons of abandoned aeroplanes which must have laid there, unwanted, for twelve years or more. The place gave the impression that nobody wanted it. The Italians who still lived there were unhappy. The British, who were now responsible for the former Italian Colony, wanted nothing so much as to get rid of it. Everything was in suspense pending the creation of a Somali government and administration capable of taking control and mustering the economic resources to make this impoverished area a going concern.

After Mogadishu, to arrive in prosperous and happy Mombasa was like coming from night to day. The authorities who had planned our tour had decided that by the time we reached this point, we deserved a rest. We were taken by road to a military families rest camp on the coast, halfway between Mombasa and Malindi. Here we spent most of our time in the sea sheltered by the coral reef, or lying on the beach, or sleeping.

After three days in Mombasa we set forth again, flying over Tanganyika, formerly German East Africa and now Tanzania, until we passed into Northern Rhodesia, now Zambia, and landed to refuel at Kasama Airfield. There was some delay here whilst a lion was shooed off the runway. Kasama, once a busy RAF aerodrome, now seldom had visitors. From Kasama we continued to Livingstone on the northern bank of the Zambezi River. Our route took us over the vast swamp area to the southeast of Lake Bangweulu, over the southeastern limb of what was then the

Belgian Congo and into Northern Rhodesia at Ndola. We followed roughly the route south of the railway line which runs from Elizabethville in the Belgian Congo, through Ndola, Broken Hill and Lusaka to Livingstone. Belgian Congo is now the Republic of Zaire, and Elizabethville renamed Lubumbashi. When we followed it, the railway line was the main artery for trade, forming a link all the way from Benguela on the South Pacific coast of Angola, in a great arc through central and southern Africa, right to Cape Town. It carried coal from the great mines at Wankie and copper ore and products from Northern Rhodesia. Other lines linked it through Bulawayo and Salisbury to Beira and Laurenzo Marques on the Indian Ocean. From the air it was possible to see the frequent freight trains upon which the trade of central South Africa largely depended.

The last part of our flight was in the gathering dusk and as it grew darker the vast bush fires, which burned in the Batoka province of Northern Rhodesia, lit up the land below and the horizon beyond. It was quite dark when we arrived at Livingstone where cars took us across the Victoria Falls Bridge, to the Victoria Fall Hotel where we were to stay two nights.

From Livingstone we flew on again to Salisbury in Southern Rhodesia, where our party from the IDC were to be guests of honour during part of the Rhodes Centenary Celebrations. We travelled via Bulawayo, landing early at Kumalo airfield in order to visit Rhodes's grave in the Matopo Hills. The heavy metal plaque which covers it is inscribed with his names and dates. From its position, at the highest point in the range of hills, the view extends as far as the eye can see in every direction, over the plains below, and over the land which Rhodes first opened up and loved. In the days which followed we were entertained with great hospitality by many local people, paid visits to the great farming and tobacco estates, attended a tobacco auction, visited schools and native villages, and again made to feel that Rhodesia was, after its first hundred years from the arrival of Cecil Rhodes, about to enter a period of rising living standards and increasing prosperity. Once again, the vital importance of the railway system linking Rhodesia to the rest of central and southern Africa was manifest. Salisbury is about 4,000 feet above sea level and the climate is mostly dry and bracing. Salisbury Kentucky Sirfield where we landed was the Headquarters of the Royal Rhodesian Air Force, commanded at that time by Air Vice Marshal Jacklyn. As Wing Commander Jacklyn he had been the Chief Flying Instructor at the Empire Central Flying School at Hullavington near Swindon during the latter part of the Second World War. Many Rhodesians served with great distinction in the RAF, not least among such men was Ian Smith, who was a Spitfire pilot. (Smith became Prime Minister of Southern Rhodesia in 1964 and on 11 November 1965 became the first Prime Minister of Rhodesia when his government declared unilateral independence. He remained premier until June 1979.)

After Southern Rhodesia, we moved reluctantly on and flew from Kentucky Airfield back to Kasama, then to Tabora in Tanganyika (now Tanzania) and on to Entebbe, flying the whole length of Lake Victoria from Mwanza in the south to the aerodrome not far from Kampala. From Uganda we flew to Malakal on the White Nile, en route to Khartoum.

At the time we were there, the Sudan was preparing for its first ever general election, supervised on behalf of the United Nations by teams, many of whom came from India. Malakal is the principal village in an area inhabited by the Dinkas. The Dinkas are very tall, some as much as 7 feet, and usually thin and bony. More often than not they seemed to appear without clothes of any sort, but with a long stick, almost a pole. Thus attired they moved around in the marsh areas in which their tribal and primitive villages are situated. Few, if any, can read or write, and the procedures of democratic election were a total mystery to them. In order to overcome this problem, the various parties, of which there were many striving to gain power, were allocated signs. Thus one was represented by a crocodile, another by a camel, and others by goats, birds, snakes and chickens. The story which came to us was that in one such Dinka village, the inhabitants, following their custom, asked their Chief what they should do. The Chief said 'Leave it to me and all will be well', and set off on the difficult journey to Khartoum. There he made enquiries and armed with new information, visited the headquarters of the various parties to find the best bids. Having concluded satisfactory deals, he returned to his village, assembled his people and instructed them that all papers would be marked with the 'Yes' mark against all the signs. He had collected useful contribution from them all, and this was the best he could do. So much for democracy!

We arrived in Khartoum and took up residence in the pleasant hotel on the west bank of the White Nile. Here we made the conventional visits to the Mahdi's tomb at Omdurman. Later, having seen the place where General Gordon was killed (the confluence of the White and Blue Niles) we were entertained by the Mahdi who was the grandson of the inhabitant of the tomb. The Mahdi made us laugh by telling us that whatever happened in the future, Khartoum could never totally rid itself of the British, because the town itself was laid out so that the streets were in the plan form of the Union Jack. And so they were, as we later saw from the air.

We left for El Adem to refuel. We continued on in the gathering darkness along the North African coast to Castel Idris, the airfield just outside of Tripoli. I took my turn at the controls along this three hour stretch of what had already been a long day's flying. I remember watching, in the midst of almost black nothing, one single tiny light on the desert 10,000 feet below. It was in sight for quite a long time and I wondered what it could be. There were no inhabited places thereabouts; was it a caravan halted for the night? A tiny, unknown settlement miles from anywhere? I don't think that I have ever seen anything that looked quite so lonely and forlorn.

At Castel Idris we piled into large cars and were taken to a fine Italian built hotel on the sea front. Next day we visited Wheelus Field, the big American Air Base on the other side of Tripoli. To me it seemed little different from the many such bases which I had visited in the United States, and could have been imported complete. The base, having been duly explored and admired, we left, on a relatively short flight across the water, to land at Luqa in Malta. This was to be a somewhat longer stay, and it began in great style when we were entertained by Lord Louis Mountbatten in this Commander-in-Chief's yacht, HMS *Enchantress*. The main harbour at Malta was filled with Royal Navy vessels, including aircraft carriers and cruisers.

From Malta we flew back, once more via Nice and so to Northolt and home. In thirty-four days we had visited seventeen different countries and flown over half a dozen more. I was very happy to get back to Rosemary and our home in Fleet.

In September we resumed our work at the IDC, and in December completed the fascinating and unique course. We had a number of farewell parties, and then dispersed for, what all of us considered, some well-earned Christmas leave.

Just before the start of Christmas leave from the IDC we began to hear where we would be going. Most of us were impatient to be back to productive work, for although the IDC course is certainly without compare, and all of us had not only learned a great deal but greatly enjoyed the manner of doing it, I felt that a year as a student at this stage of my career was too like marking time. One of the last of the announcements was my own appointment. This included promotion to Air Commodore, to become on 1 January 1954, the twenty-seventh Commandant of the Central Flying School (CFS) of the Royal Air Force, with Headquarters at Little Rissington.

CHAPTER ELEVEN
CENTRAL FLYING SCHOOL

The CFS was formed in 1912, the first organised school of military aviation in the world. It has a history older than the RAF itself, and is unique. Its original role was the initial flying training of pilots for the naval and military wings of the Royal Flying Corps. By 1919 its task had become the training of instructors to teach flying, and has remained so ever since. When I joined the Service in 1929, the highest achievement possible as a pilot was to attain the difficult A1 category as a CFS qualified instructor. The staff of CFS, then at Wittering, included such famous people as Dick Atcherley, George Stainforth, Willy Watt and Dermot Boyle. My own contacts with CFS, through Willy Watt, were confined to visits which always confirmed my opinion that CFS was my ultimate ambition, which, until 1954, remained unsatisfied.

In 1954 the posting filled me with astonished delight, combined with alarm. The alarm arose from my wartime dealings with CFS. Whilst commanding 13 OTU, we had been visited by the CFS staff to see how we taught our students to handle the Mosquito. The immediate reason for this was that, although we had no CFS qualified instructors at 13 OTU, our results were a good deal better than other schools that had instructors. I gave my opinion that the reason was that the qualified instructors taught their pupils how the Mosquito would respond if mishandled and that my pilots, all from operational squadrons, taught them how to handle it properly. This view was not well received.

Later, when the war ended, and I was in charge of the gliding schools in Germany, CFS came to fly our sailplanes. I decreed, perhaps somewhat needlessly, that they should all first be checked out by my gliding instructors. Later they found that not a single one of the gliding instructors was a qualified RAF pilot. Nothing was said but I gained the impression that a second black mark had been made against my name in CFS archives. It was therefore with mixed feeling, including the possibility that this might be CFS's revenge, that I took up my new appointment on 1 January 1954.

But I need not have feared. My first duty was to visit my new Commander-in-Chief at HQ Flying Training Command. This was Sir Lawrence Pendred who, as an Air Vice Marshal, had been my chief when I first went to Intelligence duties. I left this interview with the heart-warming knowledge that my Commander-in-Chief had specifically asked for me, and that I would have his full support in what he made quite clear, was to be a difficult and challenging task. And so it proved.

This was to be one of the happiest two years that I had in any RAF appointment. The Commandant's house at CFS was built before the war as the largest and newest type of married quarters for a Group Captain Station Commander. The reason for this was that Little Rissington was designed as the home of a large flying Training School. The Officers' Mess was a particularly commodious three-storey building. There were three big pre-war pattern hangars, workshops, stores, barrack blocks and married quarters. The whole was capable of accommodating a peacetime population, including families, of between 1,500 and 2,000 souls.

The house was the biggest we had ever lived in. It had three storeys, three main and four smaller bedrooms, an attractive drawing room overlooking the garden, large dining room, three bathrooms and kitchen, servants quarters, garage, sculleries, preparations room and, at an underground level, a boiler house like the stoke hold of a coal-burning battleship.

When we arrived, on 1 January 1954, the freezing east wind had been sweeping across the Cotswolds for several days and Little Rissinqton, which at 750 feet above sea level, was the highest occupied RAF aerodrome in the British Isles, got it all. Our house, empty since the departure of my predecessor two months earlier, like any uninhabited building, had cooled down so that coming in through the front door was not to enter a warm cosy atmosphere but more like coming into a cold store. Our first night we sat in the frozen drawing room in great coats and fur boots; it took nearly a week to warm up the house, and in the first two months of our stay we consumed the whole of our fuel ration for the next twelve months.

When the children explored the garden they found the Witches House. It was old, built of stone, and had once been thatched. It had two floors and four rooms, and an ancient stone fire place, blackened by hundreds of years of fires. Legend had it that it was last inhabited by Old Kate. She had allegedly provided sanctuary for the footpads who preyed upon the travellers passing through Burford, and using the high Cotswold road from Oxford and Witney to Gloucester. When, in the end, Old Kate's house was raided and herself removed to Gloucester gaol, legend has it that she pronounced a fearful curse to fall on whoever dared hurt her house when she was gone. And so, for over 200 years, the Witches House remained untouched until, in 1954, it was an exciting and obviously haunted house and playground for our children and their friends from the other married quarters.

Mr Streatfield was the major domo who presided over our house. Starting as a boy entrant into the Royal Marines, he had served in China and taken part in the fighting during the Boxer uprising in 1900. He refused to mention his age, but when we came to CFS in 1954, he cannot have been less than seventy. He had served his time to a pension in the Royal Marines, and then rejoined again during the Second World War, when to his intense fury, he was considered too old to serve afloat. After the war he came to CFS and took charge of the Commandant's house. I was the sixth and, as it turned out, the last Commandant he looked after. Looked after is the right expression. Streatfield had very firm ideas about the conduct of affairs in the house. Nearly all the guests who stayed were well known to him, and he knew their likes and dislikes. When we first arrived on that frozen winter's night in January 1954 Streatfield greeted us respectfully, though cautiously, and admitted some concern that he might not have got the house warmed up as we would have liked. On our side we thanked him for having it that ready, and for the supper which in due course, appeared. In the days that followed, he succumbed, like many other, to the Rosemary's inherent charm, but remained distant and carefully respectful until, in the course of some discussion, he discovered that Rosemary was not only the daughter of an Admiral but the granddaughter of one, the niece of two others, and that he, Streatfield, had served under and known two of them. The result was something like a family reunion, but Streatfield maintained his vigilance to preserve the dignity and position of the Commandant and his Lady. In our two years at Rissington Streatfield became not only a real and loved friend, but also a valuable ally in handling all the wide variety of social problems that confront the Commandant of an organisation like CFS.

Lord Trenchard's reminder, 'Always remember that quality will cut through quantity like a hot knife through cheese' might have been an apt introduction to the first major problem that I had to tackle on taking over CFS. This was the indifferent quality of many of the candidates to become flying instructors. The system was that every Monday morning the Commandant interviewed candidates. These were the result of every command being required to provide a given number and keep up the continuous flow of trained instructors into the flying training organisation. Normally, the RAF did not keep anybody on instructional duties for too long a period in one spell. Two and a half years was the desired maximum, after which the pilot concerned would be posted to other duties. It was intended that the flying instructors should never become out of touch with the main purpose of the service, which is to fight in the air, and the instruction they gave would have as its aim the production of a pilot fit to take his place in a front line squadron. In this respect, RAF requirements differ notably from civilian flying training. In clubs and similar places, instructors can spend a lifetime, solely on basic flying instruction. Moreover, the pupils they teach are for the most part paying customers who can, if not satisfied, take their custom elsewhere. Thus, although the methods of basis flying instruction may be very similar in the early stages, the conditions are different and the ultimate aim so totally apart, that the two cannot really be compared.

When considering the RAF flying instructors, their task is advanced instruction in the handling of fast jets capable of very high speeds and of imposing stresses on its pilots which are unknown in civil operation. Similarly, the infusion of experienced flying instructors into both staff and front line squadrons, serves to keep everybody aware of the needs of the training organisation. It is worth noting that, in 1943, for every pilot in a front line bomber squadron, it was necessary to have about thirty pilots, either instructing or coming up as trained replacements, to keep the front line going.

It is this very thing which created the first difficulty that I encountered in 1954.

141

During the war the demand for instructors could not be satisfied by returning enough front line tour-expired pilots to the training machine. By the time the demands of the fighting commands for experienced men to lead squadrons and flights on a second tour and to man their own operational training units had been satisfied, there were simply not enough left. In consequence, the basic training organisation was operated with a multitude of civilian instructors back in uniform. These were supplemented by a system which 'creamed off' the best pupils, and kept them back in the flying training schools as instructors. The result of the system upon young men who had volunteered for aircrew in order to fight, was that the role of flying instructor not only became exceedingly unpopular, but even in 1954 was still regarded as a second rate job. This feeling persisted in the front line squadrons of the time, for although we were now under the vastly different peacetime regimes, the RAF was going through the very exciting stage of its re-equipment with aircraft which were the equal, or ahead of, anything else in the world.

We were still reaping the benefits of Frank Whittle's pioneering work on jet engines. So who, when he might be going to fly Hunters, wanted to leave his squadron and teach on Chipmunks in a strictly disciplined Flying Training School? Most of the candidates at my first interviews reflected this outlook, and they were mostly conscripts. They were also the type of pilot I wanted, who would, I knew, instil in any pupil, the same enthusiasm for high performance flying that burned in them. The ones I did not want were mostly the few volunteers. They tended to be heavily married, often too young, and clock watchers who left for home when the whistle blew. The sort of pilot once described to me, who added ten knots to the recommended approach speed for himself, and another ten for the wife and child. These seldom did well on the course, and most of them I turned down as unsuitable.

In the end we resorted to a severe remedy and in this I must pay great tribute to my Commander-in-Chief, Sir Lawrence Pendred, who gave me the support without which it would have been impossible. For a month, or a little over, I rejected all conscripts out of hand. Naturally they were delighted, but I explained to each, for which I hope I may be forgiven, that they did not meet the exacting standards which the CFS required. The volunteers mostly eliminated themselves. When, after this slaughter, we were left with no suitable candidates and future courses likely to be empty, my Commander-in-Chief wrote to the other commands, suggesting that the quality of pilots who were sent to CFS would, in the end directly affect the quality of the newly trained products who would come to their squadrons. He added would they please cease to send to CFS, candidates who were clearly unsuited for the task. At the same time, the buzz went round that it was by no means easy to gain acceptance for training at CFS and to do so was evidently something of an achievement. This also had its effect, and very soon we began to get candidates coming to us who were genuine volunteers, and regarded becoming a flying instructor as something well worthwhile. From then on the quality improved until before long, we could pick and choose from candidates of very high quality indeed.

My second important task concerned the reorganisation of CFS courses, and their content. The war, which resulted in many short cuts, was responsible for the specialised flying instructor such as the creamed off pupil who remained on at his basic flying training school to instruct subsequent pupils. When I arrived at CFS we still made two types of instructor, designated Instructors (Piston) and Instructors (Jet). The former were trained at South Cerney which was a self-contained half of CFS. The latter were trained at Little Rissington. Until 1939, there had been only one kind of instructor and they were expected to cope with whatever aircraft came their way. It was my responsibility to preside over the restoration of the old system, essentially to initiate the production of the all-through instructor. To put this into effect, South Cerney became the basic half of the full course, and Little Rissington the advanced.

To be eligible for the CFS course, pilots had to have at least 500 hours flying as Captain or First Pilot. They also needed a current instrument rating, and to have completed not less than eighteen months in a front line squadron. Sometimes a pilot would be accepted who, for no fault of his own, had allowed his instrument rating to lapse. The Army Air Corps pilot at this time seldom had ratings.

As instrument flying was essential in order to take part in the course, one of the first tasks of the staff at South Cerney was to ensure that all pilots were rated. Those who were not were required a week or so early for instrument work. The flying units at South Cerney comprised two squadrons of piston engine Provosts, and two flights of miscellaneous aircraft for communications and use by pilots requiring practice on other types they might later have to instruct. These included some Austers for the Army Air Corps pilots. When I arrived at CFS the Commanding Officer was Group Captain Sam Lucas.

A course normally comprised about thirty students. Most were RAF, but we always had, in addition to the soldiers, some Royal Navy and a few from the Commonwealth Air Forces. Having completed his ten weeks at South Cerney, the student had a week's leave and then moved to Little Rissington for the Advance half of his course. This lasted another ten weeks. By this time, numbers had always fallen below the original thirty, partly because of the departure of soldiers who were not required to fly and instruct on advanced types, and partly because of an unpredictable number of failures. Usually we made up the numbers to thirty again by bringing in suitable instructors already qualified on piston engine aircraft so as to add their jet qualifications, or others returning to instruction after a spell away on other duties.

In 1954, the two flying squadrons at Little Rissington, now termed CFS Advanced, used the Meteor VII. In addition we had a flight of Vampire TIIs and, like Cerney, a variety of other aircraft. At any one time, South Cerney and Little Rissington each had two overlapping resident courses, necessitating a new intake of thirty every five or six weeks. This resulted in a normal student population of 120.

At the end of each course they dined at a formal guest night, when the top pupil of the course sat on the Commandant's right, and the Chief Instructor either from Cerney or Rissington gave not his formal report but his informal and often very amusing one. By the end of his course, a student would have flown about 100 to 110 hours, roughly equally divided between Basic and Advanced, and, of course, by night as well as day. Later we always endeavoured to include some extras like a few new types and, in due course, when we acquired three Hawker Hunters, this became an accepted part of the course.

Courses of instruction at CFS were very much a two-way exchange of knowledge, and we always expected to learn a good deal from students as well as to teach them. Students were encouraged to question accepted ideas and methods, and in the course of justifying them the CFS staff not only increased their own skills, often by demonstration in the air, but sometimes found that our ideas were due for a change. This kept everybody on their toes, and gave students a sense of participation in the life of CFS which the term pupil would have denied.

The arrival of our first Hunter produced problems at Rissington. On its somewhat short runway, it soon ended up with burned out brakes and tyres. So we deemed it wiser to locate the Hunters elsewhere. For this purpose they became a detached flight at the more suitable location at Kemble, the home of No 5 Maintenance Unit who looked after their day-to-day needs. The remainder of the Advanced instructor training organisation at Rissington resembled that at Cerney. The whole was commanded by Group Captain Philip Heal, with Wing Commander Frank Dodd as his Chief Instructor.

When I arrived, the Examining Wing was commanded by Wing Commander Dennis Lyster, an old hand at instructing, and formerly a much-decorated Bomber Command pilot. I can best explain the functions of the Examining Wing by quoting the charter for it, written by Air Chief Marshal Sir Ralph Cochrane when he was the Commander-in-Chief of Flying Training Command. It was to:-

(a) Provide an inspectorate of Flying Training Commands.
(b) Undertake the examination and re-categorisation: flying instructors of "B' category and above.
(c) Appoint examiners under the RAF Instrument Rating Scheme.
(d) Ensure that the latest instructional technique is being used by qualified Flying Instructors (QFIs).
(e) Provide liaison between units employing QFIs and CFS.
(f) Feed back to CFS the latest ideas on operational flying which may affect instructional technique.
(g) Provide Examiners as and when necessary to visit Commands overseas.

Item (g) was, in practice, extended to include visits to Commonwealth and Allied Air Forces. During my time at CFS, visits were paid to India, Singapore, Pakistan, Canada and the United States. In addition to the Examining Wing, commonly known as 'The Trappers' there was one further though smaller, organisation within

CFS. This was the Link Trainer Instructor School, commanded by Squadron Leader Bill Veseley. It had no aircraft of its own, but operated a battery of Link trainers. Finally, CFS had the use of two large airfields in addition to Cerney and Rissington. To the south was Blakehill Farm, with concrete runways but little else except one disused hangar and lots of hard standings. It had been one of the airfields from which the Airborne Forces in gliders were launched on D-Day for the invasion of Normandy. It was used by Cerney's Provosts who had to take some care to keep out of the way of the four-jet bombers of the USAF based at that time at nearby Fairford. To the north we had the use of Enstone, whose long runway we found useful, especially when we had one of the many types of aircraft which were borrowed by Examining Wing from time to time. These were used as preparation for their visits to operational conversion units and organisations using types which we did not possess at CFS itself.

It was from Enstone that I did my first Canberra flying. Examiners who were expected to fly anything that came their way did not often get dual instruction. My introduction to the Canberra was not unlike my first introduction some years earlier to the Mosquito. I spent some time learning the taps and reading the pilots notes, after which the Trapper, who was the current Canberra expert, gave me a thirty minute demonstration with myself in the navigator's seat. We then changed seats and I flew it; and that was that. My log book records that it was a Canberra B2, WE 112, borrowed from the Operational Training Unit then at Bassingbourne, and that this was in preparation for a visit by the Examining Wing to that unit. The Trapper was Flight Lieutenant Paddy Gilmer, and afterwards I went with them to Bassingbourne to observe how their work there went. I note that my personal call sign at this time was Reflex One.

In rather similar fashion I experienced a number of new types including the Percival Pembroke, the four-engined Miles Marathon and a Fairchild C117 Packet belonging to the 15th Wing of the Tactical Command of the Belgian Air Force. When it arrived from Belgium, it brought with it my old Gunner, Mich Jansen, who insisted on sitting alongside me whilst I flew it, and in banishing everybody else on board somewhere into the vast interior at the back.

The organisation of CFS on two separate, both large stations, each commanded by a Group Captain created some interesting problems. Not least of the causes were the directions contained in the relevant Air Ministry Order (No.A74/50). This made the two Group Captains responsible to the Commandant for everything on their station to do with flying. They were responsible to the AOC of No 23 Group for everything else. Each Group Captain had two masters, the Commandant and the AOC 23 Group. In turn the Commandant, with direct responsibility for everything to do with the Examining Wing, was responsible not to the AOC 23 Group, but directly to the Commander-in-Chief of Flying Training Command. The AOC of 23 Group was Air Vice Marshal George Harvey, a subordinate to the Commander-in-Chief Flying Training Command, and having full responsibility for all the RAF Flying Training Schools in the UK.

The advantage to me of this system was that I was free of administrative problems and able to devote my attention to the affairs of the Flying Wings at Cerney and Rissington, to the Link Trainer School, and to the Examining Wing. The system would not have worked as well as it did had not each of the four Group Captains there during my time been easy to get on with, and always helpful and cooperative. In order to emphasise the equal status of the two halves of CFS, I moved out of the building which was rightfully the Station HQ at Rissington so that the Group Captain could run his command in exactly the same circumstances as his opposite number at Cerney. I then established my own Commandant HQ in some wooden buildings which had been put up during the war and which also housed the Link Trainer School.

During the summer of 1954, we became increasingly interested in the training of helicopter instructors. At this time there were no CFS trained helicopter instructors. The Navy, who were at that time the biggest rotary wing users, trained their own and had taught numbers of RAF pilots to fly rotary winged aircraft as well. Accordingly, we would organise a helicopter convention to take place, over a period of two days, at Cerney. For this convention we acquired two very experienced RAF helicopter pilots, both of whom were already CFS qualified instructors on fixed wing aircraft. These were Flight Lieutenant Bartlett, who gave me four days introductory instruction flying a Sikorsky S.51, and Squadron Leader John Dowling. We invited about fifty people, all specially qualified in various ways to discuss the problem of setting up a helicopter instructor's element in CFS. They included designers, test pilots, operational pilots from the Navy and RAF, instructors from the Navy's school squadron, and staff officers from Flying Training Command and the training branch of the Air Ministry. We modelled proceedings broadly on the periodical instructors' conferences which CFS was accustomed to hold each year for fixed wing instructors. We at CFS learned more in the two days than could have been remotely possible in any other way. The higher staff who controlled establishments were equally convinced that the time was ripe to provide CFS with the means to get into the helicopter business.

Our first move was to acquire John Dowling to take charge of a new unit to be based at Cerney. It would comprise a small ground school and a flying instructional flight, equipped with the Sikorsky 5.51, built by Westlands. We then recruited a small team of CFS instructors who had become helicopter pilots, and collected a guinea pig course of students for them to instruct. Not to become helicopter instructors, but on whom they could practise and develop the art of instructing and, with it, incorporate the standards that CFS has always demand. We chose a newly qualified pilot who had only just gained his wings, a very experienced Coastal Command pilot who had completed over 2,000 hours on Lancasters and Shackletons, a test pilot and an assorted representation of pilots of varying experience from fighters, bombers and training schools. To these, I added myself; it was an opportunity which I could not possibly miss.

Accordingly, in January 1955, I became once more a pupil pilot, and on 27

January, twenty eight and a half years after my very first solo at Filton, I did another first solo, this time on the Westland S.51, named by the RAF the Dragonfly.

The results of our guinea pig course were fascinating. We found that the best learners were those pilots who had remained the most versatile. Thus the pilots who had flown a variety of types, and were accustomed to adapting themselves to varying needs learned the new techniques quickly and successfully. So did the least experienced pilot, the one straight from flying training school. The greatest difficulty was experienced by the pilot with the greatest number of hours and one who had become so ingrained with the skills demanded for a single type of heavy aircraft. He could not master the helicopter at all. We digested these results with great care, and shortly afterwards, with a carefully selected course of instructors already qualified on fixed wing aircraft, began to train specialist helicopter instructors.

It was also about this time that Air Ministry asked for CFS views on the instrument rating for helicopters. So far, there was no such thing as a helicopter instrument rating, and the only direct experience we possessed was obtained during an Examining Wing visit to Malaya. In Malaya at that time, the jungle warfare against the communists was in full swing, and the most skilled among the RAF's helicopter pilots were to be found there. They had become experts at the very difficult task of flying accurately into clearings in deep jungle, usually the only means of moving troops and supplies. These clearings were very small, and often among giant trees standing round the small landing pad up to a height of more than 500 feet. One pilot told me that he judged where he was when going down into such a pad by watching when his rotor blades began to clip the leaves and twigs. If he could see this happening in front then he knew that he had clearance astern. Later, I had this actually demonstrated to me. The aircraft they flew were Westland S.51 Dragonflys with reconditioned engines, many of which had spent an earlier full career propelling fixed wing aircraft. There was no room for error, little margin of power in hand, and only a pilot in practice to the point of razor sharp skill could do this work safely.

It had been decreed that when Examining Wing were there, the opportunity should be taken to enable many of the helicopter pilots to renew their instrument ratings. At that time none of our helicopters were fitted with appropriate instrumentation, and indeed were only suitable for very restricted instrument flying. It was decided that the helicopter pilots should each be allowed a period on fixed wing aircraft, in this case the Harvard, to brush up ready for testing. Few, if any of them, had difficulty in passing the test, but the effect on their helicopter flying was bad. Certainly, they were no less efficient at the ordinary day-to-day flying, but the razor edge peak of skill needed in the jungle had been blunted, and took an appreciable time to recover.

Later, at Pensacola, we found that the United States Navy never allowed any pilot under training for rotary wing to fly fixed wing. The instructors themselves were discouraged from doing so. There are pilots who fly both and seem to have few problems, but the view we eventually reached was that pilots on helicopter duties should stick to their type. The helicopter rating required the development both of suitable instrumentation as well as helicopters more suited to the task than the Dragonfly.

It was in the summer of 1954 that I accompanied the Examining Wing team on their visit to the RAF in Germany, travelling in a Vampire TII. On arrival at Jever, the Vampire was smartly appropriated for check flights, and I found myself dependent upon a borrowed Anson. In this I paid a visit to the BAFO HQ at Bad Eilsen, where I had been before. I managed to work in a long weekend at Scharfoldendorf to fly a Weihe. Sadly, my own beautiful blue Weihe, which I had flown in the BAFO Gliding contests, had been crashed and written off.

Towards the end of 1954, we were told that one of our tasks in 1955 would be to assess the suitability of the Jet Provost for flying training. It was very much with this in mind that we planned our visit to Canada and the United States for May 1955. The other two important things were to see the way in which helicopter pilots were trained in the United States Services, and to pay a visit to Pensacola. For this visit, we picked a strong team.

We flew up to Heathrow in a Varsity and there transferred as ordinary passengers into a BOAC Boeing Stratocruiser. We flew first to Prestwick and then due to adverse weather to Iceland. The Great Circle route from Iceland passes close to Cape Farewell on the tip of Greenland, and crosses the Canadian coastline in Labrador, not far from the Hamilton Inlet. It was daylight as we came in, and at a height of around 12,000 feet, the sight was breathtaking. As we approached Montreal, we descended lower and lower, keeping below the thickening layer of early morning stratus which covered the low ground towards the St Lawrence River. No instrument approaches for our Captain, however. Instead he flew a tight circuit of the airfield, seemingly as steeply banked as if he had been flying a Vampire, so that the upper wing tip appeared actually to be in the cloud, and landed off an approach which would not have been out of place in the Instructors' early morning half hour at CFS.

At Montreal Airport we had time for a quick wash and clean up before we were carried off in a Dakota by our Canadian hosts and delivered to Ottawa. The next day we spent in the RCAF Headquarters. Before going to Trenton, we were shown Ottawa.

At Trenton we were the guests of the Central Flying School of the RCAF which is very similar to our own CFS. Next day I was introduced to the advanced jet trainer used by the RCAF, the American Lockheed T.33, the two seat version of the USAF's F.80 Shooting Star. My RCAF partner was Flight Lieutenant Wilson, who allowed me to fly it first from the front seat, and then from the Instructor's seat at the back. It flew very nicely, and seemed to have no particular vices except one which it shared with both the Meteor VII and the Kranich sailplane. That was the appalling bad view for the Instructor from the rear seat. At CFS we had discussed this and were convinced that any new trainers must offer the Instructor just as good a view as obtained by the pupil. The easy solution was the side by side arrangement. Nevertheless, many of us remained unconvinced that side by side was the right answer. In one animated discussion, I recollect an instructor who had been seconded to a Middle East Air Force, declaring his preference for side by side. He said that when language failed he was still able to hit his pupils over the knuckles with the sharp edge of a ruler, which he always took into the air for the purpose. He had been instructing on light twins which, in the hot climate where they went neither high nor fast, ensured that bare knuckles were always there for disciplinary purposes. Everybody else at this particular session favoured the fore and aft arrangements of seats. The argument that carried the day was that when the pupil was sent solo, there was no empty seat alongside him to destroy confidence.

After three very full days at Trenton, three of us set off for the USA, leaving the rest of our team to continue with the RCAF. Trenton flew us in a Dakota to Toronto, where we boarded a Vickers Viscount of Trans-Canada Airlines to fly to New York and then by Super Constellation of Eastern Airlines, to Washington. We would spend two days as guests of the RAF Mission.

Our tour was diverted to go by Kansas to visit the Cessna factory that were engaged at that time in the design and development of a small jet basic trainer for the USAF. This was the Cessna T.37 with a pair of the tiny continental T.69 jet engines side by side in the lower centre part of the fuselage. The two pilots seated side by side above them. We saw the prototype, which was not yet ready to fly, so we had no chance of assessing it in the air.

We then flew in a Martin 202 of TWA to San Antonio where we were collected by the United States Army to visit their helicopter training school at Gary, near San Marcos. Next day John Dowling came into his own as we delved into the methods of helicopter instruction. I sampled all their aircraft, with all the appreciation of the difficulties of the sprog pilot which, indeed I still was. John flew everything with the same skill as their best, and between us I think we came up with a very fair appreciation of strengths and weaknesses of both their methods and their aircraft.

From San Marcos, out in the dry, dry desert, we flew, via San Antonio to New Orleans for a rest weekend. From San Antonio we travelled in a Constellation of Eastern Air Lines, in which I had the privilege of being invited up front to handle the biggest aircraft I had ever flown. Captain Eddie Rickenbacker, US Army Air Corps of the First World War founded Eastern Air Lines, and ran it on a very personal and efficient basis. At this time he seemed to have a strong preference for ex-Marine Corps pilots and one such was our captain. I remained up front, until we pulled up on the ramp at New Orleans after a very delightful ride with a most efficient crew.

New Orleans is a truly beautiful city and after two days we flew to Moody Air Force Base, via Valdosta. This journey we made as passengers in a Lockheed 14 (Electra), the civil variant of the more famous Lockheed Hudson, which made a name for itself in RAF service in Coastal Command from 1940 until the end of the war. I did not enjoy this flight. Valdosta is in the deep south of Georgia, almost midway between the eastern and western boundaries of the state. Our route from New Orleans took us over Mobile and the northwestern parts of Florida, humid and hot. The wet air from the Gulf built up in great areas of thunderstorms which reminded me of my ride some years before, from Birmingham back to Maxwell Field. As conditions became rapidly worse, the Electra was bouncing about very uncomfortably. We came suddenly to a small clear hole, beneath which ran a swampy river through a dense jungle. Here we circled whilst our Captain decided what to do next. Finally he pressed on through some nasty cumulo-nimbus, and after a very rough ride in which several passengers were unwell, we landed at Valdosta. Here the USAF from Moody Air Force Base took charge of us, and we were driven in great comfort through pelting rain to the base and made welcome.

Moody was the USAF night fighter training base and we were introduced to Northrop's twin jet successor to the earlier propeller driven Black Widow. Part of the training equipment included one of the most advanced simulators which I had yet encountered. In this, I learned the cockpit layout and functions of all controls, and was told that students were expected to find everything blindfolded before they were allowed into the real thing. They also demonstrated the full range of disasters which the instructor could feed into the system. These included failure of every system, individually, or several in succession; and horrible weather, including thunderstorms and lightning strikes which resulted in momentary blindness. Finally, I completed a simulated blind approach to the airfield and landed, not entirely successfully, but a good number of feet below sea level. This was considered a good start. After this we were to be given experience of the actual aircraft. My turn failed for interesting reasons. Having been cleared to line up for take-off, we were told to hold as a civil airliner was approaching. Strict rules said that military flying must cease when civil traffic approached. The civil flight was late due to bad weather. So, in steady rain and low cloud we sat for nearly forty minutes at the end of the runway until, patience exhausted and fuel too low, we abandoned the sortie and returned to the hangars. It was a frustrating and illuminating experience, and demonstrated how, even in spaces as large as the USA, conflicting and imperfectly coordinated flight requirements can seriously interfere with essential training.

From Moody, we flew in a USAF Dakota back to Pensacola, to be the guests of the US Navy, Admiral Doyle, the Chief of Naval Air Training and Rear Admiral Dale Harris, Chief of Naval Basic Air Training. Pensacola was first used by the US Naval Air Service in 1913. At the time of our visit it comprised a cluster of several land aerodromes, as well as the original main base on Pensacola Bay, devoted to seaplanes and flying boats. My guide was Commander JN Ball, DSC Royal Navy. Commander Ball was the resident Royal Navy Liaison Officer at Pensacola, in charge of the twenty-five or so British pilots still being taught to fly by the US Navy. This was the final stage of the very big scheme which had operated through the latter part of the war. Pensacola takes care of all basic and advanced training on landplanes, seaplanes and helicopters for the US Navy. Our particular interest lay in the basic and advanced landplane training and helicopters. We had great numbers of discussions often completed in the air and, as a result, flew between us every type of fixed, wing landplane and helicopter that was in use at that time at Pensacola. I remember being favourably impressed by the North American advanced trainer, the T-28 (Trojan) with a 1425hp Wright Cyclone engine, retracting tricycle undercarriage and fighter-like performance. It was, however, already outdated and the US Navy was interested in our use of the Meteor and Vampire as advanced trainers, and the forthcoming Jet Provost as our basic trainer. The outcome, by 1956, was a specification which resulted in the birth of the North American T-2 Buckeye. It is nice to think that perhaps Admiral Doyle's visit to CFS, and our subsequent return visit to Pensacola, helped in the development of the Buckeye. We learned a great deal about helicopter pilot training and helicopter instructor training. As a final gesture, Admiral Doyle made available to us his own personal aircraft for our flight back to the Naval Air Base at Anacostia, in Washington DC. Here we reported back to the Mission under Dick Atcherley and then returned to Heathrow via Ottawa.

In the summer of 1955 we got our first Jet Provost. This was described as a modified Provost. In fact the alterations were considerable. The piston engine, the Alvis Leonides, had been removed and a small jet engine, the Armstrong Siddeley Viper, substituted in a central position in the fuselage, much further aft. Wing, undercarriage and tail unit remained the same. As much as possible of the piston Provost air frame was used in this first version of the new trainer. The use of the old main undercarriage in conjunction with a long-legged nose wheel to make it a tricycle, resulted in a rather giraffe-like appearance, and an aircraft very different from the compact and shapely products of later developments of it. We did a lot of flying on this first version and, in spite of its appearance, it was well liked. It did, however, seem to me to introduce a number of new problems.

The intention of the Air Ministry was that the Jet Provost, like the piston Provost before it, should be the RAF's beginner's trainer and that the pupil pilot should do as much training on this jet as possible. It was very soon apparent that with a performance approximating to the earlier marks of Spitfire, the Jet Provost was capable of getting very rapidly into situations which earlier piston engine trainers could not attain. Also its performance not only enabled it to use much more of the sky including the upper air space, but that to exploit it to best advantage this ability had to be used to the full. My own feeling after some experience with it was that just as the Canadians had found with their experience of all through training on the Harvard, we might find that the Jet Provost was too much of an aeroplane for a pilot's first flights when beginning to learn. This was the last major task during my two years at CFS, and I get some satisfaction from knowing that the Jet Provost which finally resulted has served the RAF very well.

An enormous number of events took place in my two years with the CFS. When I heard that I had been awarded the honour of appointment of Commander of the

Order of the Bath in the January 1956 New Year's Honours List, I did feel that this was something that had been earned by the whole CFS.

It came as rather a nasty shock to hear, at Christmas 1955, that our very happy two years at CFS was to come to an end on 17 January 1956. With effect from 18 February I was to become the RAF Senior Air Staff Officer in Aden. It is, of course, an essential feature of service life that no one person can remain in the best of jobs all the time.

CHAPTER TWELVE

ADEN

To have lived and worked at CFS in the midst of the beautiful county of Gloucestershire, almost on the summit of the Cotswolds, inevitably spoiled one for anything else. When we arrived and were confronted by the barren rocks of Aden, we were appalled. At first sight, the place looked like the pile where, from time immemorial, the gods had raked out the dusty red brown clinker from their overheated furnaces.

The journey to Aden did little to prepare us for our arrival. After a night in London, where we surrendered ourselves to the highly efficient RAF Movements staff, Rosemary, Azalea and I left on the express from Euston to Birkenhead. The two boys, still at prep school, remained in England with Rosemary's sister. We expected to be in Aden for two years and decided to take our cocker spaniel, Ouzel, then nine years old. He travelled separately by cargo vessel. As we approached Birkenhead, the rain increased and low cloud, borne on a northwesterly wind, made the early afternoon cold, damp and dark. When the train made its tortuous way through the line into the docks and finally drew up alongside our ship, we were glad to have very little way to go before getting on board.

The ship was the *Celicia* of the Anchor Line.

We were privileged to be placed at the Captain's table. We first sailed for Gibraltar, pausing only briefly before sailing on to Port Said. We then waited our turn to go through the Suez Canal.

In early 1955, Colonel Nasser had been in power for only four months, and Egypt was still not in control of the Suez Canal. The most obvious signs of change as we passed through the canal were the absence of any signs of life at the numerous service and civilian beach clubs which had flourished on the shores of the lakes, especially near Ismalia. The building looked uncared for and abandoned. The aerodrome at Ismalia, visible from the highest deck, looked unchanged, except for one thing. Instead of RAF aircraft there were Mig-15s and a few which looked like the first Mig-19s to reach the Egyptian Air Force. Two of these were standing, tails pointed to the sky, looking as though they had overshot the long runway, and finished up in the soft sand beyond it.

We emerged from the canal, and entered the Red Sea where it became increasingly hot, with the sun blazing down out of a cloudless sky, and so continued until, on 18 February, we arrived at Aden.

In 1956 there existed the Crown Colony of Aden. This comprised the port of

Aden, the Arab town on the eastern side of the peninsular known as Crater, and the hinterland on which was located the big airfield of Khormaksar. Beyond stretched the territories of the Aden Protectorate, divided for political purposes into three; the Western, stretching south as far as the Cape of Babel Mended, opposite Perim Island at the end of the Red Sea; the Aden Protectorate, occupying the mainland adjacent to the Crown colony; and the Eastern Protectorate, extending through the Hadhramaut and Dhofar, as far north as Oman. Inland of the Protectorates lay the Kingdoms of the Yemen and Saudi Arabia, the boundaries comprised in the south deep rocky and desolate valleys, and in the north the so-called Empty Quarter, miles upon miles of featureless sandy desert. For the most part rain fell for half an hour or so a year, except in the mountains where occasional vast thunderstorms brewed up, depositing torrential downpours resulting in floods and washed out tracks and fords. Water for the Colony was piped over-ground from deep wells and a pumping station in the Aden Protectorate, at Sheik Othman. It arrived tepid and so heavily chlorinated as to wreck any drink in which it was used, and to flavour anything cooked in it. Although one became used to it, one of the luxuries of Aden was to go out to a visiting ship to have a drink of decent water.

Shipping was the main business of Aden. Perim had once been a huge coaling station and when oil took over Aden became one of the cheapest bunkering depots in the east. A thriving tourist trade also grew up in the port, so that the arrival of any big passenger liner was the signal for bustling activity in the town of Aden. In the Crescent, shops dealt in every sort of duty free goods possible. Taxis lined up at the landing stages, competing for customers to be carried off to the further and more exotic delights of Crater. When the ship left, things reverted to normal, and the residents continued to bargain and shop in their accustomed ways, at prices usually about half those extracted from transient visitors.

The Governor and Commander-in-Chief was Sir Tom Higginbottom, who had spent nearly all his working life in the Persian Gulf, Arabia and Aden. He lived at Government House, on a flat promontory overlooking the entrance to the port and harbour and looking eastward across the twelve-mile wide mouth of the bay to Little Aden. Here was a newly operational and vast BP refinery. Below Government House the beach ran across to the little Telegraph Bay, in which an old torpedo net enclosed a large shark-free swimming place used by the officers and their families who lived in the bungalows beyond, on Steamer Point. Above Telegraph Bay, on the top of the cliff of Steamer Point, was the Officers' Mess. The married quarters at Steamer Point dated back to Victorian times, when Aden was an outstation of the Indian Empire and took its orders from Bombay, 1,650 miles away across the Indian Ocean. The quarters, and indeed much in Aden, reflected Indian influence and the quarters were cool and well adapted for the climate. Unlike those more modern buildings, such as Government House and our own married quarter on the high ground 250 feet above it, which were designed in London and built very well but with small regard to the climate.

During our time in Aden, it was normal for sixteen or seventeen ships a day to use the port, in addition to the oil tankers in and out of Little Aden for the BP refinery. Under the shadow of Government House there existed a very busy and thriving business community. Firms like Cory Brothers, P&O steamships, Luke Thomas and Cowasjee Dinshaw handled vast amounts of shipping and cargo. Aden Airways, then a subsidiary of BOAC, ran routes with their Dakotas up country, as well as to Somalia, East Africa and Ethiopia. Most of the important banks maintained offices and the Besse Group of companies were controlled by a family of French origin who had been in Aden almost longer than any other trading concern. Also down in Aden was the secretariat, presided over by Evelyn Home who had first entered the Colonial Service in 1935. Because most of our tasks in Aden and the Protectorates were governed by political considerations, I had a great deal to do with him. He was, of course, a member of the Aden Legislative council, presided over by the Governor, and whose other members comprised the AOC (my immediate superior), the Financial Secretary, the Attorney General, and eighteen other members, some nominated and some elected. This was the supreme authority in the Colony and Protectorate.

Of the services, the RAF comprised the majority, with the Army represented by a Brigadier, and the Navy by a resident Lieutenant Commander who was little more than a port liaison officer. That is until the Suez Canal Crisis, when his position changed almost overnight.

At the time of our arrival in Aden, the ground forces comprised the British officered Aden Protectorate Levies, and the Government and Tribal Guards, the latter two being something in the nature of locally recruited police forces. The Aden Protectorate Levies were similar in formation and function to their better known equivalent, the Iraq Levies, and were a first class force so long as they remained under British officers. As soon as they came under their own native officers, which policy was beginning to come into effect whilst we were there, they became increasingly unreliable and undisciplined. One incident is typical. During the Suez Crisis, there was a good deal of unrest in Aden, and it was thought desirable to mount guards of the Aden Levies on some of the more important living areas and houses, including mine and the bungalow of the Brigadier immediately alongside it. One day, returning from the beach by Steamer Point we were confronted by a very wild looking Aden Levy, pointing his rifle with fixed bayonet at us. He was shouting, though what he said was totally unintelligible. Using my even louder than normal voice, I managed to get out a word of command that brought him to attention and some kind of sense.

Normally my duties kept me in the Air HQ from starting work at six each morning until we stopped at midday. Although appointed as Senior Air Staff Officer, I found myself more and more involved in administration as well. The point came when my AOC said that he would now regard my position as being that of his Chief of Staff, a position normally unknown in RAF staff organisation, but common enough in the Army. The result was that I added to my existing task as his deputy during his frequent absences, responsibility for both the operational side and administrative side of the Air HQ. For me there was no afternoon siesta. Most of our air operations at this time comprised routine transport and medical flights to landing grounds all over the Protectorate. In addition, quick reaction was needed by cannon and rocket firing fighters when one of the up-country forts, manned by Government Guards, was in trouble. These calls for help usually took place at about two or three in the afternoon, and a show of force had to be authorised, either by the AOC or myself.

Khormaksar always kept two or three aircraft, Venoms at that time, on readiness. Not all such calls were genuine. One unit of Government Guards, some hundred miles up country were frequent callers. The system was that each fort possessed an aerial survey of itself and the surrounding country. When trouble occurred, usually from marauding tribesmen, they would pinpoint the position to be attacked and signal its reference on their gridded photographs. For example, enemy firing from position X 9 Y 8. The aircraft would then attack this point using their similar photograph to identify it. Sometimes results were seen, occasionally not. This particular fort signalled regularly their thanks and nobody every saw results. So we followed up one such attack by a reconnaissance some thirty minutes later, after the Venoms had gone home. What was seen was a happy band of Government Guards foraging in the area for 20mm cannon shell cases and harvesting a good supply of brass presented to them at great cost by the British.

Another problem was the explorations of Aramco, the Arabian American oil company. Our Shackleton reconnaissance aircraft used to find drilling going on in many places miles from anywhere. Maps being what they were, it was not difficult for a mistake to result in unauthorised drilling in the Protectorate, usually in the featureless northern desert known as the Empty Quarter, north of Hadhramaut. When this happened they were asked to desist, and we maintained reconnaissance to ensure that they did. One such drilling camp, a few huts, a rig and a number of fifty gallon drums, which once contained fuel for the camp, was typical. After Aramco left, leaving everything that was not worth saving, we watched it gradually disappear. Not, as one might have supposed, buried under blown sand, but just vanishing bit by bit. It was being removed by desert Arabs.

We had many landing strips all over the Protectorates. Mostly they were swept strips of hard sand close to a village. Some strips were very good and would take aircraft like the Blackburn Beverley. Others, less good, would give trouble. One such, at Aiyad not far from Shabwa in the Hadhramaut we visited in a Pembroke to see a detachment of Aden Levies. On taxiing and turning at the end of the strip, at the end of our visit, the relatively high pressure tyres of the Pembroke broke through the hard upper crust of salty sand that formed the surface. We went through into the soft running dry sand below. When this happens, digging is a snare, for as one digs in front of the wheel, the running sand embeds the wheel even deeper and everything gets worse. We took several hours to solve this problem, eventually getting a wooden five foot mess table from the Levies under the wheel. Then, using all their remaining tables and planks, we constructed a surface hard enough on which to get up a speed at which we could be sure of remaining on top, and taking off back to Aden. The initial take-off was exciting, for the tables under the wheels tilted as each took the weight coming onto it. Most, but not all, narrowly escaped fouling the tips of the Pembroke's twin metal propellers. All this had taken place in the heat of the mid-afternoon, and the nicest thing was going up to 8,000 feet to cool off and drink quantities of lemon squash.

Other strips were more reliable. That at Beihan, close to the village of that name and the Palace of the Sherif of Beihan, would take almost any aircraft. At an elevation of nearly 4,000 feet the climate was such that the Sherif was able to grow peaches in his oasis watered garden. Once or twice when I visited Beihan, I attended the Court where the Sherif heard appellants and administered justice. The Court was in a fort-like building with a single very large chamber, and some smaller adjoining ones in which prisoners were kept. The main beam which supported the roof of the large chamber was the wing spar of a Westland Wapiti, relic of some accident on the strip in the earlier days of the RAF in Aden. The punka, which was unique, rotated. It was nothing less than the superb wooden propeller of a de Havilland 9A.

The trip to Beihan was a great favourite with the transport crews in their Valettas. We used to ferry a good deal of things up there, for the land journey, up over the escarpment which forms the rim like a saucer round the whole of Arabia, was tedious and sometimes unsafe. The excitement was that sometimes the Sherif's daughter would be part of the cargo. The procedure was that when the aircraft was ready to leave a large limousine with dark windows would come out of the Palace courtyard, drive the mile or so to the strip and pull up close to the Valetta. From the back would emerge a small figure, clothed entirely in black and veiled.

The Suez Crisis was now looming. But in Aden, at the maximum, counting the Army, Navy and RAF reinforcements, the military population increased from its customary size of 2,000 to well over 10,000. There were command problems too. Admiral Biggs, to whom the Navy in Aden was responsible, had his headquarters in the Persian Gulf. Our Cameron Highlanders were responsible to the GOC in Cyprus. In Aden, my AOC was the Senior Service Officer, wholly responsible for the RAF in Aden, the Persian Gulf and East Africa. He had the additional task of providing for the influx of visitors all that they needed to make their stay possible. He was also responsible to the Governor, whose full title was Governor and Commander-in-Chief, Aden, for the defence of the colony and the Protectorates. Later the problems were tidied up when Aden became the headquarters of a combined command, known as Middle East Command. It was headed by a single Commander-in-Chief to whom all three services in the theatre were responsible.

In my capacity as so called Chief of Staff I found the position difficult, and the fact that everything worked quite well was due far more to the goodwill of everybody concerned. This is not to forget the diplomacy of the very popular Governor, Sir William Luce. It was during this period that I attained what, in some ways, could be regarded as the highlight of my administrative career. Our sole transport squadron of Valettas was so swamped with tasks resulting from the Suez Crisis that all its usual tasks up in the Protectorates had to be abandoned. I therefore requisitioned, on half a sheet of paper, Aden Airways. With their Dakotas, they took over the task the Valettas could no longer do, and did them with such efficiency and reliability that I often wondered whether we should not have done better to keep that war proven work horse in the RAF. However, by this requisition, we doubled overnight the strength of the RAF Transport Force in Aden, and I felt that we had equalled, if not capped, the Navy's achievement in creating out of nothing, its mine sweeper squadron.

The history of the Suez Crisis is not part of my own story, except in so far as it could be watched from Aden. We were aware of the forces being gathered together in Cyprus. We were also clear about the delays and hesitations that were allowed to happen. From this point on British authority in the Middle East diminished, and unrest and fighting increased. It became a most disturbed and potentially explosive area. By the end of 1956 I was feeling distinctly exhausted, and was heartily glad when I heard that I was to be posted home, my relief being Teddy Donaldson.

Having no leave or days off for the whole of this year, I was granted permission to return home by sea. We embarked in February 1957 in the 12,000 ton ship of the Clan Line the MV *Eucadia*. The ship carried only thirteen passengers, all in great comfort. Rosemary and I shared a big double cabin with its own bath and loo; Azalea had her own cabin close by.

The Suez Canal being still closed meant that our route took us round South Africa. We were to call on the way at Durban and the Canaries, and arriving after three weeks at Avonmouth. It would be hard to imagine a more perfect and restful holiday after our exhausting and not very happy year in Aden. Almost the first delight on going on board was to drink cool clean water with no taste of chlorine to foul everything that Aden water touched.

Eucadia was a large mixed cargo carrier built just after the end of the war. The accommodation for ship's officers and passengers was all in the centre island, which also contained the bridge. Through the centre protruded the black Clan Line painted funnel. She was driven by a single screw, and the large diesel engine of some 12,000hp in four huge double acting cylinders. One cylinder gave occasional trouble, and twice during our journey down the east coast of Africa we stopped for several hours whilst the engineers did repairs. On both occasions the sea was flat calm and the ocean and sky clear and beautiful. Yet it was not unbearably hot and, certainly after Aden, positively refreshing. We all breakfasted, lunched and dined in the small saloon whose windows looked out ahead over the two forward big cargo hatches and the forecastle. The food was never less than superb. After dinner, Rosemary and I joined the Master, Captain Gibson, who treated us to his rather special brandies. On these occasions, Captain Gibson told us many things about his life at sea. He was a wonderful host.

It was shortly before our arrival at Durban that the passengers were reduced from thirteen in number to twelve. A warrant officer, returning from Aden, died suddenly in the night. He was buried at sea. The ship was stopped, the Ensign half masted, and the Master took the simple but moving service for burial at sea. All the ship's company, except those on watch, were present, and all the passengers. A short few moments pause, then the Ensign went back up to the top, the great diesel engine down below resumed its steady deep beat and life went on. After a burial at sea, there is no trace left. The sun continued to down over the still Indian Ocean, and the ship's wake stretched out astern just as before, as far as the eye could see.

We were long enough in Durban to see quite a lot of it. After breakfast, the three of us went ashore and, not knowing quite what to do, hailed a taxi cab. The driver was a nice local woman to whom we explained that we knew nothing of the place, and wanted to see as much as possible. She proved a charming and knowledgeable guide, and spent the entire morning driving us everywhere, and telling us about all the places we saw. Later, we spent a morning on the beautiful curved beach, where the huge bathing area was protected by a vast shark net. In Aden we had achieved the same protection using old naval anti-torpedo nets which seemed more durable. We were told that the Durban nets often had holes, with the resultant scares of sharks within the nets. We returned that evening to *Eucadia* and sailed that night.

Our stay in Las Palmas was quite different. The place was dirty by comparison with Durban and the taxis old and decrepit. The drivers were on the make for as much as they could get from any visiting ships' passengers. As we passed into North Atlantic the weather changed. Instead of constant sunshine, the sky became clouded. The dolphins were no longer with us, and the superb and rare Wandering Albatross, one or two of whom we were lucky to see far, far to the south, had long since gone. As the ship moved into the Western Approaches, we began to see the familiar seagulls until, closer to England, *Eucadia* had her escort of ever-ready birds waiting to swoop, fighting and screeching, for anything edible that might be thrown overboard. We began to see more and more ships, and a cold rain proclaimed that we were indeed close to England. On our last night at sea we had a superb dinner.

Next morning, as we moved cautiously up the Bristol Channel, we were enveloped in a wet clinging fog. After more than a year in Aden where we had seen rain only once and that for a bare three minutes, this damp fog was bliss. We were really home. To Captain Gibson it was the worst thing possible, and a period of strain. From then on, until we were alongside at Avonmouth, he remained on the bridge, checking and double checking, to ensure our safe arrival.

We passed back into the hands of the efficient RAF Movements Section and onto the train to Botley. After a few days there I reported to the RAF Hospital at Wroughton near Swindon for a very thorough medical check, and was sent off on a month's sick leave. This was something of a back hander for I was, in any case, due for at least that length of normal leave anyway. However, I accepted it gladly, not least because it permitted me to evade a posting in the Air Ministry which I would have had to start much sooner, and into a job which I would not have enjoyed.

After my one month of sick leave, which allowed us to get back into our house at Fleet in Hampshire, I attended a medical board. On 5 April 1957 I was declared fit for full flying duties. To my delight I was also granted a further month's ordinary leave. I was then to report on 7 May to Manby for a flying refresher course on Meteors.

CHAPTER THIRTEEN
LEAVING THE RAF AND JOINING THE AIR LEAGUE

In 1957 the RAF was coming slowly to accept that it was not always possible for pilots to keep in constant practice on modern and, compared with earlier types, complicated kinds of aircraft. I had been able to do far too little flying whilst in Aden and, since my return to England, none at all. The evolving policy was to provide refresher facilities for pilots who needed it, and Manby, the Flying College was the organisation selected to provide it. Manby was a pre-war airfield of limited size and, in consequence, most of the higher performance aircraft it used were based at Strubby, a few miles south down the Lincolnshire coastline. We refreshers lived in nice pre-war buildings at Manby, and were ferried each morning to fly at Strubby by RAF bus. We lunched there in a dilapidated Nissen hut which had been the wartime Officers' Mess of the squadrons then based there.

My instructor was Flight Lieutenant Gerry Mayor who not only handled a Meteor as though it was a Chipmunk, but also had a passion for flying in the worst possible weather. One morning I recollect, when there was no other flying, he decided to have some practice on the instrument approach system at Waddington and took me. We were in thick cloud from Strubby almost before the wheels of the Meteor had left the ground, and went up through some 12,000 feet of clag before emerging into the clear above, with further layers of stratus on top. After some conversation with Waddington, who told us that their conditions were similar, we began our descent and approach. It was an extraordinary demonstration of absolutely accurate flying; airspeed, rate of descent, lining up to the runway all immaculate and done with a precise unconcern as though the whole thing was in clear air with thirty mile visibility. At hangar height, the runway appeared exactly in the right place and, after a touch and go the whole thing was repeated with the same exact unconcern and accuracy.

Looking back, I think that this was the moment when I first conceded that the new generation of pilots were better than me. This must always be a landmark in one's life as a pilot. I had, perhaps with too little modesty and too great pride, continued to believe that what any other pilot could do I could do better. Certainly, had I thought more objectively about it, I ought to have realised at CFS, when I became reduced to one eye that my young men could do better than I. But this is always, I suppose, something very hard to admit. At Strubby I did, very belatedly perhaps, have to admit the truth. I hope that Gerry Mayor will accept my honest assurance that, far from making me unhappy, he gave me the certain belief that the new generation of pilots in the RAF are, as indeed they must always be, superior in every way to their predecessors. Nowadays, when I am privileged to visit squadrons I have known I find them commanded by the sons of my own commanders, or even contemporaries, I am confirmed in this belief. My much-loved RAF is indeed in good hands.

So, at Strubby, I enjoyed flying Meteors, acknowledged my limitations, and returned to a job at the Air Ministry on 1 June 1957 as the Director of Operational Training. My immediate superior, as Assistant Chief of Air Staff for Training, was George Harvey who, as Air Vice Marshal Harvey, had been my immediate administrative superior when I was Commandant at CFS.

At that time the offices of the Assistant Chief of Air Staff for Training were in the fine old buildings in Richmond Terrace, off Whitehall. The title was misleading because his responsibilities were for training in the air, whilst the equally vast responsibility for all technical and ground training was in another branch of the Air Ministry altogether. George Harvey had a fine office on the second floor. I, as the Director of Operational Training, lived on the floor above with my own staff. It was a time of great changes in the RAF. The Suez affair was over and resolved, if it could be said to be resolved, in a thoroughly unsatisfactory way. All three services were under great pressure to save money. On the one hand the services demanded of the government that sufficient resources be provided to them, to achieve specified jobs. On the other hand, the Treasury was constantly telling the services that no more money was available. As is almost always the outcome of such difficulties, the services are told to spend less, and to discover how to do the jobs required without the cash.

The first impact of this situation arrived in Richmond Terrace in the form of papers discussing how to retain what was regarded as the minimum essential front line strength without the cash to do it. The eventual hard fought decision was to cut down elsewhere. The first cuts were made in a variety of training and communication aircraft. Up until this point, there had been on most big RAF stations, a Station Flight, usually comprising two or three light aircraft and used as an appropriate means of making official journeys without waste of time, or using larger aircraft more costly to operate. These were abolished, and at the same time a variety of other communications flights, used by Staff Officers at the various headquarters, were done away with. The total saving thus effected was reckoned to be of the order equivalent to half a front line squadron of Valiants. The cost was that the pilots employed on staff duties were deprived of any means of keeping in some sort of flying practice. Other means had to be found of refreshing them when they returned to a spell of regular flying. The refresher facilities at Manby soon ceased to be adequate. Later still it became the custom for refreshing pilots to be sent for training back into the normal flying training organisation, usually to join it at the advanced training stage. In the end, there was no saving.

Another problem of great interest was the introduction of the first Lightnings into the service. This was the first aircraft of such performance to come into RAF service, and the plans for introducing it provided a great deal of work and interest. A bonus from this was that I was required to make a tour of inspection of possible aerodromes on which to locate the new Lightning Operational Conversion and Training Unit. This involved visits to a number of far-off aerodromes, mostly in Scotland, and some unused since the war.

Then there was also the introduction of the Folland Gnat. At this time Sir Richard Atcherley, having retired from the RAF, had become Folland's military aircraft adviser. He was actively interested in the Gnat as a future two-seat advanced trainer for the RAF. The aircraft would achieve fame as Central Flying School's Red Arrows (later superseded by the Hawk).

The fourth major problem was helicopter training and this, in effect, was a continuation of the work which I had begun at CFS, when we set up the first helicopter instructor courses. In this task, I chaired an inter-Service committee to study and recommend the future organisation in all three services of helicopter training. I find it very satisfactory to know that the arrangements in existence much later are not vastly different from those which our committee recommended.

Whilst all this was going on, I managed to get some flying at the still existing Elementary and Reserve Flying School at Fairoaks, who used Chipmunks. The CFI was Wing Commander Cyril Arthur. Cyril Arthur began flying in the Royal Flying Corps in 1916, and had been at it ever since. In 1917 he was flying Camels in a Home Defence squadron based at Throwley in Kent. The remains of this old aerodrome can still be found. After the First World War he went to Canada and flew seaplanes and boats for the newly emerging Royal Canadian Air Force on the west coast. From there he went to the Far East, and became a commercial pilot flying charters in small aircraft. Later, Cyril Arthur returned to England and to Fairoaks where, in 1939, he once more put on uniform and was CFI at Fairoaks throughout the Second World War, and of the shrinking school that remained after it. When the school finally closed, he remained as the CFI of the Club until finally, with something like 15,000 hours of flying instruction in his logbook, and a continuous record as a pilot since 1916, he retired after over fifty years as a pilot. Later, when I had left the RAF and kept my own small light aeroplane at Fairoaks, I got to know Cyril Arthur very well.

My Chipmunk flying whilst I was DTO was chiefly memorable for a visit to Boscombe Down in an aircraft whose last two letters were EL. The phonetic alphabet current in 1957 was not that in use now, but an earlier version, which caused me to announce my arrival in the Boscombe circuit as Chipmunk EASY LOVE. For a moment there was no response. And then came a horrible coarse female giggle, presumably from the duty WAAF in the Air Traffic Control. I felt very embarrassed.

As the year progressed, the contraction of the three services continued. The RAF was hit particularly hard. Early in 1958 the Air Ministry introduced a new early retirement scheme designed to encourage people to go. The essence of this was a sort of graduated golden handshake, calculated according to rank and length of service. In October 1958 I retired under this scheme, receiving a big enough handshake to pay off my children's school fees, and to manage one or two other desirable things which would otherwise have been impossible.

I retired on 6 October 1958 and two days later took up the civilian appointment of Secretary General of the Air League of the British Empire. I was sad to leave the service though looking back I still think it was the right time to go. Since I first flew as a Reservist in 1927, the changes had been enormous. Then we had been flying the same sort of aeroplanes, and using the same weapons as had been used in the First World War. The Second World War saw enormous advances, especially in radio aids and instrumentation. The performance of aircraft increased very greatly. Nevertheless we were still, for the most part, relying on free fall bombs, guns and cannon, and engines which were developments of earlier years. It was only right towards the end of that war that the forerunners of a new age in air armaments appeared. These, with the single exception of the devastating atom bombs dropped on Japan were too late to affect the final outcome. Until 1945 we lived in an age in which the dominant weapons were the ones used in previous wars, or developments of them. It has been an amazing period in the world's history, unlike anything in so short a space before. Sometimes I have been asked if I had my time again, would I want it to be different. My answer has to be, No. I hope that this sounds neither self satisfied nor smug. I am only too well aware of my own shortcomings, of opportunities missed, of failures that I could have avoided, and of times when my performance was second or third rate. But, during my career, I was privileged to meet, and sometimes to know well, many remarkable people. Some of them were people whose genius was leading us through these astonishing times. Some, like my AOC Sir Basil Embry, were outstanding war leaders and national heroes. Others, like Cyril Arthur, had unshakeable foundations upon which they built. There is my own splendid crew in 98 Squadron and Jock Campbell who taught me to fly. To all of them I owe a debt of gratitude for something which has made life richer, more colourful, more worthwhile, and sometimes terrifying. This last experience is, in my view, most important, for it is my conviction that until you have been in great fear of losing your life, you cannot truly value it.

When I retired in late 1958 I was aged fifty-one years old. At the same time many other officers of similar same rank and experience were leaving the three services. They were all seeking civil employment. The Air Ministry set up a special office under the direction of Air Marshal Sir Victor Goddard to help RAF leavers find jobs. It was not very successful, and I avoided it. But as my retirement pension, after tax, amounted only to a little under £1,200 a year, a job to supplement this was essential.

To this end, as soon as my retirement had been approved, I started work on my own and, after some sixty applications for what I hoped might be suitable jobs, was shortlisted to join the Royal Institute of Chartered Surveyors, based in London in

Birdcage Walk. At an interview with their full council, I found them a singularly pleasant company, who brushed aside as irrelevant my protestations of total ignorance about surveying. The chairman explained my duties, which were mainly administration in charge of an office of some twenty staff. And the pay was generous. All seemed fine, except for one horrid little niggle in my own mind. Would this be, could this be allowed to be, the end of my flying?

It was at this point that Air Marshal Sir Francis Fogarty, himself now retired and having become Director of the English Speaking Union, as well as Chairman of the Air League of the British Empire, offered me the job of Secretary General of the Air League. Such an invitation could not be refused, even though the money was a good deal less. Was I being stupid? But when flying is involved, inevitably the heart rules the head. Two days after leaving the service, I became, under Joe Fogarty, Secretary General of the Air League still in close touch with my service and able to continue flying.

The Air League needs some explanation. In 1912 the French led the world in flying. The aviation meeting that summer in Rheims was, in size and prize money, not equalled again until twenty-five years later. In Germany, Count Zeppelin was operating a commercial airship service. The armed forces of both France and Germany were greatly interested. In Russia Igor Sikorski was designing military aircraft of a kind which he developed for the Imperial Russian Air Service, to become the world's first multi-engine heavy bomber. In Britain, the Chief of the Imperial General Staff (CIGS) had not long since opined that he could see no future use for aeroplanes in the Armed Forces. The English still believed that the English Channel secured us against continental enemies, and that, beyond that, the Royal Navy, more powerful than any other navy in the world, was still as it had been for centuries, this country's Sure Shield. When Blériot flew across the Channel, it was a nasty shock.

In 1912, at a meeting at the Mansion House in London, chaired by the Lord Mayor and attended by many prominent people, foremost among whom was the then young Winston Churchill, that the Air League was founded. Its objectives were the promotion of an air mindedness among the population and, above all, to persuade the government of the day that military and naval aviation must be given a priority in the armed forces, no less than it had already gained on the continent.

I doubt if the Air League can claim full credit, but it is fact that in 1912 the Royal Flying Corps was formed. It comprised a military wing controlled by the War Office, a naval wing controlled by the Admiralty, and a Central Flying School to train pilots for both. The same Central Flying School which, as CFS, it was my great privilege to command many years later.

The military wing of the RFC soon merged with the Army. The naval wing became part of the Navy. By 1914, when war broke out, each had become embodied as parts of the army or navy. It was not until the creation of the Royal Air Force in 1918 that the two air services, somewhat reluctantly, reunited. Only CFS remained distinct.

In 1914, the Air League went into hibernation. In 1919 it emerged to fight for the continued existence of the RAF which both Army and Navy did their utmost to dismember and take back. How nearly they succeeded is history. The Air League played its part in public and political propaganda in preserving the RAF. It is relevant that the Air League derived its funds, not only from membership subscriptions, but from the subventions of the many independent aircraft firms which then existed. During this interwar period, the Air League acquired its most famous and effective secretary, Air Commodore Chamier.

As the Second World War approached, Chamier devoted all his great skill and energy to the creation of the Air Defence Cadet Corps. This was the nationwide youth organisation which in 1941 was taken over by the RAF lock, stock and barrel, together with Air Commodore Chamier, to become the Air Training Corps (ATC). The ATC would remain the best source of recruits for the RAF. I doubt if Air Commodore Chamier has ever been given the credit he deserves for this great and enduring creation.

During the Second World War the Air League again went into hibernation, to be revived once more in 1950. Its role by this time had changed. No longer was there the same need as in 1912 and again in 1919 to publicise the need for a separate Air Service. Instead the Air League devoted its resources to propaganda aimed at making public and government aware of the need to maintain a strong RAF. They also encouraged the development of civil aviation.

By the time I went to the Air League in 1958, the aircraft industry was undergoing great changes. The multitude of firms who had previously given generous support was disappearing, or being amalgamated to create fewer but larger organisations. Ultimately only one big aircraft firm remained, British Aerospace. The Air League's main source of funds was rapidly drying up. Membership, which was minimal, provided nothing.

The organisation comprised a council whose chairman, Sir Francis Fogarty, had recruited me. There were twelve members representing RAF, Navy and Army, Industry and Civil Aviation. All were very senior in their respective spheres. I remember particularly Sir Percy Hunting, Chairman of the Hunting Group of companies and an old friend of Sir Francis from Royal Flying Corps days. There was also Peter Masefield (later Sir Peter) and our President, The Duke of Hamilton and Brandon. The council met once a month. I had frequent meetings with Sir Francis, and also the Duke of Hamilton. Both were able and charming, and meetings with them were always both helpful and a pleasure.

Besides myself the full time paid staff were Miss Neill, its efficient secretary and Accountant, one or sometimes two typists, and the editor of the Air League's monthly journal, called at that time *The ATC and Air Reserve Gazette*. Our offices were in the old Londonderry House, at that time rented by the Royal Aero Club to supplement their clubhouse in Piccadilly. We paid rent to the club and worked closely with their Secretary, Colonel Preston. All this cost rather more than our declining income.

In consequence, I found myself with three major tasks. First, to put into action the various decisions made by the Air League Council in pursuit of its particular role. Secondly I had to increase membership, and thirdly to revive the Air League's income. Not that all this was immediately apparent, for it took me a good twelve months to work myself into the job and to see clearly how to set about it. In the meantime the council members were both patient and supportive for which I was deeply grateful. It was during this period too, that I learned one great difference between service and civil life. In the service, one's first responsibility is to look after your subordinates, and to rely on your superiors to look after you. In civvy street it tends to be the reverse. Naturally neither of these generalisations are always true, but I did find that many of the powerful and successful people I was now required to meet seemed to have got there by putting number one first, and sometimes trampling on subordinates on their climb up the ladder. I learned, too, to detect them and deal cautiously.

As part of my golden handshake from the RAF I was able to buy, for £650, a little aeroplane. This was a Druine Turbulent, built by Rollasons at Croydon, and powered by a converted Volkswagen 32hp engine. It was a single seater with a small locker for overnight kit. I fitted a sliding cockpit canopy and wheel spats. With these embellishments I could cruise at a little over 60 knots and manage about 30 miles per gallon. By doing all my own maintenance I avoided a good deal of the normal running costs and, with a wing span of only 18 feet, hangar charges at Fairoaks (near Woking) where I kept it were small. Because the work of the Air League involved a lot of travelling, I was able to do much of it by air, generally at no greater cost than that of running a Morris Mini. This was a great delight and in the course of such duties, I covered most of England and Scotland, recruiting new members for the Air League. I can't remember exact figures, but certainly several hundreds.

Besides membership, Air League income was a problem. It was Colonel 'Mossie' Preston (of the Royal Aero Club) who suggested what was to become the solution. He pointed out that the Air League's journal, *The ATC and Air Reserve Gazette*, was an unexploited and potential asset. We managed to install David Dorrell as the new editor and changed the title to *Air Pictorial*. David Dorrell remained its editor for twenty-five years and, by the time he retired, was the longest serving editor of any aviation periodical in England. During this time he became an accepted authority on aviation affairs, and built up a team of regular contributors covering civil and military aviation, engine and aircraft industries, airlines of the world, and history. *Air Pictorial* became the best of the non-technical flying papers and with its all round coverage and good pictures, built up its circulation to a monthly peak of 32,000.

My part in all this was to become the manager of *Air Pictorial*. I also wrote and photographed for it. In particular I developed my so-called Air Tests of interesting aeroplanes, describing their technical features, handling in the air, virtues and faults. In all we published 114 of these air tests. They covered a whole range of types from the four-engine Vickers Viscount to the tiny 200 mile an hour Formula racer Cosmic Wind named Ballerina, some seaplanes and amphibians, and a variety of sailplanes. There were also two autogyros and a helicopter. As the series became known, I received invitations from manufacturers, some of whom ordered large numbers of reprints of the articles for publicity purposes, for which the Air League received good payments.

As *Air Pictorial* sales improved, so did its revenue. After five years, I was able to cover the entire running costs of the Air League, rent, wages, heating, lighting and the lot from *Air Pictorial* revenue, and still have a little in hand. In this I was guided by the skilled hand of our Treasurer, Anthony Cayzer.

Three important routine activities were meetings with Ministers and Members of Parliament, the annual Air League Ball at the Dorchester, and the annual lunch at the Mansion House. For meetings with Ministers and MPs we usually arranged a small reception with drinks at the Royal Aero Club. This was the period when Dennis Healey was Minister of Defence in the Labour Government. Under his direction the TSR2 (developed by the British Aircraft Corporation) was cancelled in April 1965. This deprived the RAF of the most advanced aircraft of its time, together with many lost orders notably from the Royal Australian Air Force (in fact the RAAF chose to buy the F111 in 1963 but had to wait ten years for delivery). The Navy lost its projected new aircraft carriers, and it was decided that the Fleet Air Arm would no longer operate fixed wing deck landing aircraft. In consequence the Air League had a series of meetings with Healey and his supporters at which discussions were frequently animated and usually frustrating. My duty was to keep both drink and questions flowing. Generally speaking we were no match for Healey. I remember one very searching query put by my good friend, Admiral Ben Bolt. After a pause and general silence, Healey replied, 'A very good question', he said, 'May I just re-phrase it for you?' This he did, answering his own re-phrased query with irrefutable logic, and leaving Ben Bolt's unanswerable one in the air.

I sometimes attended meetings of the Conservative Parliamentary Defence Committee of which the Secretary was Admiral Morgan Giles, and the Chairman, Enoch Powell. Powell, a master of logic and apparently never swayed by emotion, seemed a very cold fish. Morgan Giles, later my near neighbour in Old Alresford, was well acquainted with the Fleet Air Arm and RAF and their problems. He was always both sympathetic and understanding, but my overall impression of Members of Parliament was that while many were former soldiers and sympathetic to the Army point of view, few had either naval or air experience and their understanding and sympathy were lacking. The Navy, the senior service, but by no means the silent service which it once claimed to be, could still get away with quite a lot. The RAF, in the 1960s, was still regarded by some older MPs as new upstarts.

While intensely interesting, these political encounters usually took place in the late evening, and often, instead of returning home to Fleet, I had to stay at the RAF Club. Much later after many, in my view, undesirable changes in Air League Council membership, the emphasis on political encounters increased, but at a lower level. I was expected to hang around Westminster and lobby MPs. This I refused and it became one of the reasons for my eventual departure from the Air League in 1971.

Of course the Air League Ball had a propaganda purpose. Besides the distinguished and hopefully Royal guest of honour invitations went to senior Air Marshals and their wives, Ministers and MPs who were concerned with aviation. Other guests, who always included many members of the aircraft industry and their families, as well as suitable socialites were expected to pay high prices of tickets. Each year it was hoped to make the ball self supporting, but this seldom happened and the loss was a charge on Air League funds.

The Air League Ball became our occasion for a family party. My privilege was tickets at half price. At this time, son Simon had left school and was in the Durham Light Infantry in Berlin. He then spent a year in London before joining the Bank of London and South America and, in 1964, was sent by his Bank to Argentina. Timothy was at Dartmouth and then at sea, but Azalea was at home and working, initially in London and then in Winchester. We were therefore able to organise a family table with the children's friends as our guests. It was an occasion to meet many friends from the service and for them to meet my family. For the Air League I think it attracted favourable attention, and enabled it to press its views among important people. And once my official duties were discharged, it was fun. It's a sad thought though, that since then I have never again worn white tie and tails. They reside in the attic, smelling of moth balls.

The third established event in the Air League's calendar was the Mansion House lunch in November. This sprang from the Air League's own founding meeting at the Mansion House in 1912 and was a highly prized privilege granted by successive Lord Mayors ever since. The Lord Mayor himself presides, and introduces the Guest of Honour. In my time these included Lord Louis Mountbatten, various Chiefs of the RAF, the American Commander in Chief of NATO forces and, on one very special occasion, Prince Philip. The setting, the prestigious Guest of Honour and the ceremonial of the occasion commands an important audience. I remember two speeches in particular: Lord Mountbatten's because of his claim that he had learned to fly in 1918 (his biography contradicts this, putting it as 1926 at the Aero Club at Hamble), and Prince Philip for personal reasons. I had just changed my Druine Turbulent for the slightly more potent but equally small Tipsy Nipper. His reference to the Air League Secretary General 'Nipping about the country in a turbulent manner' baffled many but delighted my friends and myself. Prince Philip had not long since been flying a Turbulent. This was from White Waltham aerodrome, near Maidenhead. It came about because John Severne had piloted a Turbulent entered by Prince Philip for the King's Cup Air Race. It won, at a speed never before or since equalled by a Turbulent and, on the lap of honour, the engine tuned to a hair's breadth for the course, found it too much and blew up. John Severne became the Commandant of the Central Flying School not long after me, and finally retired as Air Vice Marshall Sir John Severne KCVO OBE AFC DL after a distinguished tour as Captain of the Queen's Flight.

At White Waltham I was present with my Turbulent (G-AJCP) as the reserve aircraft, whilst the one HRH was to fly was spanking brand new and specially prepared by Norman Jones. He was the owner of Rollasons who made it and Chairman of the Tiger Club who owned it. Also present was the Belgian Tipsy Nipper 00- NIP flown by their Chief Test Pilot. As we waited, with a space all cleared on the perimeter track for the Royal entourage to arrive, we were surprised when a small red Mini drew up and a large man began to emerge, backwards. We were just about to hustle away this trespasser when it was realised that the emerging posterior was Royal, and that HRH had arrived, unaccompanied in a borrowed Mini, and was searching on the back seat for his flying kit. He was then duly briefed on the Turbulent, took off and disappeared for forty minutes. Later, we learned that he had gone off to Windsor, shot up the castle containing his admiring wife and, in fact, behaved like many other young pilots before him.

Having, as Commandant of the CFS, had something to do with the selection of instructors who taught Prince Philip to fly, I was well aware that he was a pilot of exceptional ability. His son, Prince Charles, has the same skill, and I remember one of his instructors reporting that Prince Charles was just the sort of officer we needed to command one of our fast jet squadrons. At the Mansion House, Prince Philip went on to say, 'There are few things more enjoyable than to fly in a small aeroplane over our beautiful English countryside'. With this comment, I can only concur.

Apart from the routine administration of the Air League and the three major tasks described, two other things stand out. One was purely administration. When Londonderry House was sold, the Air League and the Royal Aero Club lost our homes. The Royal Aero Club lost its long time Club House in Piccadilly and finally ended up in a shared office with the British Gliding Association in Leicester. For a couple of years the Royal Aero Club occupied rooms in the basement of Artillery Mansions in Victoria Street. There, presided over by John Blake, it maintained a presence in London and preserved something of its status as the oldest and premier flying club in the United Kingdom. It was also the representative of this country in International Sporting Aviation. Finally, the Royal Aero Club lost its place in Artillery Mansions, and disappeared to what was little more than an accommodation address in Leicester. The Royal Aero Club had once ranked in status and prestige with the Royal Aeronautical Society. The Royal Aero Club was organised at its school at Eastchurch, the flying training of the founder pilots of the Royal Naval Air Service. It had been the national authority until 1918 for the granting of both service and civil pilot licences. The Club had supervised the British entries and eventual win in perpetuity of the Schneider Trophy Races and conducted its affairs from one of the best clubs in London.

With the decline of the Royal Aero Club, my own involvement in the various sections of amateur and sporting flying increased. From being a member of the

Royal Aero Club Committee I became involved as their representative with the popular Flying Association with my old friend. Group Captain Johnny Kent, DFC, AFC had been the Commander of the Polish Wing at Northolt in 1942-43 and had been awarded the Polish equivalent of the Victoria Cross. Our task was to investigate the disappearance of some thirty small Aeronca-Jap engines, which the RAC had obtained for the PFA. We never solved that mystery.

I was still closely involved with the RAF Gliding and Soaring Association. Because of this I was invited by Philip Wills, National Gliding Champion and Founder President of the British Gliding Association (BGA), to become a member of the BGA council. My special duty was accident investigation. This was a fascinating analytical task which also enabled me to visit and to fly with most of the gliding clubs in the country. Many I could visit by air in my own little Druine Turbulent. In the course of such visits I could indulge in Air League propaganda to recruit not a few new Air League members. Accident prevention is closely allied to training standards and flying discipline. It was in part due to my work that the BGA enforced its constituent clubs to improve training and to insist upon better discipline. Some years later the BGA took on a national coach. This was a full time paid appointment for a specialist and experienced gliding instructor whose duties among gliding clubs are not unlike those of the CFS examiners of the RAF, and from which source the idea originated.

Work which occupied a good deal of my time came under the heading of Air Education. This stemmed from two roots. The first was in the person of Mrs Gwen Alston, an HM Inspector of Schools. She had worked as a scientist at the Royal Aeronautical Establishment at Farnborough. Her husband, a flight test observer, had been killed in the course of some hazardous wartime work, to the best of my belief flying aircraft into balloon cables to test cable cutting services. Thereafter, Gwen Alston devoted her great abilities to interesting young people in schools in aviation. In this campaign, she sought help from the Air League.

In my earlier career, first in Air Ministry Intelligence, and later as Manager of the Air League's *Air Pictorial* I had become interested and impressed with the French attitude to Air Education. In 1912, when the Air League was founded, the French led the world in flying. In the First World War the French Air Force, with aces such as Guynemar, Nungesser and Fonck became the pride of France. In the interwar years the French Air Force, and its supporting industry, were regarded as pre-eminent in Europe. In the post-Second World War period the French sought to rebuild their national pride in many ways. These included their education system, a stern rebuilding of their armed forces, and an emphasis on the flying service and its traditions. The practical effects of this policy were to be seen in the establishment at Government expense, of a system of flying and gliding schools throughout France. The elementary flying schools provided instruction in aviation activities and elementary gliding training, corresponding roughly to that available for our own Air Training Corps Graduates from these many schools could proceed, at government expense, to advanced schools where they could take courses in mountain and wave soaring, or parachuting, or lay the foundations of becoming aircraft engineers and designers. It was upon such foundations that the new and efficient French Air Force was rebuilt, and firms like Dassault producing such aircraft as the world-beating Mirage fighters.

Gwen Alston foresaw all this. My part was to help in the creation of the Air Education and Recreation Organisation, for which I later received the Air League Founders Medal. This organisation by the Air League sought to achieve its aims via three main routes. The first, largely through Gwen Alston and the HMI's, was to introduce into school curricula, aviation examples to illustrate everyday subjects. More directly, a school would be studying the development of Roman England or industrial England. As part of this study, an aircraft would be chartered to fly the students over the area of study, pointing out old Roman roads, the natural features which led to the establishment of ports, roads and, in much later years, railways, conurbations, and the shape of England as it became. Another activity was sponsored flying training. A number of county councils were persuaded to put up money to help selected students to learn to fly. After a good start with some six councils and flying clubs taking part, the scheme lost impetus. Out of this, however, grew the independent Air Education and Recreational Organisation (AERO) under the initial Presidency of Clive Hunting. It revived the Flying Scholarships schemes, work in schools, and continued the work of Air Education.

It was because of the Air League that I became involved in the amateur side of civil flying, concerned with sailplanes and gliders, light aircraft of all sorts, and the clubs, schools and individuals who flew them. One organisation of importance was the Tiger Club. It was based at Redhill and operated under the benevolent dictatorship of the redoubtable Norman Jones, owner of Rollasons Aircraft at Croydon. The club had a vast stock of Tiger Moth parts, spares and whole aircraft. Originally devoted to Tiger Moths, the Tiger Club and Rollasons went on to introduce a whole series of excellent French light aircraft, some of which they built under licence. One of these was my own little single seat Druine Turbulent, with cockpit, instruments and seat specially tailored to my own needs.

The popular Flying Association came to life shortly after the end of the Second World War. It had the object of making possible cheap flying by group co-ownership of small aircraft, coupled with special licensing arrangements permitting group owners to do much of their own maintenance. This was made feasible when the Civil Aviation Authority granted powers to the Popular Flying Association (PFA) to issue its own permits to fly in lieu of the more restrictive and costly Certificate of Airworthiness. The Permit to Fly system was limited to small aircraft only and never permitted for any aircraft flying for hire or for clubs giving flying instruction.

In due course the PFA applied this licensing system to homebuilt aircraft. Under the early leadership of Group Captain Edward Mole, Frank Parker and the technical expertise of John Walker, at that time an engineer with Miles Engineering at Shoreham, the PFA became leaders in Europe in home building. They were second only to the much bigger and more commercial Experimental Aircraft Association (EAA) in the United States, led by Paul Poberezny.

It was in December 1967 that the Chairman of the PFA, Frank Parker, invited me to become its President. This was an honour which I gladly accepted, and was formally installed on 1 January 1968. Thereafter I attended nearly all PFA Council meetings held usually at the Royal Aero Club in London. An exception was one held in the basement of the Army & Navy Club in Pall Mall. At this we found ourselves in competition with a Ghurkha Pipe Band working up for their performance that evening at the Ghurkha Reunion upstairs. The club basement, with echoing tiled lavatories on a Victorian baronial scale constitutes an unequalled noise chamber. Our meeting was quite unable to match the squeaks, howls and the thunderous din of the Ghurkha pipers. The problem was resolved with copious whisky and it was then we discovered that the pipes were not the only Hibernian custom taken up by those very brave and loyal men from Nepal.

The PFA had about 400 members, and owned between them some 150 small aeroplanes, many of them home built. Membership comprised an amazing collection of designers and craftsmen whose handiwork in wood, metal, fabric and engines equalled the best to be found in any aircraft factory. Often one man would spend four years or more building his own aeroplane. Quite early on the PFA began to organise an Annual Rally at which the most prestigious award was for the best home build.

These annual PFA rallies tied up very conveniently with the interest of the Air League in Air Education and the creation of the Air Educational & Recreation Organisation. In October 1964 we had already established a number of Flying Scholarships at various flying clubs. The object was to provide up to thirty hours flying training for boys and girls selected by three Local Education Authorities in conjunction with the committee of the club concerned. The flying was paid for jointly by the Local Education Authority, the parents and local benevolent sponsors. The Air League and AERO were at pains to emphasise that we were not in competition with the RAF oriented Air Training Corps. Our object was to interest the brightest and best boys and girls in all aspects of aviation and, in particular, its importance in the future development of our own country. In this we were, at first, notably successful. I note in my flying log book that at a Flying Scholarship Air Day at Swanton Morley in October 1964 I flew with a number of our scholars. They were impressive apt pilots, intelligent, and were in equal numbers of boys and girls. Early in 1965 we bought an autogyro for the Swanton Morley scholars. After a promising start, this proved unsuccessful and they reverted to flying conventional light aircraft. I remember with delight being one of a trio taking part in an Air Day display at Swanton Morley, flying Wallis Autogyros. Later I did some test flying at Shoreham on a similar autogyro in which both the RAF and Army Air Corps were interested. It was being demonstrated for the makers (Beagle Aircraft) by my good friend Pee-Wee Judge. Sadly at the Farnborough Air Show the following year it killed him.

The problem with autogyros is that the rotor depends upon positive G to keep its rotation and thus its lift. Negative G destroys this rotating force. This is quite unlike a helicopter in which the rotor is driven by the engine. I have experienced engine failure on more than one occasion flying an autogyro. The automatic instinct of a fixed wing pilot when the engine fails is to stuff the stick forward (i.e. nose down) to maintain speed. In an autogyro this instinctive response imposes negative forces on the rotor, which loses speed, and so loses lift. I was lucky. On one such episode, climbing out and at about 250 feet, the engine seized solid. I followed the fixed wing pilot's instinct to stuff the stick forward and, of course, the rotor speed decayed, but its rotational inertia kept it going long enough for me to collect my wits, and I landed, undamaged, in a field of carrots.

It was in July 1969 that we organised the first big popular Flying Association Rally in conjunction with AERO. The aerodrome at Sywell, under the direction of Mike Newton and in conjunction with the long established Northamptonshire Aero Club, had been among those prominent in helping the Air League start its Flying Scholarships. At that time some ten boys and girls were learning to fly under the scheme. Mike Newton's father, Charles, a former Mayor of Northampton, was one of the founders in 1920 of the Northamptonshire Aero Club and an enthusiastic member of the Air League Council. We launched what we called the F3 Rally (Flying for Fun). About 250 aeroplanes flew in, many of them home built. I helped judge the competition for the best home built, and flew several of them. The following year we repeated the two day event under the title of F4 (Further Flying for Fun). In further years the event grew and grew until it outgrew Sywell and moved to Leicester East. From there it moved to Cranfield, and on it's twentieth anniversary, in 1989, over 1,100 visiting aircraft flew in. This made it the biggest gathering of amateur aviators in Europe since the great event in Rheims in 1910.

It was during the 1960s that my three children were married. In 1966 Simon married Maria Elvira in Argentina and provided our first grandson, Azalea married Philip Mayhew and the following year Timothy married Deborah Boyd Martin.

It was after 1966 that I became increasingly unhappy about the Air League and my position in it as its Secretary General. Joe Fogarty had retired, and it seemed to me that the Air League was losing its sense of direction, becoming less interested in flying and more interested in lobbying. AERO became a separate organisation, with Clive Hunting as its President. Finally, the Air League gave me the sack and on 12 February 1971 I ceased to be its Secretary General.

CHAPTER FOURTEEN
THE LAST YEARS

Leaving the Air League had a number of benefits amongst which was the fact that I became President and Chairman of the Winchester Division of the Soldiers, Sailors and Airmen's Families Association (SSAFA). I was able to do more flying and to write Air Test Reports for the now independent *Air Pictorial* (the Air League had sold the magazine).This earned me a bit of valuable extra income so, in effect, I was still getting paid to fly. Sometimes manufacturers would buy extra copies of these reports for publicity purposes, but on other occasions products were submitted for test which I had to criticise severely. One such was a small amphibian flying boat which I condemned as unsafe. I was proved right when it later suffered a bad accident.

Finally, of course, I was able to spend more time at home; in the garden, in the house and with my family. It was during the summer after my retirement that Rosemary became seriously ill. This was in July 1971. Being at home I was able to look after her, but in the end there was nothing for it but hospitalisation. By the autumn of 1971 it seemed that all was well again and things returned to normal, or so it seemed. But looking back, I think it was at this time that her final illness was beginning. It was cancer and by the autumn of 1974, it was evident that something was seriously wrong. In early the next year a prolonged hospital visit and investigation resulted in the shattering verdict of inoperable cancer. I remember in 1939 Winston Churchill's memorable phrase as war became inevitable 'The lights are going out all over Europe'. As 1975 continued into the spring and early summer, my dearly loved Rosemary's light flickered and dimmed until, on 16 July 1975, it was finally extinguished.

After the funeral I went away for three weeks, motoring through the west and south of the country until it seemed time to come home again. I had, earlier in the year, resigned from several jobs; from the Parish council, from the local Committee of the RAF Association; and from SSAFA. I continued as Chairman of our School Managers, and President of the Popular Flying Association, and did a lot more flying.

I continued to fly until May 1978. Flying provided a lonely but effectual solace. I was able to become totally absorbed in the exploration of the qualities of some new aeroplane, or sailplane, and in writing about it afterwards. The resulting articles for *Air Pictorial* provided a useful supplement to my pension, but the real benefit was therapeutic.

Then, in 1978, a British Airways Trident, taking off from Heathrow, suffered an appalling accident, killing everybody on board (in fact the Trident flight BE548 had crashed on 18 June 1972). The subsequent enquiry established that the captain, despite having recently passed a full medical, had suffered a massive and fatal heart attack (it was not possible to conduct a post-mortem to confirm this). I never did understand why his two assistant pilots, both of whom had not long before qualified at the College of Air Training at Hamble, were unable to take over. This concerned me, for I had been a severe critic of Hamble methods and standards, and the accident reinforced my opinions. The direct effect on me was that the authorities imposed much stricter medicals on those they termed 'elderly pilots', and seemed determined to fail anybody over seventy. Caught in this trap were my friends Alan Wheeler and Douglas Bader and myself. Legless Douglas Bader's survival for so long was a miracle of determination anyway and (to make a bad pun) he had not a leg to stand on.

Alan Wheeler spent a lot of money on specialist doctors to argue his case, and won a reluctant and costly one year's remission. They condemned me as having 'an irregular heartbeat', only one eye and various bits missing, including parts of my left arm, and being decrepit.

It was a great blow and, for a long time, I could not bear to go near or see an aeroplane. I resigned as President of the PFA because I could no longer practice what I preached. I gave my firm opinion that the President of the PFA must always be an active pilot. Finally I consoled myself to some extent by remembering that I had been an active pilot for over fifty years. I also discovered that when it finally expired, my civil license, No 1179, was the oldest still current. The PFA was kind enough to make me an Honorary Life Member.

It was during the black time too that I lost all three members of my 98 Squadron crew. Bill Williams in 1979 and after him both Zdenek Kokes and Mich. There were sad memories too of other close friends of earlier days: Harry Burke, Daddy Emms and Josh Braithwaite, to name only three.

Life became dull, flat and rather aimless. I owed much to my Sussex spaniels and of course my daughter Azalea. She still found time to pay frequent visits and when in 1981 I became ill it was Azalea who took me to hospital in Winchester. It was also her home that I went to for convalescence. After a fortnight I returned home. Hospital had made me think and to realise that however bad one's own state there were always many others so much worse. In the ward there were many such and when I became mobile my job became assistant tea boy. This resulted in getting to know my fellow patients. The ward contained all sorts and experience in it convinced me that seclusion in a private room, unless in intensive care, is to be avoided. I felt myself welcome in a small, tight community where I could be useful and, in particular to William Stanley.

William Stanley was a former RAF Corporal who had served in Burma. He returned to civil life after the war. He was in hospital having undertaken a sponsored parachute jump for charity. The training given in the civil school was abysmal and the drop, made in adverse conditions, had broken both his legs. One was repairable, but despite six hours on the operating table the other proved too shattered to mend and was amputated. I became his personal tea boy and wheelchair chauffeur. More than others in that ward he taught me not to moan in adversity and to make the best of it. Later William became Secretary of the Portsmouth branch of the Burma Star Association and we stayed in touch.

When I came home I was shamed if you like into taking a grip on things. My first job was to recover the dogs from the kennels and then to get the house and garden going again. I then settled down to a task I had wanted to do for some time. This was to recreate the last working drawings of the First World War Short 184 seaplane. This was the same plane whose remnants resided in the Fleet Air Arm Museum at Yeovilton. My old friend and shipmate Dennis White was the director there. The task involved much reading, visits to firms that had built great numbers of the type and research into all sorts of archives. The results, after three years hard work, were complete working drawings from which a similar aircraft or replica could be built. I hope that one day a true full-size replica may indeed be made.

From this absorbing task developed another. The engine of the Short 184 was a 225hp Sunbeam. It was a fascinating 1914 design and quite new to me. It led to the discovery that about half of the front line aircraft used by the Royal Naval Air Service in the First World War were powered by Sunbeam aero-engines. They had been designed by the Frenchman Louis Coatalen.

This led to another period of lengthy and widespread research. In this I was much helped by the Fleet Air Arm Museum, the RAF Museum, the Science Museum and many others. The work took three years to complete. The Royal Aeronautical Society, by paying for their copies, covered the production costs and I was indebted to Avril Turner, who was able to turn my jumbled writings into proper shape and made a good final product.

In parallel with these tasks I returned to duty with SSAFA and other ex-service organisations. In particular I became involved in the creation of the 90 Squadron Association, whose architect was Jim Munro. We held our first reunion at Mildenhall in September 1980. It was attended by over 200 former squadron members and their families, including many from overseas and crews who had not met together since 1945. It was an amazing gathering and has been repeated every September since. I was greatly honoured to be elected as the first Association President with my good friend Alan Scott as its most able Chairman. Later Alan succeeded me as President and his place was taken by Eric Richardson. Much to my surprise and delight, I was then elected Patron in succession to the great Australian Hughie Edwards, VC who in 1938 was our squadron Adjutant.

It was shortly after becoming Patron that we investigated the possibility of producing a squadron history. We could find no publisher who was interested, nor could we find, after a multitude of enquiries, any reputable author willing to tackle it. After hanging fire for two years I offered, as a last resort, to have a go myself. At the AGM in September 1985 the Association invited me to proceed.

Years before, with the intention of producing it himself, Jim Munro had accumulated rooms full of letters, personal reminiscences, photographs and battle orders; an overwhelming wealth of information from sources all over the world. Jim's plans were frustrated by his long illness and death, leaving his school teacher wife, Kay Munro, to care for this collection. I took over the papers, whilst George Jeffery later took over the photographs. Meanwhile Kay patiently transcribed much of Jim's records which were on tapes, many dictated during his final illness when writing became impossible. In the autumn of 1985 I began the daily task of sorting, cataloguing, analysing and selection from this mass of information.

It was about this time that I became aware that life was no longer an uphill effort. In fact the future began to look rather exciting. The cause of this was one Mollie Denise Samuels. I met Mollie in 1985. She had just bought a cottage in our village. I pushed my luck at a garden party and asked if she might consider coming to have a bite to eat. She turned me down, but undaunted she agreed to see me the following year and on 4 July 1987 we were married.

My grandson, Angus, was my best man and Mollie was given away by her cousin, Jack Starr. Jack served in the RAF during the war as an Air Navigator. We later discovered that he and I must have been operating within a few miles of each other over Normandy on D-night. Mollie looked quite superb and the speeches were much enjoyed and appreciated. The principle speaker was Mollie's long term friend John Harris (Lord Harris of Greenwich).

The following day we flew to Skiathos to begin our honeymoon properly in the Aegean where we had a hillside villa for a fortnight. We left Gatwick in a BAC1-11. It was the first time I'd been airborne since losing my licence, and whilst crossing Germany at 36,000 feet (to avoid thunderstorm tops) I realised that I'd never been so high before. Mollie, a seasoned long haul air traveller, took it all in her stride, and over a glass of wine told the stewardess that I used to like flying but was now a trifle nervous. This got me free whisky.

At the 1987 Squadron Reunion in September I presented Mollie to the assembled Association members as the reason for my inability to finish the squadron history on time. Later, Mollie gave me much help, and together with the processing skills of Avril Turner, the final draft was completed. We found a printer and David Dorrell helped with the editing. It was published by the 90 Squadron Association entitled *Sing High* and was ready and on sale at the 1989 reunion. The final result was a sell out. In consequence the Association was, after keeping a small sum for its funds, able to present a cheque for £1,500 to the RAF Benevolent Fund and a further £560 to the RAF Association for new furniture in its convalescent home at Sussex Down. We had already given a special orthopaedic bed to Sussex Down in memory of Jim Munro.

In the autumn of 1988 Mollie and I went to Australia via Hong Kong. The object was to visit Bill Meecham (ex RAAF) in Perth, relations and friends in Melbourne and Sydney, and to see the Barrier Reef. We left Heathrow in a British Airways Boeing 747 Jumbo on 20 October 1988 to fly direct and non-stop to Hong Kong.

Boarding at 07.45 am in the dark, via a door in the side was more akin to departure by sea than anything which I had previously experienced by air. I also found the tight packed seating not altogether to my liking. On the other hand, there were compensations. My experienced wife got the best available seats, with a window, on the port side near the tail. Here, in the morning we were treated to breath-taking views over the northern Plains of India. The snow covered Himalayas, icy-bright in the sun, formed the back drop to this scene in which Mount Everest stood out quite clearly above all the rest. The first surprise, however, was when, during pre-supper drinks, Captain O'Grady announced that we were over the Frisian Islands and would soon be over the Baltic and crossing into Russia. We were then at 39,000 feet and I thought of all the RAF Stirlings of Bomber Command which, forty-five years earlier, had struggled through cloud and ice across the North Sea, unable to get much higher than 13,000 feet. In our 747 all the weather was far below.

Our route, just south of Leningrad over central Russia and the Aral Sea revealed, at first light, the brown grey hills of Afghanistan. At midday local time, we flew across India, Burma and into China. At Canton, we began our descent and landed, again in the dark, in Hong Kong on the runway of what was once the small grass aerodrome of Kai-Tak, used mainly by the pre-war Fleet Air Arm. I was terrified to see our wing tips brushing past skyscrapers, and the captain's use of full reverse thrust to prevent our Jumbo from continuing off the far end of the runway. This only added to my feelings of apprehension but needless to say we landed perfectly safely.

Eventually we landed in Perth and after making our visits we headed for Sydney, where we were able to enjoy a flight in a small float seaplane. We flew up the coast and all round the vast harbour where, at one moment, I thought our pilot was about to take us under the Sydney Harbour bridge. The seaplane was a de Havilland of Canada (DHC) Otter, and my first ride in a seaplane since the Sea Tiger at Lee-on-the-Solent.

From Sydney we flew once more by Qantas to Cairns in Northern Queensland, and then Brisbane before returning home to Heathrow.

In 1989 Mollie and I were officials at the Country Landowners Association (CLA) Game Fair at Stratfield Saye, home of the Duke of Wellington. 1989 was also the year in which I was invited to become President of the Central Flying School Association. Personally, I considered it should have been somebody younger but was persuaded to accept, and indeed it would have been difficult to refuse such an honour. The President is always a former Commandant and holds office for five years. The Chairman is the current Commandant and the Patron a very senior Officer who has served on the CFS staff. The Patron was Air Chief Marshal Sir Alastair Steedman who, as Wing Commander Steedman, was Chief Flying Instructor at South Cerney when I was Commandant.

The annual event is the reunion, always held at CFS. At this we hold the AGM of the Association and there is a flying display in which the CFS aerobatic team, currently the Red Arrows, always take part and a dinner. At this dinner, it is traditional that the Chief of the Air Staff is invited as Guest of Honour in his first year in that appointment. In other years it has been men of distinction such as Sir Raymond Lygo (Head of British Aerospace), the Prince of Wales and, when I was commandant, Lord Trenchard, father of the RAF. It is always a very special occasion, both privileged and private. The Commandant-in-Chief was Her Majesty, the Queen Mother.

The Queen Mother's ninethieth birthday was on 4 August 1990. Naturally CFS and the CFS Association wanted to give her a birthday present. Through her Private Secretary, Sir Alistair Aird it was found that Her Majesty would be delighted to accept an awning to go over the sunbed on the balcony at Royal Lodge, her home when at Windsor. The size, shape, colour and design were duly decided and approved. It would be Royal blue and, on the front fringe, there would be the CFS coat of arms.

It was with surprise and delight that I found myself summoned to accompany Sir Alastair Steedman and the Commandant, Bruce Latton, to make the formal presentation at Royal Lodge. Accordingly, the three of us duly met at the park gate where we were admitted, and presented to the Royal party. Looking back I think that wonderful day at Royal Lodge marked both the climax and the beginning of the end of my RAF orientated life.

The change was gradual, of course. I completed my five year tour as President of the CFS Association, dutifully attending the annual reunions. Two of our guests on these occasions were Marshal of the RAF, Sir Peter Harding, and his successor as Chief of the Air Staff, Sir Michael Graydon.

My final year was saddened by the sudden death of Frank Dodd, my former Chief Flying Instructor at CFS and predecessor in office as President of our Association, of Sir Alastair Steedman, our Patron; and of Marshal of the RAF Sir Dermot Boyle. I had the great honour of being one of the three who escorted the Cranwell cadets who carried the cushion bearing Sir Dermot's decorations, honours and awards in a slow march up the aisle of St Clements Dane where they were placed on the altar.

At Frank Dodd's funeral I was invited by his family to give the address. I accepted with misgivings for it seemed to me difficult to do justice to a man of such distinction and achievement. In 1939 he had been reading agriculture at Reading University, planning to become a farmer. Like so many similar young men, when the war came, he promptly joined up and was selected for pilot training. He proved very good and was the pilot whose reconnaissance from northern Scotland at extreme range discovered the hiding place of the German ship, *Tirpitz*, in a fjord in Norway. His aircraft actually ran out of petrol as he landed back home and was unable to taxi back to the hangars. Frank waited while his photographs were developed, offering to go again at once if they were not good enough. Fortunately they were. As my Chief Instructor at CFS he proved himself exceptional, with wonderful skills as a pilot and even more important, a sympathetic understanding of his pupils' difficulties and problems; a rare combination.

Alastair Steedman's sudden death set me a problem for, coming near the end of my five year term as President of the CFS Association, I had to find not only his successor but mine as well. The search for a Patron became a farce when I discovered that Sir Alastair, not long before he died and without telling me, had invited another Air Marshal to take over. This one, waiting in the wings, was peeved with me because I had failed to make contact. It was therefore, with some relief, that I found my old friend, Sir John Severne, former Captain of the Queens Flight, willing to take over from me. I was happy and thankful to leave everything in his capable hands and so it was that, in 1994, I attended my last CFS reunion, with John Severne installed in my place as President.

On 1 March 1990 Mollie and I left the UK bound for Egypt. We landed in Heliopolis. The RAF aerodrome I had known in 1938 had now become a vast international airport. We arrived with, we were told, 4,000 other tourists on that same day and took hours to get through immigration and customs. One day we shared a guide with two charming Americans. Led by our tour guide we visited the magnificent but very crowded Cairo Museum, the Citadel and the Pyramids. Mollie and the American lady climbed up inside the big one, queuing with a thousand others to share the claustrophobia, smells and fetid air inside. The American and I sat outside where I listened to his tales of the Pacific war as an US Marine officer. At one point he and his patrol were cut off by Japanese and in a bad situation. He told me how, completely surrounded on all sides, the Japanese commander had emerged from the jungle demanding the Marines to surrender. They refused. The Japanese commander then challenged him to single-handed combat. In a fight to the death he disarmed his opponent and strangled him, at which point the Japanese melted away silently into the jungle and he and his Marine patrol made good their escape. The Colonel was a big man and attributed his victory to having been a well-trained American footballer.

After a fortnight we embarked for home in a BOAC Tri-star manned by a former British Caledonian crew, and commanded by Captain Albrecht. Mollie rapidly found us the best seats in the aeroplane in the very front on the starboard side. Nothing in front and lots of leg room, but shortly after this I realised that she was missing. I became worried, but she re-appeared just before the doors were shut. The explanation came soon. It happened that the BOAC resident engineer at Heliopolis was an old gliding acquaintance. He had greeted us on first arrival and was there again to see us off. Mollie, having noted this, had gone to ask him to ask the captain if I could visit the flight deck. Unbeknown to me all this was arranged by radio between the engineer and the captain. The first I knew of it was an invitation to the flight deck where I sat in the rumble seat for the push out from the parking bay, through start up and take-off, and until we were over Crete. After a brief supper and drink I was allowed to return there and stayed until final shut down after landing at Gatwick.

At first everything looked familiar. But it wasn't. What looked like the familiar artificial horizon turned out to be part of the flight director system. It can be told the course, height and speed to maintain, to fly to a particular beacon, to climb, to maintain a given Mach number and much else. Another installation was the radar. This one, a development of the old wartime H2S gave a plan view of the ground and sea below. From 36,000 feet it showed most of the eastern Mediterranean, with the African coastline astern, and Crete and the Greek mainland ahead.

Albrecht and his crew, the second pilot and the flight engineer, took great pleasure in explaining everything to me. It was, as you can imagine, a memorable experience. But more than this, for it was a clear fine night. From over Paris, itself a blaze of lights, the south coast of England became visible. There was a line of silver and gold lights from each town and village all the way from Portsmouth to Thanet. Nearer to us was the coast of France, and in between the darkness of the Channel, with only the faint pinprick of lights of ships and sometimes other aircraft visible. It was an unforgettable sight and, thanks to Mollie, an amazing climax to a marvellous holiday. It was only the second time I had sat in an aircraft cockpit, or I should say flight deck, since I lost my licence in 1978. I enjoyed it enormously.

About a month after our return, we went to see the aviation artist Edmund Miller on completion of his picture, commissioned by Mollie, for me. It is a magnificent composition depicting 98 Squadron in an attack on a German fortified position near Caen during the Normandy landings in 1944. I led this attack and so the picture shows my Mitchell with its special insignia in the lead. The painting was exhibited at the show for aviation artists before we got it, where it won an award.

After a couple of enjoyable holidays with Mollie in 1991 and 1992, the fiftieth anniversary of the end of the Second World War loomed in 1995. This was a particularly poignant year for many of us, especially those of us who took part in the 1939-45 conflict. We never can or will forget our comrades or our experiences and memories of these difficult times.

At the VE Day Service held on Sunday, 7 May at St John's Parish Church, Alresford, I read the following to the congregation.

At 8.00 am on the 5th May fifty years ago, the German forces in Holland surrendered. I was with my crew in Brussels. One of them came from Amsterdam. He had not seen his family since 1940. All we knew was that they were still there and, like all Holland, near starvation.

By 9.00 am we were on the way in a borrowed jeep loaded with food. Brussels to Eindhoven to Nijmegen, over the river and on to Arnhem, the Bridge too Far. All around remains of burned out tanks, broken gliders, wrecked houses. Out of one stood the tail of a Spitfire that had plunged into it. After Oosterbeck we picked our way through lone convoys of sullen, grey clad German troops, all still fully armed.

By 6.00 pm we were in Amsterdam and present at a wonderful family reunion. That evening we learned how they had lived. No coal, no heat, no electricity through the coldest winter of the war. All they had was a tiny stove. It burned chippings from the wooden paving blocks pulled up from the road outside. All the trees had long since gone. For food, two sisters, aged twelve and fourteen, scoured the countryside on bicycles. No bicycle tyres, they wound rope onto the wheel rims, concealed in the rope they carried messages for the Resistance.

Their father had an aerial concealed in a chimney, and a radio hidden in a cellar. Their lifeline was the BBC. All this despite their house being only a few doors away from the Gestapo Headquarters.

The next day we met a few family friends. One in particular I can never forget. A girl of about twenty. Very beautiful, and ashamed of being well fed when all around were starved. She was Jewish. She had that day got out of a prison camp. A camp where people like her were prepared for unspeakable medical experiments in Germany. She was lucky. Those before her were not.

This meeting brought home to me as never before the total evil of Hitler's Nazi Regime. And what could have happened here if we had lost the war.

We did not lose because many thousands gave their lives to fight that evil. The debt we owe them can never be repaid.

But fifty years on we can think of the survivors. Elderly, and sometimes lonely veterans. Those left permanently damaged in mind or body. The widows who can no longer care for themselves. This is the special task of the Service Associations here today, and all minded to help them.

For me it is well summed up in something I want to read to you now, it was written by John Pudney:

> 'Do not despair
> For Johnny Head-in-Air
> He sleeps as sound
> As Johnny under ground
> Fetch out no shroud
> For Johnny in the Cloud
> And keep your tears
> For him in after years
>
> Better by far
> For Johnny the Bright Star
> To keep your head
> And see his children fed.'

This is what I have strived to do. So it was a very moving and indeed humbling, experience for me to find that the full congregation were clapping and applauding as I returned to my seat.

And so, dear family, it is at this point that I cease to write history and hope that you may find something in my story which will interest, entertain or amuse you. I have been granted a most wonderful life and as I approach my ninetieth birthday, I look back with gratitude to a life filled with action and personal fulfilment. I would just like to pay special tribute to you all who have played such a large part in this, and in turn wish you good health, a richness of life, and the giving and receiving of love such as you have given me. I thank you and bless you with all my heart.

Finally to Mollie. There is no way I can ever express in words my feelings for her. The best I can do is to try by total devotion and love to show how much I treasure the new life she has given me, and hope that I will always be able to give her something like the wonderful happiness she makes for me. Bless Her!

Now my Love, what's the plan for TODAY?

Let's get on with it!

G.J.C. Paul – in the year 1997

Sadly, Mollie, the driving force behind getting this book published, died unexpectedly on January 8, 2012.

APPENDIX 1
RECORD OF RAF SERVICE

SERVICE ROLE	DATE COMMENCED	DATE ENDED
Reserve of Air Force Officers	25 June 1927	31 August 1929
Cambridge University Air Squadron	1 September 1927	26 July 1929
No 1 FTS Netheravon	1 September 1929	11 February 1930
No 13 (Army Cooperation) Squadron	12 February 1930	31 June 1930
RAF base Gosport and attachments to Leuchars and Calshot	1 July 1930	1 January 1931
446 Flight Fleet Air Arm (HMS *Courageous*)	1 January 1931	1 November 1931
RAF base Gosport	2 November 1931	4 August 1932
Home Aircraft Depot Henlow	5 August 932	1 June 1934
Lee-on-the-Solent	2 August 1934	5 June 1936
HQ Flight HMS *Furious*	6 June 1936	2 May 1938
No 90 (Bomber Squadron) Bicester	2 May 1938	23 January 1939
RAF Staff College Andover	24 January 1939	26 August 1939
HQ AASF Rheims	26 August 1939	1 February 1940
Air Ministry	2 February 1940	8 July 1940
No 1 (Bomber Group) HQ Hucknall	9 July 1940	30 November 1940
No 150 (Bomber Squadron) Newton	1 December 1940	22 June 1941
HQ Bomber Command	23 June 1941	12 November 1941
HQ Flying Training Command	13 November 1941	1 January 1943
Air Staff College Camberley at Minley Manor	2 January 1943	27 February 1944
No 13 OTU Refresher	28 February 1944	18 May 1944
No 98 (Bomber Squadron) 2 Group to Command	19 May 1944	18 September 1944
HQ 2 Group (2TAF)	19 September 1944	20 October 1944
No 2 Group Support Unit to Command	20 October 1944	3 March 1945
No 13 OTU to Command	30 March 1945	6 November 1946
HQ British Air Forces of Occupation Germany	7 November 1946	13 June 1948
British Joint Services Mission Washington, USA	30 July 1948	4 August 1948
USAF Air War College, Maxwell Field, Alabama, USA	10 August 1948	14 June 1949
Air Ministry, London, Intelligence Branch	22 August 1949	31 December 1952
Imperial Defence College	1 January 1953	31 December 1953
Commandant RAF Central Flying School, Little Rissington	1 January 1954	17 January 1956
HQ British Forces in Aden	18 February 1956	14 February 1957
Air Ministry, Director of Operational Training	1 June 1957	6 October 1958
Secretary General of the Air League	8 October 1958	12 February 1971
President Popular Flying Association	1 January 1968	July 1978

APPENDIX 2

BATTLE FLIGHTS WHILST LEADING 98 SQUADRON

Extract of flying log book. Flying Officer I. M. Williams. Pilot on all operational sorties Wing Commander G. J. C. Paul.

DATE	HOUR	AIRCRAFT	DUTY	REMARKS
20/05/44	1115	Mitchell FW189A	Navigator/bomb aimer	Operation – formation leader/6 aircraft. Target – 3 x 240mm railway guns, SANGATTE. 8 x 500 MC bombs. Slight flak – Calais. Bombs on right of target area.
22/05/44	1845	Mitchell FW189A	Navigator/bomb aimer	Operation – formation leader/6 aircraft. Target – railway engine sheds, DOUAI. 8 x 500 MC bombs. Direct hits and overshoot.
24/05/44	1000	Mitchell FW189A	Navigator/bomb aimer	Operation – formation leader/6 aircraft. Target – EVREUX airfield dispersal areas. 8 x 500 MC bombs. Slight flak en route. Dispersal covered and hangar hit.
24/05/44	1810	Mitchell FW189A	Navigator/bomb aimer	Operation – formation leader/6 aircraft. Target – LILLE-VENDEVILLE airfield dispersal areas. 8 x 500 MC bombs. Flak barrage over airfield. Dispersal covered.
27/05/44	1800	Mitchell FW189A	Navigator/bomb aimer	Operation – formation leader/6 aircraft. Target – coastal guns LONGUES near BAYEUX. 4 x 1,000 MC bombs. All bombs in target area.
28/05/44	1405	Mitchell FW189A	Navigator/bomb aimer	Operation – formation leader/18 aircraft. Target – coastal guns QUEND near RUE 4 x 1,000 MC bombs. All bombs in target area, except own bombs which hung up. Later jettisoned in sea.
29/05/44	1435	Mitchell FV976S	Navigator/bomb aimer	Operation – formation leader/6 aircraft. Target – coastal guns DIEPPE. 8 x 500 MC bombs. Moderate accurate flak. 6 holes in fuselage. Some bombs in target remained at overshoot.
05/06/44	0215	Mitchell FW201C	Navigator/bomb aimer	Night operation – individual. Target – road/railway defile near THURY-HARCOURT. Abortive owing to 10/10 low cloud.

DATE	HOUR	AIRCRAFT	DUTY	REMARKS
06/06/44	0125	Mitchell FW201C	Navigator/bomb aimer	Night operation – individual. Target – road/railway defile near THURY-HARCOURT. 4 x 1,000 MC bombs dropped on target indicators. Target identified and hit.
07/06/44	2300	Mitchell FW201C	Navigator/bomb aimer	Night operation – individual. Target – VIRE railway station. 4 x 1,000 MC bombs dropped on estimated position of target. Many fires already burning in Vire.
16/06/44	1740	Mitchell FW189A	Navigator/bomb aimer	Operation – formation leader/18 aircraft. Target – ammunition dump NE of ALENCON. 8 x 500 MC bombs. Bombs in target area and overshoot.
17/06/44	1940	Mitchell FW189A	Navigator/bomb aimer	Operation – formation leader/24 aircraft. Target – MEZIDON railway marshalling yards. Bombed by GEE/H. 4 x 1,000 MC bombs. Slight flak en route. Target area covered. Many explosions observed through broken cloud.
18/06/44	1750	Mitchell FW189A	Navigator/bomb aimer	Operation – formation leader/18 aircraft. Target – ammunition dump NE of ALENCON Bombed by GEE/H. 8 x 500 MC bombs. Moderate flak en route. Two holes. Results not observed.
20/06/44	0745	Mitchell FW189A	Navigator/bomb aimer	Operation – formation leader/18 aircraft. Target – NOBALL SE of ABBEVILLE. 8 x 500 MC bombs. Moderate flak over bombing run. Target area covered.
21/06/44	1810	Mitchell FW189A	Navigator/bomb aimer	Operation – formation leader/6 aircraft. Target – NOBALL N of NEUFCHATEL Abortive owing to 10/10 low cloud in target area.
22/06/44	1800	Mitchell FW189A	Navigator/bomb aimer	Operation – formation leader/6 aircraft. Target – steel foundry NE of Caen. Converted into fortified strongpoint 1,000 yards ahead of our own troops. 8 x 500 MC bombs. Moderate heavy flak in target area. Bombs straddled aiming point.
25/06/44	1540	Mitchell FW102M	Navigator/bomb aimer	Operation – formation leader/6 aircraft. Target – Chateau E of BEAUVAIS headquarters of NOBALL commander Colonel Wachtel. 8 x 500 MC bombs. Some bombs on aiming point, remainder overshoot.

DATE	HOUR	AIRCRAFT	DUTY	REMARKS
27/06/44	2330	Mitchell FW189A	Radar navigator/bomb aimer	Night operation – individual. Target – troop concentrations at AMAYE SUR ORNE. Abortive owing to radar failure near target area.
06/07/44	1205	Mitchell FW189A	Navigator/bomb aimer	Operation – formation leader/6 aircraft. Target – fuel dump at CERENCES. 8 x 500 MC bombs. Slight flak, Coutances. All bombs in target area. No fires observed.
12/07/44	1700	Mitchell FW189A	Navigator/bomb aimer	Operation – formation leader/6 aircraft. Target – fuel dump at CHARTRES. 8 x 500 MC bombs. Slight extremely accurate flak SE of Dreux. Slight inaccurate flak over target. Cloud covered exact aiming point. Estimated target position bombed. Results unobserved.
15/07/44	2000	Mitchell FW189A	Radar navigator/bomb aimer	Operation – leader of first box of 6 aircraft, 3 boxes in all. Target – troop concentrations at EVRECY. Abortive owing to bad weather at beachhead.
20/07/44	1920	Mitchell FW189A	Radar navigator/bomb aimer	Operation – leader of first box of 6 aircraft, 3 boxes in all. Target – fuel dump at ARGENTAN. Abandoned over Channel. Impossible weather.
23/07/44	1510	Mitchell FW189A	Radar navigator/bomb aimer	Operation – leader of first box of 6 aircraft, 3 boxes in all. Target – rail yard at MONTFORT-SUR-RISLE. 8 x 500 MC bombs. Bombed by GEE/H through 10/10 cloud. Results unobserved.
24/07/44	1950	Mitchell FW189A	Navigator/bomb aimer	Operation – leader No 2 box of 6 aircraft, 3 boxes in all. Target – anti-tank concentrations holding up our troops in LA HOGUE WOOD, BOURQUEBUS SE OF CAEN. Abortive as No 2 of leading box received direct hit from flak, splitting up the formation. Intense flak from enemy battle line. Two holes, one in front cockpit.
25/07/44	0610	Mitchell FW189A	Navigator/bomb aimer	Operation – leader of first box of 6 aircraft, 3 boxes in all. Target – LA HOGUE WOOD. 8 x 500 MC bombs. Slight flak at target. All bombs in target area.

DATE	HOUR	AIRCRAFT	DUTY	REMARKS
26/07/44	0855	Mitchell FW102M	Navigator/bomb aimer	Operation – leader of first box of 6 aircraft, 3 boxes in all. Target – fuel dump at ALENCON. 8 x 500 MC bombs. Slight flak at TROUVILLE. All bombs on aiming point. Large fires indicate at least 4 large containers hit.
28/07/44	0020	Mitchell FW189A	Radar navigator/bomb aimer	Night operation – individual pathfinder. Target – wood near BOURQUEBUS SE of CAEN. Retiring point of enemy's armour by night. 4 x 500 MC bombs and four target indicators, laid by GEE/H over 10/10 low cloud for squadron main force.
31/07/44	1650	Mitchell FW189A	Radar navigator/bomb aimer	Operation – leader of first box of 6 aircraft, 3 boxes in all. Target – fuel dump at LIVAROT. Abortive. Impossible to achieve and maintain GEE/H approach line.
02/08/44	1800	Mitchell FW189A	Navigator/bomb aimer	Operation – leader of No 4 box of 6 aircraft Target – ammunition dump NW of ANGERS. 8 x 500 MC bombs. Aiming point obscured by bomb smoke. Bomb burst on aiming point and overshoot onto main dump.
04/08/44	1900	Mitchell FW189A	Radar navigator/bomb aimer	Operation – leader of first box of 6 aircraft, 18 aircraft in all. Target - railway yards at GLOS-SUR-RISLE. 8 x 500 MC bombs. Bombed by GEE/H through 8/10 cloud. Observed results. First bomb burst on aiming point. Remainder overshot.
05/08/44	1700	Mitchell FW189A	Radar navigator/bomb aimer	Operation - leader of first box of 6 aircraft, 18 aircraft in all. Target – railway yards at VERNEUIL. 8 x 500 MC bombs. Bombed by GEE/H through 9/10 cloud. Observed results. Bombs straddled target area.
06/08/44	1045	Mitchell FW189A	Navigator/bomb aimer	Operation – leader of No 4 box of 6 aircraft. Target – ammunition dump at LIVAROT. 8 x 500 MC bombs. Difficult bombing run with 9/10 cloud obscuring target until last minute. Results not observed.
09/08/44	1010	Mitchell FW189A	Navigator/bomb aimer	Operation – leader of first box of 6 aircraft, 3 boxes in all. Target – ammunition dump W of GOURNAY. 8 x 500 MC bombs. Scattered heavy flak in NEURCHATEL area. All bombs on target. Large fires and explosions. Smoke up 6,000 feet

DATE	HOUR	AIRCRAFT	DUTY	REMARKS
11/08/44	1825	Mitchell FW189A	Navigator/bomb aimer	Operation – leader of first box of 6 aircraft, 3 boxes in all. Target – enemy concentrations in wood at OUILLY-LE-TESSON. 6 miles NW of FALAISE. 8 x 500 MC bombs. Slight accurate flak from enemy lines. Bombs in target area.
12/08/44	1135	Mitchell FW189A	Navigator/bomb aimer	Operation – leader of first box of 6 aircraft, 3 boxes in all. Target – ammunition dump at MARSEILLE-EN-BEAUVAIS. 10 miles NW of BEAUVAIS. 8 x 500 MC bombs. First bombs burst on target. Remainder overshot.
12/08/44	2310	Mitchell FW189A	Navigator/flare dropping by GEE	Night operation – individual. Target – bridges over River ORNE between FALAISE and ARGENTAN to cut roads in use by German army in retreat. We dropped flare, by which remainder of squadron bombed bridge targets.
14/08/44	1035	Mitchell FW189A	Navigator/bomb aimer	Operation – leader of second box of 6 aircraft, 4 boxes in all. Target – enemy strongpoint and troop concentrations in wood at SOUMONT NW of FALAISE. 8 x 500 MC Slight accurate flak after bombing. All bombs in target area.
16/08/44	1135	Mitchell FW189A	Navigator	Operation – leader of first box of 6 aircraft, 3 boxes in all. Target – road/river bridge at LIVAROT. Recalled shortly after take-off – bridge already destroyed.
17/08/44	2250	Mitchell FW189A	Radar navigator/bomb aimer	Night operation – individual Target – road bridge over River RISLE at BERVILLE-SUR-MER. 8 x 500 MC bombs Bombed by GEE. Nuisance raid over 2 hour period on 4 bridge targets. No results observed.

AIRCRAFT TYPES FLOWN AS CAPTAIN OR FIRST PILOT

(CHRONOLOGICAL ORDER)

AIRCRAFT TYPE	ENGINE
Bristol Preliminary Training Machine (PMT)	Lucifer
Bristol Jupiter Fighter	Jupiter
Avro 504K	Armstrong Siddeley Lynx
Bristol Fighter	Rolls Falcon
DeH 60 Moth	Cirrus
Blackburn Bluebird	Armstrong Siddeley Genet
Avro Avian	Cirrus
DeH 9J	Jaguar
Armstrong Whitworth Atlas	Jaguar
Bristol Bulldog	Jupiter
Hawker Hart	Rolls Kestrel
Blackburn Lincock	Armstrong Siddeley Lynx
Fairey 3F (landplane)	Napier Lion
Fairey 3D (seaplane)	Napier Lion
Fairey Flycatcher	Armstrong Siddeley Jaguar
Blackburn Dart	Napier Lion
Fairey 3F (seaplane)	Napier Lion
Armstrong Whitworth Siskin 3A	Armstrong Siddeley Jaguar
Avro Tutor	Armstrong Siddeley Lynx
Blackburn Ripon IIC	Napier Lion
Hawker Horseley	Rolls Condor
Cutty Sark Amphibian	2 x Cirrus Major
Avro Bison	Napier Lion
Blackburn Blackburn	Napier Lion
Hawker Nimrod	Rolls Kestrel
Hawker Fury	Rolls Kestrel
Miles Hawk	Cirrus
Avro Sea Tutor (seaplane)	Armstrong Siddeley Lynx
Fairey Seal (landplane)	Armstrong Siddeley Panther
Fairey Seal (seaplane)	Armstrong Siddeley Panther
Hawker Osprey (landplane)	Rolls Kestrel
Hawker Osprey (seaplane)	Rolls Kestrel
Blackburn Baffin	Bristol Pegasus
DeH Hornet Moth	Gypsy

Airspeed Envoy	2 x Wolseley Aries
Avro Cadet	Armstrong Siddeley Genet Major
Gloster Gauntlet	Bristol Mercury
BA Swallow	Pobjoy Radial
Blackburn Shark (seaplane)	Armstrong Siddeley Tiger VI
Blackburn Shark (landplane)	Armstrong Siddeley Tiger VI
Fairey Swordfish (seaplane)	Bristol Pegasus
Walrus Amphibian	Bristol Pegasus
Percival Vega Gull (Proctor in RAF)	Gypsy Six/Gypsy Queen
Hawker Tomtit	Armstrong Siddeley Mongoose
Fairey Seafox (seaplane)	Napier Rapier
Fairey Swordfish (landplane)	Bristol Pegasus
Miles Magistor	Gypsy Major
Comper Swift	Pobjoy Radial
Bristol Blenheim I and IV	2 x Bristol Mercury
Tipsy (2-seater)	Gypsy Minor
Hawker Hurricane (Marks I and IIC)	Merlin
Spitfire (Marks I, II, V, IX, XVI)	Merlin
Spitfire (Marks XII, XIV, XIX)	Griffin
Farman F200	Salmson Radial
Westland Lysander	Bristol Mercury
Miles Mentor	Gypsy Six
Blackburn Skua	Bristol Perseus
Fairey Battle	Merlin
Gloster Gladiator	Bristol Mercury
Heston Phoenix	Gypsy Six
Miles Master	Kestrel
Miles Martinet	Bristol Mercury
Miles Whitney Straight	Gypsy
Avro Anson	2 x Armstrong Siddeley Cheetah
Hendy Heck	Gypsy Six
Wellington IC	2 x Bristol Pegasus
Wellington II	2 x Merlin
CW Cygnet	Gypsy
Harvard	Pratt and Whitney Wasp
Handley Page Hampden	2 x Bristol Pegasus
Airspeed Oxford	2 x Armstrong Siddeley Cheetah
DeH Moth Minor	Gypsy Minor
Martin Maryland	2 x Pratt and Whitney Twin Wasp
Whitley	2 x Merlin
Havoc II	2 x Pratt and Whitney Twin Wasp
Boston III, IV and V	2 x Wright Double Cyclone
Fairchild Coupe	Ranger
Boulton and Paul Defiant	Merlin
Miles Monarch	Gypsy Major
Westland Whirlwind	2 x Rolls Peregrine

Miles M38 Messenger	Gypsy Major
DeH Leopard Moth	Gypsy
DeH Puss Moth	Gypsy
Stinson 105 Voyager	Lycoming
Vultee Vigilant	Lycoming Radial
North American Mustang Mk I	Allison
North American Mustang Mks III and IV	Packard Merlin
Hawker Typhoon	Napier Sabre
Auster	Gypsy Major
DeH Dominie (Rapide)	2 x Gypsy Queen
DeH Mosquito II, III and VI	2 x Merlin
Hawker Henley	Merlin
North American Mitchell II and III (B25C and D)	2 x Double Cyclone
Stinson Reliant	Lycoming Radial
DeH 82 Tiger Moth	Gypsy Major
Hawker Tempest II	Bristol Centaurus
Hawker Tempest V	Napier Sabre
Kirby Tutor Glider	
Supermarine Sea Otter Amphibian	Bristol Mercury
Vickers Warwick	2 x Bristol Centaurus
Kirby Falcon III Glider	
Gloster Meteor Mk I	2 x Rolls-Royce Welland
Gloster Meteor Mks III, IV, T7 and VIII	2 x Rolls-Royce Derwent
Kirby Kite Glider	
Kirby King Kit Sailplane	
Kirby Gull II Sailplane	
DeH Horne	2 x Rolls-Royce Merlin 130/131
DeH Vampire	DeH Goblin
Weihe Sailplane	
Kranich Sailplane	
SG38 Primary Glider (Broomstick)	
Grunau II Intermediate Sailplane	
Fieseler Storch	Hirth Inverted V8
Mu13 Glider	
Meise (Olympia) Sailplane	
Condor Sailplane	
Minimoa Sailplane	
Rhonsperbber Sailplane	
DeH Chipmunk	Gypsy Major
Ercoupe	90hp Continental
Piper Cruiser	90hp Continental
Republic F84 Thunderjet	Westinghouse Allison J35 (4000lb st)
Fairchild BT19 (Cornell)	150hp Ranger
Beechcraft C45 (Expeditor)	2 x 225hp Jacobs
Schweizer 1-23 Sailplane	
Slingsby (Sedbergh) T21 Glider	

Slingsby Prefect Glider	
Supermarine Attacker	Rolls-Royce Nene III
Slingsby Sky Sailplane	
Nord NC859	105hp Walter
Arsenal Air 100 Sailplane	
Slingsby Gull IV Sailplane	
Dart Kitten	36hp Aeronca/Jap
Hiller 360 Helicopter	175hp Franklin
DeH Devon (or Dove)	2 x 250hp Gypsy Queen
Percival Provost	550hp Alvis Leonides
Jet Provost	Viper
Canberra B2	2 x Rolls-Royce Avon MkI
Percival Pembroke	2 x Alvis 550hp Leonides
Miles Marathon	4 x 310hp Gypsy Queen
Sikorsky Dragonfly Helicopter	550hp Leonides
Lockheed T33 Shooting Star	J33 Westinghouse
North American T26	1800hp Wright Double Cyclone
Slingsby Motor Tutor	65hp Aeronca/Jap
Percival Jet Provost	Armstrong Siddeley Viper
Slingsby Gull Mk I Sailplane	
Slingsby Skylark 15m Sailplane	
Percival EP9 (Prospector)	225hp Continental
Slingsby T31 Glider	
Fairey Tipsy Junior	60hp Walter Mikron
Eon Olympia 401 Sailplane	
Eon Olympia 415 Sailplane	
Thruxton Jackaroo	Gypsy Major
Slingsby T42 Eagle	
Rollason Turbulent	30hp Arden
Curric Wot	32hp Aeronca/Jap
Slingsby Swallow Glider	
Meta-Sokol	140hp Walter
Tipsy Nipper	40hp Hepu
Piper Tri Pacer	160hp Lycoming
Jodel D117	90hp Continental
Piper Super Cub	150hp Lycoming
Miles Aries	2 x Cirrus Major III
Cessna 301C	2 x 260hp Continental
Piper Comanche	2 x 250hp Lycoming
Garland Linnet (Piel Emeraude)	90hp Continental
Sesna 210	260hp Continental
Piper Apache	2 x 160hp Lycoming
Sesna 175	175hp Continental
Aero 145	2 x Walter 140hp
Cessna 150	2 x Continental 100hp
DeH C2 Beaver	550hp Alvis Leonides

Jodel DR 1050 Excellence/Ambassadeur	100hp Continental
Slingsby Skylark 3 Sailplane	
Eon Olympia 419 Sailplane	
Piper Colt	108hp Lycoming
Piaggio P166	2 x 340hp Lycoming
Fornaire Aircoupe	90hp Continental
Piper PA28 Cherokee and variants	
Bolkow-Klemm KL107C	150hp Lycoming
Handley-Page Herald	2 x Rolls-Royce Dart DA7
Druine/Rollason Condor	75hp Continental
Piper Aztec	2 x 250hp Continental
Aero-Commander 560F	2 x 350hp Lycoming
Jodel D140B Mousquetaire	180hp Lycoming
Schleicher Ka6 Rhonsegler Sailplane	
Cessna 185 Skywagon	260hp Continental
Cosmic Wind Ballerina	85hp Continental
Slingsby Skylark 4 Sailplane	
Breguette Fauvette Sailplane	
Beagle Airdale	180hp Lycoming
Beagle Terrier	145hp Gypsy Major
Pzl Mucha Standard Sailplane	
Beagle M206	2 x 260hp Rolls-Royce Continental
Beagle AOP Mk II	260hp Rolls-Royce Continental
Beagle D5/180	180hp Lycoming
Tiger Moth Seaplane	140hp Gypsy X
Slingsby T49 Sailplane	
Morane Rallye	100hp Continental
Morane Super Rallye	240hp Franklin
Morane Rallye Commodore	180hp Lycoming
Wallis Beagle Wa116 Autogyro	72hp McCulloch
Pilatus Porter	350hp Lycoming
Scheibe SF26 Sailplane	
Blanik L13 Sailplane	
Morava L200D	2 x 210hp M337 Walter
Jodel D150 Mascaret	100hp Rolls-Royce Continental
Slingsby T51 Dart Sailplane	
Piper PA30 Twin Comanche	2 x 160hp Lycoming
Bensen (Campbell) B11-2 Gyroglider	
Victa 115 Air Tourer	115hp Lycoming
Bölkow Junior 208C	100hp Continental
Miles Gemini	2 x 90hp Cirrus Minor
Piper PA15 Vagabond	65hp Continental
Fournier RF3	35hp VW Conversion
Gardan Horizon	160hp Lycoming
Dornier Do28 B1	2 x 290hp Lycoming
Jodel DR250	160hp Lycoming

Slingsby Dart 17m Sailplane	
Wassmer Super (Mk IV) Baladou	180hp Lycoming
Rollason Turbulent Seaplane	45hp Arden
Piper PA32 Cherokee and variants	260hp Lycoming
Aero Commander 200	285hp Continental
Mitchell Proctor Kittiwake	100hp Continental
Britten Norman BN2 Islander	2 x 260hp Lycoming
Piper PA25 Pawnee	150hp Lycoming
Pzl 104 Wilga-32	0470 Continental
Beagle Pup 100 and 150	100 and 150hp Continentals
Cessna 172	145hp Continental
Diamant Sailplane 16.5m	
Rollason Beta	Continental C90
Scheib Falke Motor Glider	45hp VW
Schemp Hirth SHK Sailplane	
Bölkow Phoebus Sailplane	
Schemp Hirth Cirrus 18m Sailplane	
Szd-30 Pirat Sailplane	
Schleicher ASW-15 Sailplane	
Jodel D9 Bebe	45hp VW
Piper J3 Cub	65hp Continental
Siai-Marchetti F260	260hp Lycoming
DeH Canada Twin Otter	2 x PT6A 260hp turboprops
American Aviation Yanqui	180hp Lycoming
Britten Norman Trislander	3 x 260hp Lycoming
Jodel DR253B Regent	180hp Lycoming
Wassmer WA52 Europa	160hp Lycoming
Wassmer WA51 Pacific	150hp Lycoming E320
Champion Type 7AC	75hp Continental
Piper PA34 Seneca	2 x 200hp Lycoming
Robin HR200/100	108hp Lycoming
Evans VP1	45hp VW
Stolp Starlet	90hp Continental
Robin DR400/140	140hp Lycoming
Grumman AA-5 Traveler	150hp Lycoming
Cessna 337 Skymaster	2 x 195hp Continental
Finnish Viima	160hp Siemens Halske 7-cylinder radial
Luton Minor	36hp Aeronca/Jap
Jurca Tempête	65hp Continental
Robin DR400	108hp Lycoming
EAA Biplane	140hp Lycoming
Spitfire 6/10 Replica	100hp Continental
Taylor Titch	Continental C90

Grand total of 276 aircraft types and variants.

Index